T0293689

The Art of Commitment Pacing

The Art of Commitment Pacing

Engineering Allocations to Private Capital

THOMAS MEYER

WILEY

Registered Office(s)
John Wiley & Sons Ltd, The Atrium, Southern Gate, Chichester, West Sussex, PO19 8SQ, UK
John Wiley & Sons, Inc., 111 River Street, Hoboken, NJ 07030, USA

Editorial Office
The Atrium, Southern Gate, Chichester, West Sussex, PO19 8SQ, UK
For details of our global editorial offices, customer services, and more information about Wiley products visit us at www.wiley.com.

Library of Congress Cataloging-in-Publication Data is Available

ISBN 9781394159604 (Cloth)
ISBN 9781394159611 (ePDF)
ISBN 9781394159628 (ePub)

Cover Design: Wiley
Cover Image: © Baac3nes/Getty Images

Set in 10/12 pts Stix Two Text by Straive, Chennai, India

SKY10073370_042224

Contents

Acknowledgements

'MBAs once scoffed at the thought of relying on a scientific and systematic approach to investing, confident that they could hire coders if they were ever needed. Today, coders say the same about MBAs, if they think about them at all.' Zuckerman (2019)

To a large degree, this book and the concepts described here build and follow on from the cooperation and discussions with my co-author Pierre-Yves Mathonet. We wrote our first book *Beyond the J-Curve* (John Wiley and Sons) in the years after the dot-com bubble during the early 2000s, documenting our experiences from building up the European Investment Fund's risk management function and developing methodologies for managing portfolios of private equity funds. As we found out at the time, many ideas are, in fact, quite difficult to implement as a functioning piece of software.

I am grateful for the opportunity SimCorp A/S has given me to turn these ideas into reality. I am greatly indebted to Hugues Chabanis and Marc Schröter, without whom the portfolio management solution for alternative assets would never have seen the light of day. I am extremely grateful for the support of my colleagues Catherine Le Caranta, Ross LeBlanc, Jan Aarre Midtgaard and Jacob Perner.

I particularly thank Emilian Belev from Northfield Information Services for our joint work and the discussions on private capital fund exposure.

A fund cash-flow forecasting model is at the core of portfolio management for private capital funds. Here, the main insight is that it is even better to run a less detailed model and to analyse its results frequently than interrogate a complicated model rarely. Building a sophisticated solution that generates forecasts with a high degree of automation, consistently, and – thanks to intensive testing – reliably, requires working across several development teams. I am greatly indebted to their current and previous members:

Team 'Air Croissants'

Ivan Artamonov, Oleksii Fedoruk, Jensjakob Kristiansen, Jeppe Sidenius, Danyang Wang

Team 'Alf'

Pietro De Caro, Jesper Rønning Dalby, Marie Dufva, Jozsef Gáspár, Mads Thorstein Roar Henriksen, Juni Kuriakose

Team 'Asset Kickers'

Mateus Volkmer Nunes Gomes, Nikhila Maddipatla, Prasad Tarikere Murthy Rao, Daniel Secrieru, Ole Sieling, Oliver Simon

Team 'Bynars'

Udo Dittmayer, Alin Gabriel Eremia, Masoud Hoore, Maria-Cristina Ionita, Bogumiła Jelito, Michael Röhrs, Maria Vasylieva

I am also much obliged to Richard Ballek and Kai Weber for their help.

Acknowledgements would not be complete without expressing my gratitude to Gemma Valler and Alice Hadaway at John Wiley and Sons, without whom this book would not have happened. Aravind Kannankara has done an outstanding job as copy editor and Vithusha Rameshan as leader of the production process.

I reserve the last acknowledgement to my most important supporter: once more, my heartfelt gratitude goes to Mika Kaneyuki, my wife and best friend, who is my strength and purpose in life.

Luxembourg, January 2024

CHAPTER 1

Introduction

This book is about commitment pacing for private capital. As Preqin describes, what now is termed 'private capital' originally emerged as an offshoot of private equity.[1] It comprises a wide range of assets that are not available on public markets and, therefore, are highly illiquid. This also includes, but not exclusively, venture capital (VC), private debt, real estate, infrastructure, commodities, timberland, and other natural resources. The organised market for this asset class is dominated by funds as principal financial intermediaries. Private capital has a long history, from an institutional investor perspective starting with the leveraged buyout boom in the 1980s.[2]

Practically, commitment pacing is the most relevant way for managing the exposure to private capital. It is the process by which an investor plans the timing and size of future commitments to funds, and the choice of the funds' strategies to reach and maintain a targeted allocation. Jeet (2020) stated that a 'good commitment pacing plan is often seen as the lynchpin of a private capital program and can account for much of the dispersion in performance across LPs'.

SCOPE OF THE BOOK

A lot has been written about investing in this asset class, particularly private equity, so let us start with clarifying what this book is not about. It is not dealing with the question whether it is now a good time to increase or decrease allocations to private capital. Like in all markets, there are boom and rather depressed periods, limits to growth, etc. This will not be discussed here. Investing in private markets is here to stay.

It is not dealing with financial returns and the attractiveness of private market strategies, like what returns are buyouts delivering, or whether their risk-return ratio is better than that of VC. All data decay over time, and it is dangerous to rely on outdated market trends. We are, therefore, not discussing current market statistics, as results are likely to look different in other periods and economies anyway.

This book will also not deal with the question of how to select funds. Rather, it takes as core assumption that an individual limited partner (LP) has no systematic advantage in selecting funds. This will raise eyebrows, but the famous claim 'we only invest in first-quartile funds' requires the belief that an investor is better than others in selecting funds. Investors need to ask themselves the (uncomfortable) question how much better their selection skills can be than that of the average institutional investor who has experienced professionals and established a proper due diligence process as well?

The focus of this book is the methods for commitment pacing and the reasoning behind them, to demystify this process and to describe a state-of-the-art approach to building up and maintaining allocations to private assets. The book aims to strike a balance between not taking a view that is too broad and not getting bogged down in more detail than is needed.

The figures and examples are for illustrative purposes only. Unless specifically pointed out, all examples are based on expected contributions, distributions, and net asset value (NAV) projections. The examples' assumptions may not be realised, and thus, cash flows and valuations of a real investment programme may significantly differ from the projections presented here.

QUICK GLOSSARY[3]

When referring to 'investors' in this book, we mean institutional investors – like insurers, pension funds, banks, endowments, sovereign wealth funds, and family offices – and the organisational entities they have set up for managing allocations to private capital. These investors either employ professionals as 'investment managers' to directly invest in private assets or invest through funds where professional management is provided by intermediaries.

'Funds' in the private capital context are usually structured as a limited partnership and are investment vehicles for pooling capital. Here, institutional investors mean the fund's 'LPs' who commit a certain amount to the fund and do not take an active role in its management. The term 'general partner' (GP) refers to the firm as an entity that is legally responsible for managing the fund's investments in private assets and has unlimited personal liability for its debts and obligations. Such 'fund management firms' regularly raise funds.

'Fund managers' are the professionals involved in the fund's day-to-day management. They form the fund's management team that includes the carried interest holders, i.e. those employees or directors of the GP who are entitled to share in the carried interest of the super profit made by the fund.

An LP's 'commitments' are drawn down as needed. There is little, if any, opportunity to redeem the investment before the end of the fund's lifetime. A significant part of the capital remains as 'undrawn commitments' in the hands of the LP. This capital waiting to be called is also referred to as 'dry powder' and carries opportunity costs. When and how much of these commitments are called, invested in what private assets, and when these investments are exited and the resulting proceeds returned to the LPs, is decided by the fund managers only.

THE CHALLENGE OF PRIVATE CAPITAL

After unabated 'triumphalist money making' since the 1980s, in the 2020s, private capital firms worldwide were sitting on about $2 trillion worth of dry power committed by their LPs but not invested. With more and more capital being allocated to private assets, returns increasingly have been coming under pressure. The 'first quartile' label attached to 'institutional quality' firms ceases to make sense.[4] The ability of private equity investors to turn a company they buy and improve its efficiencies is, in the words of one industry observer, largely illusory: 'This is, after all, the leveraged-buyout industry, and not the operational wizard-genius industry'.[5] This may be exaggerating, but in all industries that are coming of age, successful practices spread and are adopted by companies outside the industry as well. As a consequence, the number of attractive investment opportunities appears to be in decline.

Institutional investors fear – not the first time in the industry's history – that future returns on private capital will be mediocre and again some LPs accept high discounts when selling to the secondary market.[6] Crises like COVID-19 and the wars in Ukraine and the Middle East look like Black Swans,[7] events of the highest improbability but with large consequences in the financial markets, that look as if they would change the industry's dynamics forever.

However, over the past decades, private capital regularly has survived Black Swans and thrived despite or maybe even because of them. There are no indicators why the real economy's core dynamics that drive private market – entrepreneurship, innovation, technological obsolescence, industrial restructuring, and societal change – should not continue to be of relevance in the future. Private capital will continue its long-term outperformance compared to public markets.

Risk and uncertainty

Since private capital, by definition, does not regularly trade on an open market and is held over several years, there is typically no recent third-party-determined quotation by which to calculate a fund's market value and that of the private asset it holds. When talking about 'risk' in this context, we are mainly looking at situations of 'uncertainty' in the definition of University of Chicago economist, Frank Knight, where there is no valid basis for quantifying the probabilities of outcomes.[8]

Volatility, therefore, is a controversial indicator for private equity risks. In the (relatively) early days of private equity, *The Economist* once quipped 'to say that private equity is less volatile and thus less risky is a bit like saying that the weather does not change much when you stay inside and rarely look out of the window'.[9]

For private capital, the fund managers' reaction to an adverse market environment will be different than in the case of hedge funds or traditional assets. Funds structured as limited partnerships essentially protect companies from adverse market developments by giving them a lifetime in the form of the funds' dry powder.

All transactions in private markets are negotiated, and any reaction to short-term market developments cannot be instantaneous. When the market is in crisis, funds hold on to their portfolio companies as long as possible until it has recovered. There are no early redemptions, and rather than selling at lower price, exits are delayed, often significantly for years.

To keep with *The Economist*'s witty analogy, fund managers are looking out of the window, see the rain, and decide to stay inside. In fact, the funds' limited partnership structure can be viewed as the response to uncertainty rather than risk.[10] For forecasting and measuring risks, uncertainty is an undesirable characteristic of the process to be assessed, but in the real economy, the domain within which private capital investing is taking place, it is considered a necessary condition for profit, and here, the assumption that the absence of data means higher financial risk is wrong.

Why do we need commitment pacing?

For private assets, a target allocation cannot be bought like in the case of public equity or bonds. Rather, LPs commit to funds, and then, these commitments are called over time by the fund managers and gradually turned into investments in private asset. Commitment pacing is primarily applicable to allocations to limited partnership funds as these are cash-flow assets – which we would describe, in the absence of a common definition, as assets that during some market periods cannot be traded at fair prices, need to be sustained through a timely provision of liquidity, and are characterised by their cash-flow streams of uncertain amounts and at unpredictable times.

Commitment pacing is not needed for liquid assets or hedge funds that operate in public markets.[11] Here, investors can increase and decrease allocations quickly through trading at prices that are close to valuations – where essentially, value is synonymous to cash flows.

Illiquidity

The commitment is waiting to be called and invested by the fund managers, but the LP's financial exposure is also limited to the amount. Controlling exposure is difficult, as it is driven by a number of factors, such as the timing and the amount of commitments, the number of years during which the commitments will take place, and the growth rate of the different assets.

If the LP commits too little, the real investment in private assets will not be sufficient for generating returns commensurate with this asset class. On the other hand, committing too much lead to liquidity shortfalls and can, therefore, result in the need to liquidate valuable positions or forgo attractive opportunities. This is complicated by the fund's J-curve, their tendency to post negative returns in the initial years and only turn into positive return territory in later years (see **Box 1.1**).

In contrast to asset classes available in public markets that may become illiquid during periods of financial turmoil and heightened risk aversion, private capital is structurally illiquid and its LPs are aware ex ante of the risk they are taking. It is precisely this risk, and more specifically the associated risk premium, that attracts investors to these asset classes. As a matter of principle, only long-term investors, whose liability profile allows them to lock capital in for a prolonged period of time, can harvest this risk premium.[12]

The siren song of the secondary market

Secondary markets are often viewed as a panacea for the illiquidity related to primary fund commitments and suggested as a means to accelerate the build-up of portfolios with an acceptable vintage year spread and to mitigate the portfolio's J-curve. Should opportunities appear, secondaries have a real-option character and as such can create

Box 1.1 J-Curve

Typical reasons why LPs pursue secondaries are as faster route to liquidity and for reducing the impact of the so-called 'J-curve'.[14] The J-curve refers to the pattern of interim returns between the inception and the termination of a fund. This pattern – also referred to as the 'hockey stick' – is explained by the funds' structure with set-up costs and management fees that depress early returns.

The 'classical' fund performance J-curve is mainly caused by the fact that valuation policies followed by the industry and the uncertainty inherent in private assets lead to promising investments being revaluated upwards quite late in a fund's lifetime. As a result, private capital funds tend to apparently decline in value during the early years of existence – the so-called 'valley of tears' – before beginning to show the expected positive returns in later years of the fund's life. This period is generally shorter for buyout than for VC funds, where many early-stage investments fail before eventually the few winners emerge.

value, but they are impractical for swiftly rebalancing a portfolio of funds or as a reliable route to liquidity. LPs are faced with severe limitations to managing their exposure to private capital in this way.

The size of the secondary market is a fraction of the amounts committed to primary stakes in funds, and therefore, it will be difficult to significantly accelerate the build-up of a portfolio.[13] To manage exposure through acquisitions, the secondary market often is unable to provide the targeted stakes with the desired strategy, vintage year, and remaining exposure.

Reducing the exposure through secondary market sales is possible but, particularly when trying to sell under time pressure, difficult to execute on advantageous terms. Liquidity tends to dry up precisely when LPs would prefer to sell and, even under normal circumstances, LPs will find it difficult to dispose of or acquire stakes in funds that match their desired portfolio composition, at least for an attractive price.

How does commitment pacing work?

According to the Chartered Financial Analyst Institute (CFA), commitment pacing enables investors in private alternatives to better manage their portfolio liquidity and set realistic annual commitment targets to reach the desired asset allocation.[15] How does commitment pacing work?

We take as a simple example a fictitious small insurer who wants to build up an allocation to private capital over the coming years and plans to make an amount of not more than €100 million available for this purpose. The timing and the amounts of the fund's cash flows are highly uncertain, but the total called capital is not supposed to exceed the committed amount. Risk is an important consideration, so the portfolio should be spread over several funds and, importantly, over several vintages.

The insurer's pacing plan quantifies the amount and timing of capital commitments to achieve and maintain a targeted exposure to private assets over a specified period of time. The cause of exposure (the commitment to a fund at one time) and the resulting effect (the amounts actually invested in private assets and then their performance on maturity) are separated by years.

Let us look at three different pacing plans (see **Figure 1.1**) for committing the €100 million of available resources to a portfolio of funds. **Pacing plan 1** foresees accelerating commitments over three years to quickly achieve a targeted exposure. Here, the peak exposure to private assets in NAV terms of around €58 million is already achieved after six years. Compared to liquid assets, this looks 'glacial' but underlines that private capital is only for very long-term-oriented investors. The other two pacing plans are even less aggressive. **Pacing plan 2** foresees equal commitments spread over five years, and **plan 3** slows down commitments and stretches them over seven years, with the expected maximum NAV exposure not exceeding €50 million.

With any of these pacing plans, it looks as if the insurer does not even need €100 million and, in fact, we therefore can expect that she will have put much less capital aside for this purpose. But how much capital is really needed? All three plans foresee a total of €100 million in commitments, but the resulting peak NAV exposures are reached later, and these maxima vary in size. Which pacing plan would we prefer? **Plan 1** looks obvious, but this overlooks an important constraint: the liquidity needed to honour the funds' capital calls in time (see **Figure 1.2**).

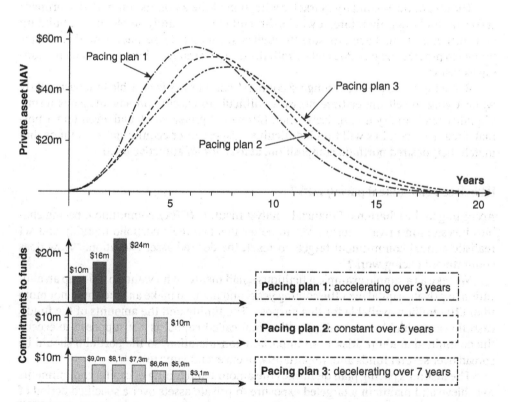

FIGURE 1.1   Examples for commitment pacing strategies

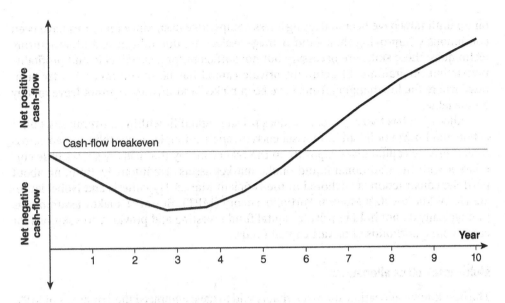

FIGURE 1.2 Cash-flow J-curve

The cash-flow J-curve depicted in **Figure 1.2** represents the evolution of the net cash flows from the LP to the funds. During the early years of a fund's existence, these cash flows are negative before making a U-turn to become positive in later years of the fund's life. The pacing model needs to reflect the liquidity constraints this J-curve implies to determine the appropriate timing and weighting of future commitments to new funds to keep the portfolio at or near its target allocation.

To phrase the commitment pacing problem differently, how could the insurer engineer reaching a target exposure as quickly as possible and minimise opportunity costs while respecting constraints? What makes this a complex undertaking is that not all resources allocated to private capital can be committed to funds right away, that not everything that is committed to funds is also invested in private assets, and that older funds have begun to return capital to the LP.

Significant allocations needed

A significant allocation is necessary for private capital to have an impact on the overall portfolio's returns. Assuming simplistically that private capital can outperform the public markets by about 500 basis points, at least 5% of the entire portfolio needs to be allocated to the asset class. Auerbach and Shivananda (2017) found that portfolios with higher shares of private investments – at least 15% – have outperformed portfolios with lower allocations. In fact, the late David Swensen suggested less than about 15% be difficult to justify.[16] 20% is consistent with average allocations for large US public pension funds.[17]

With such sizeable allocations, LPs are reaching the limits of rule-of-thumb-based portfolio management techniques. The practices that institutional investors have relied on up until now have been reflecting a less competitive past. Since then, LPs have been continuously improving their fund manager selection, due diligence, and structuring techniques; these skills are necessary but not sufficient for a sustainable and profitable investment programme. Structurally, private capital has become a much harder business, where the low-hanging fruits have been picked and investors cannot leave money on the table.

Allocation has two aspects: how does private capital fit within an overall asset allocation and how to build an intra-asset class diversification, i.e. a portfolio spread across funds? Private capital gives exposure to the real economy that usually shows little correlation with the traditional liquid public market assets. Traditionally, thinking about portfolio construction is anchored in the Efficient Market Hypothesis and Nobel laureate Harry Markowitz's Modern Portfolio Theory (MPT). But MPT makes assumptions that typically do not hold in private capital fund investing and provides no solutions for constructing portfolios of private capital funds.

Multi-asset-class allocations

The best-known allocation approach that is said to have embraced the principles of MPT, albeit in simplistic but robust way, is the 'Yale model', also known as the 'endowment model' of a multi-asset-class investment strategy.

It was pioneered by the Yale endowment's Dean Takahashi (whom we will meet again in the context of forecasting models) and David Swensen and is based on diversification across asset classes with dissimilar correlations to maximise risk-adjusted investment returns. This endowment model divides a portfolio into five or six roughly equal parts and invests each in a different asset class. The novelty of this approach was that liquidity is to be avoided rather than sought out, since it comes at a heavy price through lower returns and that it has a relatively high exposure to alternative asset classes, private equity, real estate, hedge funds, and natural resources, compared to more traditional portfolios.

Intra-asset-class diversification

According to MPT, risk-averse investors can construct an optimum portfolio that maximises expected returns for a given level of market risk. As markets are continuously in flux, what is an optimum portfolio is also changing. Therefore, investors need to periodically buy and sell assets to bring the portfolio's allocations back to the optimum. Updating the optimisation and rebalancing is a constant and ongoing process.

For portfolios of funds, under simplifying assumptions, it may be possible to define an optimum, but the instant criticism is that such a plan will be impossible to implement: the deals foreseen are not accessible at the time, the quality of available opportunities is not right, or funds raised by firms with whom relationships are to be maintained do not come to the market at the right time.

Therefore, commitments to funds tend to be suboptimal from a portfolio management perspective, and once they had been taken, they are practically irreversible. Due to the illiquidity of private assets, LPs cannot rebalance their portfolios. Decisions that may have been optimal in a stable and predictable environment can be detrimental in the changing environment of private markets characterised by uncertainty.

ENGINEERING A RESILIENT PORTFOLIO

For illiquid private assets, a portfolio needs to be resilient, to meet objectives without having to rebalance, and to be able to recover and bounce back after shocks in the economy. LPs need to find a balance between resilience and efficiency. If a system, in our case a portfolio, is not resilient, it could collapse rapidly; if it is inefficient, it will with certainty die gradually. To build a resilient portfolio, LPs need to forecast and assess how it will behave under the typical market conditions and how it responds to various stress scenarios.

Here, actions chosen cannot be guaranteed to lead to the intended results. Instead, risks are addressed through applying experience in the form of engineering principles as accepted basic truths that explain how private markets work. Examples for such principles are giving funds a time-proven structure, i.e. the limited partnership, selecting competent and trusted fund managers, to be flexible in identifying opportunities and assure quick reaction to changing market conditions, and provide them proper incentives and align their interests with those of their LPs. Another important engineering principle is that LPs need to build efficiently diversified portfolios of funds where 'big hits' compensate for the unavoidable underperformers.

The academic literature on building portfolio of private capital funds remains sparse. Most work on this subject is still done by practitioners at various specialist asset managers. Also, the modelling of securitisations of private equity fund portfolios through the so-called 'collateralised fund obligations' (CFOs) is highly relevant to this subject. These securitisations are probably the most practical route to liquidity, to overcome the limitations of secondary markets, and to address risk measurement. CFOs are regularly analysed by rating agencies, but they are complex to model.

LPs manage the efficiency of their portfolios through various levers. Traditionally, the ability to pick top funds is perceived to have the strongest impact. A lot has been written on this subject already; however, with no silver bullet found. Relevant for this book are tools like building portfolios where diversification offers protection for the lowest cost, i.e. a minimum number of funds, a cash management that minimises opportunity costs for uncalled and uncommitted capital, and over-commitments to leverage the resources available for commitments.

The private capital industry is to a large degree organised around decentralised decision-making. Decentralisation uses funds as intermediaries, to allow faster growth of portfolios and wider diversification, also in regard to decision-making. Here, LPs balance between resilience and efficiency, whereas GPs can focus on efficiency and are incentivised accordingly. The often-surprising resilience of private capital fund investment programmes even during economic downturns may also come from LPs being forced to cling on to their commitments. Fund managers are committed to their portfolios of private assets by virtue of being repeat players in the market and the need to preserve their reputation.

ORGANISATION OF THE BOOK

So far little has been written on commitment pacing, and this process is not very well known outside the institutional investment world.[18] It is mainly practitioners coming up with techniques, but simplistic approaches are still the norm.[19] Pacing tools are typically in-house built applications and comprise the following main components:

- A forecast model for the funds' cash flows;
- A portfolio model that describes how the funds interact;
- A market model that provides realistic and specific assumptions for the funds' expected performance;
- An investor model that captures the LP's fund-selection skills.

Depending on the use case, commitment pacing relates to a short-term (monthly or quarterly), medium-term (semi-annually or one year), or long-term (annual or spanning several years) time horizon. The major use case is the 'glide path' describing how the portfolio of existing funds will develop over the medium term. A long-term-oriented use case is to set the 'flight path' for maintaining exposure by adding new commitments. The main use case over the short term is to determine the probability density function for the portfolio's cash flows as basis for the management of treasury assets.

Exposure

LPs commit to funds that are 'blind pools', i.e. the fund initially holds no portfolio of private assets. In the case of traditional asset classes, capital is put to work immediately, but in the case of commitments to funds, the 'true' investments into private assets follow, usually with a significant delay. During the fund's early years, this portfolio is insignificant compared to the undrawn commitments. What is then the LP's 'exposure'?

One view is to only consider the investments into private assets as exposure. On the other hand, the committed capital is what the LP puts at stake over the fund's lifetime. Therefore, an alternative perspective is to consider the undrawn commitments as a significant liability for the LP to cover when called and thus part of an exposure to manage.

Forecast modelling

The basis for commitment pacing and for assessing the impact of potential new deals in the pipeline on an existing and planned portfolio is a model that forecasts how much and when capital is called by the funds and when and how much they will be repaying it.

Aalberts et al. (2020) expressed surprise when observing that after decades of booming private equity markets, the literature on cash-flow modelling for funds has 'remained sparse'. To this day, LPs interested in forecasting their exposure to private assets and their liquidity needs mainly revert to the model proposed by the Yale Investments Office's Dean Takahashi and Seth Alexander.[20] It is also often called the 'Yale model' but in the following will be referred to as the Takahashi–Alexander model (TAM).[21]

Models are built by looking for and identifying variables that offered some predictive value. The major predictive value is the lifecycle characteristics of the fund. With the TAM, we can model the stylised pattern of capital calls, value creation, and distributions for primary, secondaries, and co-investments. This model has been tried and tested over many years, in various economic environments and geographical settings. It was found to stack up well against more complex approaches. The TAM's main advantage is that its logic is simple to understand, so that analysts and decision-makers intuitively trust its results.

Private market data

Commitment pacing requires meaningful assumptions regarding performance expectations. Data that reflect a risk profile similar to the funds to be modelled are provided by a number of commercial private market data providers. However, model outputs can only be as good as its inputs; in other words, it is 'Garbage-In-Garbage-Out'. While private market data suffer from a range of deficiencies they are all we have. Models are, therefore, rather constructed as 'Uncertainty-In-Stress-Out', with stresses applied to the model outcomes and the lack of complete and reliable data being mitigated through judgement in the form of qualitative parameters.

Augmentations of the TAM

The forecasting models presented in this book, the A1*TAM and A2*TAM, are augmentations of the TAM for producing stochastic cash-flow scenarios for funds that are, however, reconcilable with the expected cash flows and NAVs forecasted by the simple original TAM.

The precise timing and amount of cash flows is unpredictable, but their stochastic properties, such as expectations, frequency, and volatility, can be modelled through the A2*TAM. This model provides more granularity, i.e. it does not just consider annual cash flows but quarterly and monthly, as needed, as well as offering more differentiation between the various types of cash flows.

Avenues into private capital

There are various avenues into private market relevant for institutional investors. Cash-flow models need to differentiate between primary fund investments, secondaries, and co-investments – all of these have highly idiosyncratic cash-flow patterns. We assume that institutional investors will delegate secondaries and other more complex strategies like co-investments to specialist fund managers. The TAM and its augmentations can capture these dynamics, and a portfolio model is super-positioning such funds' cash-flow patterns.

Diversification

Diversification is the LP's main control for resilience and efficiency, and therefore, this will be looked at in detail. Most LPs do not look beyond the number of funds to commit to in each vintage year when looking at their intra-asset-class diversification.[22] However, this is just giving an incomplete picture.

Apart from the vintage year spread, geographies and sectors are viewed as key to a well-balanced portfolio. A portfolio model, therefore, needs to capture similarities of funds across these dimensions and the resulting dependencies in their behaviour. A high degree of diversification also smooths the cash flows and, thus, can mitigate the risk that the LP's funding needs overshoot.

However, diversification in private capital is expensive. Due diligence, legal expenses for structuring, fees, and incentive compensation are typically substantially higher than in portfolios of publicly traded assets. Back-office operations also require additional systems and resources because reporting and data collection is not standardised in the same manner as for public securities. The impact of these costs put limits on efficient diversification for smaller allocations to private capital. This is of course not the full story as larger LPs need to commit more than a theoretical optimum number of funds could possibly absorb.

Model input data

Diversification for managing risk is mainly a protection against lack of knowledge. The near perfect data we are used to from public markets do not exist for private markets. We need to work with the data we have, but we should not be discouraged by their absence. A lack of widely available data in private markets is an advantage to those who can merge information from various sources and apply judgement to their interpretation. Judgement in the form of a qualitative scoring plays a strong role in a fund rating methodology.

Fund rating/grading

Many research findings suggest that, unlike many other asset classes, the performance of a superior private equity manager dominates all other criteria. Outcomes materialise only over the long term and are highly uncertain. Therefore, the link between risk and return ex ante is unclear and controversial, with deal makers being most vocal in the discussion and convinced that their latest proposal is 'top quartile'. Within an appraised asset class valuations are highly subjective, and the ability to pick winners, i.e. funds that outperform their peer group, depends on judgement and experience as well.

Moving away from a general assumption of 'institutional quality' of GPs, fund ratings can refine forecasts based on what is known on the fund, its managers, and the private assets it holds. This fund rating, here referred to as 'fund grading', evaluates the compliance with engineering principles that based on experience should be respected. It additionally measures deviations of the individual fund's development against the average development of its aggregated peer group of funds with similar characteristics.

This grading technique uses qualitative as well as quantitative inputs to categorise funds according to their expected performance and their risk. A scoring can be forward looking and is particularly important if no reliable data are available. With increasing fund age and information on the fund's investments becoming available, quantification becomes more relevant compared to the qualitative scoring.

For LPs that are convinced of their selection skills, it is rational to forgo diversification and aim for a highly concentrated portfolio. The question is how much better in selection have LPs to be to justify ignoring diversification. The impact of the LP's assumed selection skills can be assessed through the grading technique as well.

Bottom-up forecasting models

The forecasting models introduced are top-down and could arguably ignore inside information on the fund. Pure bottom-up forecasting models that can capture such details, on the other hand, cannot be maintained as the regular data collection is too cumbersome to do this often enough. The way out of this dilemma is to improve top-down models in those exceptional situations where superior insights are available through so-called 'overrides'.

Commitment pacing

Funds are self-liquidating, so LPs must actively build and maintain a desired level of their exposure. Commitment pacing needs to consider various factors: the composition of the existing portfolio, the current allocation in a multi-asset context, the allocations and compositions to be targeted going forward, the current deals identified and under evaluation, the LP's risk appetite, and the assessment of scenarios for potential for market downturns.

A pacing plan needs to meet several other objectives and constraints: it should not lead to liquidity shortfalls caused by capital calls that exceed what the LP has reserved for this purpose, and the plan should assure diversification, notably over vintage years, strategies, and fund management firms, in line with the portfolio's target risk profile.

Stress scenarios

Stress scenarios address potential model failure, uncertainty in data, and prudence. The burst of the dot-com bubble, the Great Financial Crisis from 2007 to 2009, and COVID-19 created the fear that 'this time it is different'. Essentially, we are forecasting the past; in other words, we are basing our assessment of what will happen in the future on what has happened before. A market model answers the question which historic vintage years are most representative for the situation to be assessed?

Models can provide useful insights but will be sensitive to the underlying assumptions that may create a false sense of certainty. Institutional investors will be concerned and ask what will happen if we have another global economic crisis? What if there is another pandemic? It is good practice to model uncertainty by adding stresses to the commitment pacing model.

Let us start

Most of commitment pacing's technical complexity is caused by the fact that institutional investing in private capital is intermediated through funds structured as limited partnerships, which have been criticised as 'archaic' and 'spectacularly ill-suited' for long-term investing.[23] As we will discuss in the following chapter, nothing could be further from the truth, and limited partnership funds are the time-proven structure of choice for long-term investing under extreme uncertainty.

NOTES

1. See https://www.preqin.com/academy/lesson-2-private-capital/what-is-private-capital, [accessed 13 March 2023]
2. For more details, particularly on limited partnership funds, see Meyer (2014).
3. See also **Glossary** and **Abbreviations** for additional definitions.
4. See Gottschalg (2021).
5. See Teitelbaum (2018).
6. See Plender (2023).
7. See Taleb (2007).
8. See Knight (1921).
9. The Economist 'Once burnt, still hopeful'. 25 November 2004.
10. See Meyer (2014).
11. 'Hedge funds are typically open-ended investment funds with no restrictions on transferability. Private equity funds, on the other hand, are typically closed-ended investment funds with restrictions on transferability for a certain time period.' See https://corporatefinanceinstitute.com/resources/equities/private-equity-vs-hedge-fund/, [accessed 14 March 2023]
12. See Cornelius et al. (2013).
13. Mende et al. (2016) estimated that merely 1.5–2.0% of commitments made to funds in 2001–2005 had translated into secondary transactions. By 2015, this conversion rate had reached approximately 6.2%. According to Auerbach and Shivananda (2017), between 2002 and 2016, the secondary transaction volume averaged between 1.6% and 8.4% of primary fund commitments.
14. 'Simulations by BlackRock showed that a co-investment allocation of 20% to 30% can shorten the J-curve by 12–18 months.' See https://www.tfoco.com/en/insights/articles/coinvesting-in-private-equity#, [accessed 10 March 2023]
15. See https://www.cfainstitute.org/en/membership/professional-development/refresher-readings/asset-allocation-alternative-investments, [accessed 31 December 2023]
16. See Swensen (2009).
17. See Brown et al. (2021).
18. See https://analystprep.com/blog/financial-models/, [accessed 23 June 2022]
19. See Jeet (2020), Pangburn and Green (2021), PitchBook (2020), Pazzula (2021), and Saket (2022).
20. See, for example, Burgiss blog, 'Best Practices: Creating Scenarios and Analyzing the Takahashi–Alexander Forecast Model Results'. July 2021. https://www.burgiss.com/best-practices-using-takahashi-alexander, [accessed 3 August 2022], Lenz et al. (2018), Jeet (2020), and Karatas et al. (2021)
21. See Takahashi and Alexander (2002). Note that several authors, for example Fraser-Sampson (2006), mean the multi-asset-class investment strategy pioneered by the Yale endowment's David Swensen (see Swensen, 2000) when they confusingly also refer to the 'Yale model'.
22. See Brown et al. (2021).
23. See Love (2009).

CHAPTER 2

Institutional Investing in Private Capital

The organised market for private capital is dominated by funds as principal financial intermediary. In fact, McKinsey (2020) defines private markets in general as closed-ended funds, as well as related secondaries and funds of funds (FOFs). These funds are structured as limited partnerships with a contractually set lifetime.

Funds fulfil several functions. They allow the pooling of capital for investing in private assets, such as start-up companies, real estate objects, airports, etc., and delegating the investment process to fund managers with significant experience and the proper incentives to screen, evaluate, and select potential companies with expected high growth opportunities.

Fund managers have the necessary expertise to finance, for instance, companies that develop new product and technologies and to foster their growth and development by controlling, coaching, and monitoring these companies' management. Finally, the fund managers source exit opportunities and realise capital gains on disposing portfolio companies.

LIMITED PARTNERSHIPS

Funds in a private market context are usually set up as an asymmetric limited partnership. Here, institutional investors are the fund's 'limited partners' (LPs) who commit a certain amount to the fund and do not take an active role in its management. In this book, LPs are referred to as the institutional investors that provide the capital for commitments to private capital funds. To avoid the potentially significant liabilities, the LPs relinquish their ability to manage the business in exchange for limited liability for the partnership's debts. Also, regulatory and taxation-related requirements drive the structuring of these investment vehicles.

The term 'general partner' (GP) refers to the firm as an entity that is legally responsible for managing the fund's investments and who has unlimited liability for the debts and obligations. The funds are raised every few years on a blind pool basis, i.e. they are formed for investing in a designated strategy but hold no assets yet. 'Fund managers' are the investment professionals involved in the fund's day-to-day management. They form the fund's management team that includes the carried interest holders, i.e. those employees or directors of the GP who are entitled to share in the 'super profit' made by the fund.

STRUCTURE

While limited partnerships are widely perceived as typical for private equity, also infrastructure funds are usually structured in this way,[1] and, according to Arnold et al. (2017), private equity real estate (PERE) funds organised as limited partnerships play an important role in real estate capital formation and development.[2]

While terms and conditions, and investor rights and obligations, were defined in specific non-standard partnership agreements, the limited partnership structure – or comparable structures used in the various jurisdictions – has evolved over the past few decades into a 'quasi-standard' (see **Figure 2.1**). A detailed discussion of the legal aspects of this structure is beyond the scope and purpose of this book; the relevant points for this discussion are as follows:

- The fund usually has a contractually defined limited life of 7–10 years. The fund manager's objective is to realise all investments before or at the liquidation of the partnership. Often there is a provision for an extension of one to two years.
- Investors – mainly institutions such as pension funds, endowments, FOFs, banks or insurance companies, or high-net-worth individuals or family offices – are the

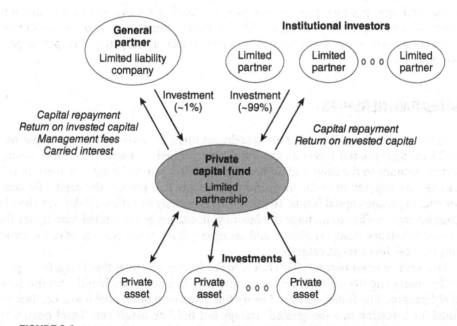

FIGURE 2.1 Limited partnership structure (simplified economic perspective)

LPs and commit a certain amount to the fund. There is little, if any, opportunity to redeem the investment before the end of the fund's lifetime.

- The main part of the capital is drawn down during the 'investment period', typically four or five years, where new opportunities are identified. After that, during the 'divestment period', only the existing and successful portfolio companies will be further supported, with some follow-on funding provided to extract the maximum value through exits. The manager's efforts during this time are concentrated on realisations through selling the investments.

- 'Committed capital' is the total amount that the LPs promise to deploy to a fund over its lifetime. Commitments are contributed as needed, i.e. 'just-in-time' to make investments or to pay costs, expenses, or management fees.

- Because funds typically do not retain a pool of un-invested capital, their managers make capital calls when they have identified an opportunity to invest in. LPs who default on their contributions risk penalties and legal action. If no suitable investment opportunities are found, funds may even end up returning some of the capital to the LPs.

- Paid-in capital is how much money the LPs have put into the fund. The difference between committed capital and paid-in capital is called 'undrawn commitment', representing the amount that LPs are still obliged to contribute to the fund.

- When realisations are made, or when interest payments or dividends are received from the assets held by the fund, they are distributed to the LPs as soon as practical. Thus, from the LP's perspective, the fund is 'self-liquidating' as the fund managers realise the underlying investments. However, LPs typically have no right to demand that realisations be made, and these returns are coming mostly in the second half of the fund's lifetime up to its liquidation. Distributions can also be 'in kind' as securities of a portfolio company, normally provided that these securities are publicly tradable.

- The management fees depend on the size of the fund and of its investment focus. In the case of private equity, they generally range from 2.5% of committed capital for funds of less than €250 million to 1.5% for the largest buyout funds. To incentivise exits, the fees are often scaled down once the investment period has been completed and adjusted according to the proportion of the portfolio that has been divested. There are, however, considerable differences from one fund to the next, particularly relating to what the managers do with income and expenses from their investment activity, such as directorship fees or transaction costs. These can have an impact on the returns and often account for material differences between gross and net returns.

- The main incentive for the fund managers is supposed to be the 'carried interest' of, typically, 20% of the profits realised by the fund. Usually carried interest is subject to a 'hurdle rate', so that it only applies once investors have received their capital back and a minimum pre-agreed rate of return.

- The 'distribution waterfall' sets out how distributions from a fund will be split and in which priority they will be paid out, i.e. what amount must be distributed to the LP before the fund managers receive carried interest.

- Fund managers also often invest a significant share of their personal wealth into the fund to put themselves at risk in case of underperformance and to signal thereby their belief in their success. These incentives motivate fund managers to take large risks only when they believe that the potential returns are high, and thus align their interests with those of the LPs.

- The interests of the LPs are aligned with those of the fund managers mostly by the managers' own commitment into the fund and by the profit share or carried interest of the manager.
- From a strictly legal viewpoint, limited partnership shares are illiquid, while in practice secondary transactions occasionally take place.

As discussed in more detail in Meyer (2014), the limited partnership has ancient roots and is a time-proven structure for skilled and risk-taking professionals to pool funding from relatively risk-averse deep-pocket parties for investments in an environment of extreme uncertainty. Co-investments complement the limited partnership structure and form an important component in LPs' private capital portfolios.

CRITICISM

Institutional investors as well as the fund management firms regularly criticise the limited partnership structure. Their concerns mainly relate the costs the intermediation through funds implies and, from the firms' perspective, the effort to continuously raise follow-on funds.

Costs of intermediation

Some estimates put the cumulative costs of a closed-ended fund's compensation structure, including fees and carried interest, at five to seven percentage points per year. In theory, that makes cutting out the fund as middle-man and investing directly into private assets attractive. For a small investment programme, investing directly may be advantageous. But for larger allocations, the potential for cost savings will be less than widely expected. Investing directly comes with significant diseconomies of scale, and with increasing capital allocated to private markets, investors have no choice but to seek intermediation through funds.[3]

Inefficient fund raising

Open-ended 'evergreen' funds are often promoted as the solution to the alleged inefficiency associated with the regular need to fund raise, but they are also criticised as there is no mechanism for them to return capital to investors and they provide little incentive to managers to force exists from their investments. The periodical liquidation of closed-ended funds is essential for the LPs, because the exit and re-investment cycle allows them to withdraw capital from less competent fund managers or managers whose industry expertise has become obsolete. It also allows setting back the clock for new investors, who do not need to value and pay for an existing portfolio.

ADDRESSING UNCERTAINTY

Funds organised as limited partnerships are the vehicle of choice to deal with the extreme uncertainty of private market investing. Funds shield vulnerable projects and portfolio companies in their early stages and those being restructured in turnaround situations from disruptive market influences and through the undrawn commitments assure these private assets continued financing. Similar considerations apply to explorations and green field projects that are particularly susceptible to sudden changes in investor sentiment and are at risk of being cut off from sources of financing. To allow the value of private assets to increase, financial resources need to be provided on a sustained and predictable basis over a reasonably long time frame.

Moreover, private assets do not trade easily; also because they are difficult to value, a valuation is not a price with a market being 'obliged' to transact on. Creating exits with proceeds in line with the valuations requires private market networks, deal-making expertise, and incentives that most institutional investors are not able to provide. In an environment of uncertainty where valuations are largely appraisal based, the only way to give an investor confidence is by liquidating private assets and thus showing that valuations are 'real'.

CONCLUSION

The limited partnership structure has, for right or wrong reasons, been repeatedly criticised. With its success, it has been increasingly applied to situations where it makes less sense and where then workarounds and special structures (evergreen funds, NAV-based facilities, credit lines, GP-led transactions, pledge funds, etc.) emerge.

To paraphrase Sir Winston Churchill, the limited partnership may be the worst form of investing in private markets, except all those other forms that have tried from time to time. Cases where the limited partnership model has been argued as 'broken' or 'dead' are more likely to be describing a misapplication or an absence of the conditions that make this structure efficient. Variants such as co-investments aim to address some of its weaknesses, while other approaches such as open-ended evergreen structures or direct investments are either replacing one ill with the other or are even aggravating the problems.

NOTES

1. See Bitsch et al. (2010).
2. McKinsey (2019) observed that real estate assets had grown faster in open-ended vehicles. However, while the traditional drawdown vehicle has lost ground to more flexible structures, they saw the private-equity-style closed-end structures as 'not dead'.
3. See Meyer (2014).

CHAPTER 3

Exposure

Measuring exposure helps an investor to determine the composition of a portfolio and understand the consequences of such decisions. The meaning of the term 'exposure' appears to be so obvious that, to the best of our knowledge and as we discussed in Belev and Meyer (2022), which this chapter is based on, neither academic literature nor the industry has put forward a commonly accepted formal definition in the context of limited partnership funds. Some studies have focused on the risk aspect of exposure and, in particular, the market beta-related exposures of private equity.[1] Other works, like Mathonet and Meyer (2007), have focused on measuring exposure based on the distinction of invested versus committed capital.

For private assets, a target allocation cannot be bought like in the case of public equity or bonds. Rather, limited partners (LPs) commit to funds, and then, these commitments are called over time by the fund managers and gradually turned into investments in private asset. This, in combination with the illiquidity of private markets, creates confusion around the definition of *exposure* and requires taking a closer look at this.

For private equity, it takes on average five years for 80% of the LP's commitments to be called. This is approximately two years less in the cases of private debt and private real estate. Over time, the fund portfolio's net asset value (NAV) increases due to additional investments and its organic growth. Longer duration of the fund leads to a higher invested capital and NAVs and, as Schneider et al. (2022) pointed out, the impact of this delay on returns can be substantial.

As the fund matures, its managers are divesting the portfolio until it is fully liquidated and the called capital plus its gains (or minus its losses) is returned to the LPs (see **Figure 3.1**).

EXPOSURE DEFINITION

According to the Cambridge Dictionary, *exposure* is 'the fact of experiencing something or being affected by it because of being in a particular situation or place'.[2] Two aspects matter in this context: the position already taken and making changes to this position subsequently.

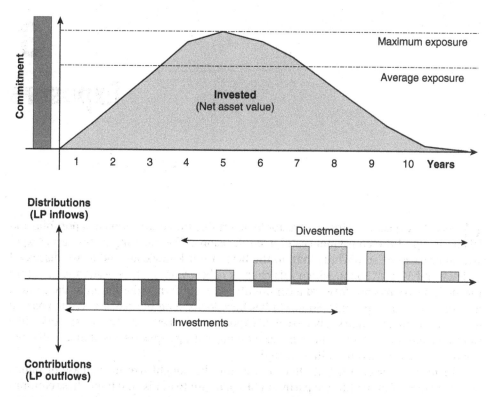

FIGURE 3.1   Commitments, investments, and cash-flows

- **Position:** Exposure is a measure for the investor's position in an asset at a given point in time. Through investing in one asset, investors take a position and thus forgo the opportunity to earn a higher return through another investment. By building a portfolio with exposures to various assets, the investor aims to 'stack a deck of cards' to benefit as much as possible from anticipated developments in the market. Investors can magnify their exposure through leverage[3] or reduce it through hedging.
- **Changing position:** Investors would prefer to be able to measure and manage their exposures actively. This is because an investor needs to have the toolset to respond to changing views and market circumstances, comparable to both rebalancing and active management familiar with the public asset portfolio management. For reference, there are no readily available passive investment vehicles in private asset investing comparable to ETFs for public equities. While some academics and managers claim to accomplish broad replication of private equity using public investments, this practice is not part of the mainstream private asset investment process.[4] Therefore, the LP both has to build the portfolio of funds and adjust it over time.

Financial exposure is commonly viewed as 'the amount an investor stands to lose in investment should the investment fail'[5] and basically describes the fact of being exposed to a risk.[6]

Exposure to liquid assets is occasionally also referred to as the market value of a position.[7] For liquid markets, this is consistent with the definition of *exposure* as the invested amount and thus at risk. Here, an asset can be sold off and bought back at any point in time at market value; holding on to a position is equivalent to liquidating the asset and investing in it anew. For illiquid private assets, this does not work. We, therefore, define *exposure* as the capital remaining at a given point in time from the originally invested amount that an investor stands to lose should the investment fail.[8] Actually, what is termed 'investment' differs depending on whether this is looked at from the LP's or from the fund manager's perspective.

LAYERS OF INVESTMENT

There are two layers of investing: the LP is 'investing' by committing to a fund and then the fund is investing in private assets. A fund at the beginning of its lifetime will have no portfolio and, therefore, has nothing invested yet. At the same time, its LPs are exposed to the total committed amount into the fund (see **Figure 3.2**).

The principal components that comprise a fund's exposure are its NAV and its undrawn commitments.

Net asset value

The fund's NAV reflects its managers' best estimate of the current market value of the portfolio companies held and other assets of the fund, less any fund liabilities. Market values can only be approximated through appraisal techniques. Being an estimate, it is subject to the biases and incentives of the manager.

Arguably, this is one of the biggest challenges to the quantification of exposure, as it implicitly assumes a metric that is derivable for both public and private assets. While definitions appear to be similar, they are not comparable. Public asset valuations are largely synonymous to price, whereas for private assets there is no market that is 'obliged' to transact on the NAV.

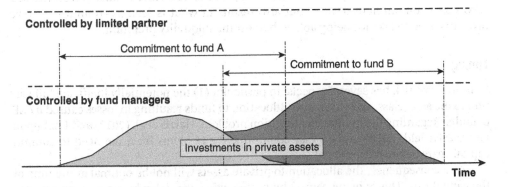

FIGURE 3.2 LPs indirectly controlling investments in private assets

Undrawn commitments

Many LPs, especially the larger ones, and also regulators view undrawn commitments as irrelevant. In this view, each individual asset – uncalled capital as well as the investment in private assets – is considered to be priced correctly; therefore, no opportunity costs arise and there appears to be no need for investors to take unfunded commitments into account. This, however, needs to be questioned.

Investors often fail to realise that internal rates of return (IRRs) published for funds only give an incomplete picture. The IRR ignores the undrawn commitments and implicitly assumes that distributions are reinvested at the same rate of return as the overall portfolio. Just because the fund had achieved an 'X% IRR', the individual LP will not have realised the same result. These returns may be lower if distributions are reinvested in lower returning assets or remain in cash. Schneider et al. (2022) calculated that, based on the average pacing of capital calls and distributions and a low and negative real yield environment for treasury assets, the 'cash drag' from undrawn commitments would be upward of 5% for a fund with an IRR target of 15%.

The impact for the LP is rather related to how the commitment to the fund is financed. We can model a fund as two instruments: the LP's undrawn commitment to the fund and the corresponding loan by the fund to the LP.[9] In this view, the undrawn commitments are un-invested and with opportunity costs, reflecting the fund's future investments and thus also the fund manager's quality.

Consistently achieving and maintaining a targeted exposure to private assets is the key to reaping the expected rewards. That the LP has no control over how the fund invests and divests creates commitment risk.

COMMITMENT RISK

Not being forced to redeem and being able to rely on funding in the form of the LPs' committed capital allows fund managers to pursue long-term-oriented strategies that have a higher chance to generate excess returns. However, the differences between commitments that the LP controls and the amount of private assets actually invested by the fund – what the LP actually wants – can be substantial. The closed-ended fund structure serves as a commitment device[10] but also results in what is seen as commitment risk investors need to take for being able to harvest the illiquidity premium.

Timing

Commitment risk has several aspects, in particular (1) the potentially inefficient allocation to the asset class, and (2) an over-allocation to funds resulting in losses caused by LP defaults. Regarding the inefficient allocation problem, Harris et al. (2012) and Phalippou and Westerfield (2014) explain that commitment risk stems from the need to commit capital years before it is invested.

As a consequence, the allocation to private assets will not be optimal at the time of the capital call. This is being caused by timing risk – the delay being the commitment and the actual investment being stochastic – and by quantity risk: during this delay, other sources of investor's wealth face random shocks, due to the uncertain time profile of capital calls and realisations that are outside the LP's control. To calculate the premium associated with commitment risk, Phalippou and Westerfield (2014) looked at the implications of being able to turn on and off timing certainty and to adjust commitments at the time of capital calls. They conclude that for private equity, this premium can be significant and equivalent to increasing investment returns by up to 1.63% per annum.[11]

Classification

How is the exposure to be labelled? Again we are faced with the question on whether to classify exposure on the fund or the private asset level. As practically LPs rely on primary commitments, they base their diversification on the self-proclaimed strategy stated by the fund managers (see Chapter 9).[12] Here, investors are taking the view that a fund's risk and return profile is mainly determined by this initially declared investment strategy and the fund manager's quality. This is because at the beginning of the fund existence, the fund strategy and the resulting composition of the portfolio only exist as the stated intentions of the manager and only become apparent after the fund starts calling capital and its portfolio of private assets evolves.

Such classifications, however, can only be very coarse, either by a specialist focus, e.g. by the majority of investments to be undertaken, or by broad labels like 'generalist'. Markets, strategies, teams, and portfolios evolve, and the true fund exposure will regularly deviate somewhat from the manager's initially declared strategy, which anyway often allows for some flexibility or has broad focuses (e.g. multi-country). This classification is 'through-the-lifetime', reflecting intention rather than the fund's current situation.

The mismatch between the initially declared strategy for a fund and the actual classifications of the private assets held is part of the commitment risk. One could argue that, in a large portfolio, this mismatch is to some degree diversified away, but when there are 'trendy strategies', which is often the case, this is probably not true anymore and even unexpected concentrations may emerge.[13] One could also see this as 'style drift'. For hedge funds, style drift is one of the areas that cause concerns for investors as it is seen as one of the major causes of investment failures in this asset class. A too close parallel to hedge funds is misguided as LPs of private capital funds need to follow a different modus operandi. In the hedge fund world, investors control and regularly rebalance their portfolios of funds – it is them who react to markets, and style drifts of a hedge fund clearly weaken their control. In private capital, a rebalancing of a portfolio of funds is clearly impractical. Because LPs cannot react to new information, they need to assure the portfolio's resilience by giving the fund managers flexibility and allowing them to adapt to changes in the market environment.

EXPOSURE MEASURES – LP'S PERSPECTIVE

From the LP's perspective, the exposure is the investment in a fund and 'consists of contributed capital, minus capital returned from exits and any write-downs of investment value'.[14] Practically, however, various LPs are using different definitions.

Commitment

In the context of private equity, Brown et al. (2020) define *exposure* as 'capital commitments to newly raised funds' (see **Figure 3.3**).

The commitment reflects what the LP made available from resources dedicated to private capital. Measuring the portfolio's exposure by commitments is obviously easy to apply, as exposure remains the same from the initial commitment until the full liquidation.

Brown et al. (2020) argue that the commitment size is the right measure for exposure 'in part, because investors can only time their commitments to funds; they cannot time when commitments are called or when investments are exited'. One stage of the investment process where the commitment size is particularly applicable as a measure of exposure is for constructing portfolios ex ante, i.e. before implementation.

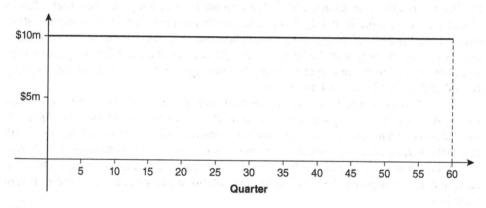

FIGURE 3.3   Commitment

When fund exposures are measured on a commitment basis, they keep a high weight even if close to expiry and until after all private assets have been fully realised and the resulting proceeds repaid to the LPs. This assumes that the exposure remains constant during the fund's lifetime and therefore provides no signal to add commitments to new funds to the portfolio.

The total commitment is a poor proxy of a fund's investment in private assets in absolute terms (only about 60% of the commitment will be truly invested; see **Figure 3.1**) but in relative terms, i.e. as percentage of a portfolio of funds, it can be a reasonable approximation.

Commitment minus capital repaid

'Commitment minus capital repaid' is another *exposure* definition commonly used by LP investors. Exposure measured in this way is decreasing over the fund's lifetime.

Defining exposure as commitment minus capital repaid has the advantage that this can easily be measured and does not require any subjective inputs. The problem with this measure is that that either the exposure can become negative or that an exposure remains, even after all the fund's private assets have been liquidated and the proceeds have been repaid to the LP (see **Figure 3.4**).

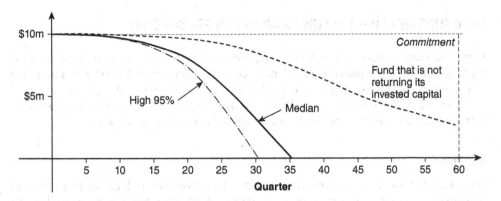

FIGURE 3.4 Commitment minus capital repaid

Repayment-age-adjusted commitment

To get around this problem, we can instead approximate the LP exposure at time t by looking at the fund's percentage (measured against accumulated repayments RP_t until time t) of total commitment that is still tied up in the fund at time t (see **Figure 3.5**):

$$Exposure_{LP,t} = Commitment * \left(1 - \frac{\sum_{i=0}^{t} RP_i}{NAV_i + \sum_{i=0}^{t} RP_i} \right).$$

From the LP's perspective, this can be good model for the exposure to a fund. It is easy to measure, is continuously declining, and, by definition, reaches zero precisely when the fund is mature, i.e. fully liquidated.

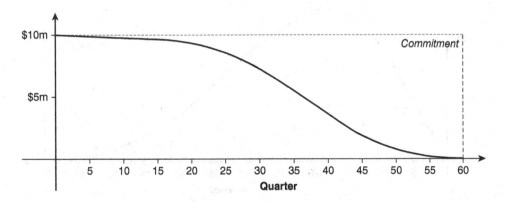

FIGURE 3.5 Repayment Age adjusted commitment

EXPOSURE MEASURES – FUND MANAGER'S PERSPECTIVE

From the fund manager's perspective, exposure to investments in private assets is the aggregate amount of capital contributions made to the company, reduced by the amount of distributions constituting return of capital, minus any write-downs of investment value.[15]

The following examples are based on the Takahashi–Alexander model[16] with $10 million committed to the fund, and an annual expected growth of 8%.

IPEV NAV

IPEV (2018) finds that, historically, the NAV 'based on the underlying Fair Value of Investments held by a Fund, as reported by the Fund Manager, has been used as the basis for estimating the Fair Value of an interest in an underlying Fund' (see **Figure 3.6**).

Private assets are difficult to value because they do not change hands often enough to reliably generate current market prices comparable with those of publicly traded securities. In the case of private assets, guidelines encode a market consensus on how to approach valuations under clearly specified assumptions. IPEV (2018) requires for the fair value measurement of unquoted investments to assume that 'the Investment is realised or sold at the Measurement Date whether or not the instrument or the Investee Company is prepared for sale or whether its shareholders intend to sell in the near future.' LPs often use the IPEV NAV measure for exposure, too. This practice is arguably anchored in the desire to assure comparability within a multi-asset class portfolio.[17]

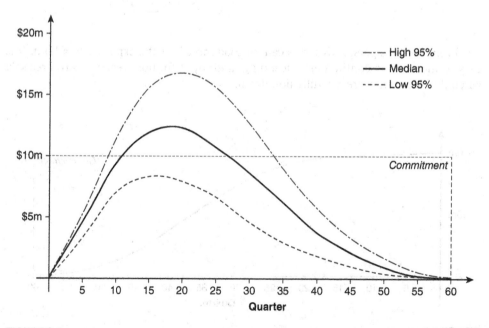

FIGURE 3.6   IPEV NAV

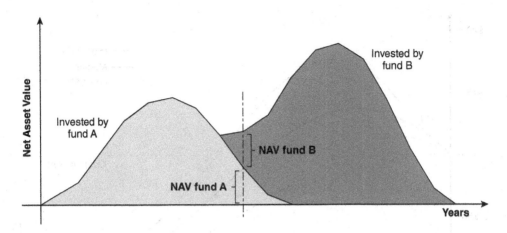

FIGURE 3.7 NAV and fund's age structure

What is problematic with this measure of exposure is that at the time of the first commitment, an IPEV NAV is zero. However, this is also the time when actually the LP's funding risk is highest as the fund is expected to call capital soon for its first, often substantive, investments in private assets.[18] As the NAV tends to exceed the capital drawn, it is not the capital invested by the fund. Another conceptual flaw of managing exposure on the private asset level is that the funds' maturity structure is ignored (see **Figure 3.7**).

Trying to change the existing portfolio composition and thus essentially driving the portfolio in the rear mirror resembles the situation of the age pyramid of a human population.[19]

IPEV NAV plus uncalled commitments

Another approach is to measure the portfolio's exposure by the IPEV NAV plus the uncalled commitments.[20] When investors use this approach, they take the view that the fund is characterised by the value of the private assets held and by uncalled commitments, reflecting the fund's declared investment strategy and the value added by the fund management team (see **Figure 3.8**). This is one way of how secondary markets for interests in private limited partnership funds look at exposure, factoring in the uncalled commitments in the pricing.[21]

Note that current financial regulation does not properly reflect the impact of the uncalled commitments. This weakens incentives to LPs to assess risk ex ante, i.e. before committing to the blind pool and can result in detrimental behaviour. According to Studer and Wicki (2010), Solvency II does not focus on liquidity requirements. For an insurer, in order to meet the solvency capital provisions, it is however important to analyse liquidity requirements stemming from its private equity commitments. In a stress scenario, the surplus capital will most likely decrease. Capital calls from undrawn private equity commitments will further increase the required solvency capital, while at the same time reducing the surplus capital.

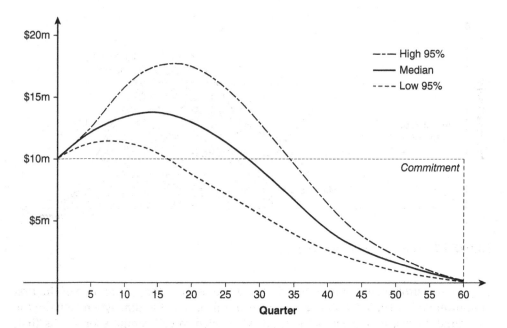

FIGURE 3.8 IPEV NAV plus uncalled commitment

Also, under Basel III, the minimum capital requirements for funds are not related to undrawn capital. Requirements for regulatory capital are split between private equity assets and undrawn commitments. The private-equity-specific treatment is related to the portfolio companies.

Repayment-age-adjusted accumulated contributions

The previous measures from the fund manager's perspective express exposure as market value of fund's portfolio instead of its invested capital. Murphy (2007) suggested that invested value (also referred to as 'unrealised cost basis') is a more appropriate metric for pacing commitments. Compared to the NAV, it is a more stable metric – thus dampening the impact of short-term market fluctuations – and less influenced by subjective valuation practices. Practically, measuring the fund's capital invested in private assets requires a look-through approach and data that are difficult to collect (see **Box 3.1**).

Instead, the invested capital can be approximated by looking at the percentage (measured against accumulated repayments RP_t until time t) of the accumulated capital called CC_t that is still tied up in private assets held by the fund at time t (see **Figure 3.9**):

$$Invested\ Capital_{Fund;t} = \left(\sum_{i=0}^{t} CC_i \right) * \left(1 - \frac{\sum_{i=0}^{t} RP_i}{NAV_i + \sum_{i=0}^{t} RP_i} \right).$$

Box 3.1 Approximating invested capital

According to ILPA, invested capital is the 'total amount of drawdown capital which has actually been invested in companies. In practice, this will be equal to the amount of drawdown capital less amounts which have been used to pay fees, or which are awaiting investment'

When trying to calculate the invested capital based on the logic that capital call is turned into private assets, which subsequently is turned into a realisation, we are faced with several problems:

- One capital call is turned to one or more private assets by the fund.
- Typically, one repayment relates to one private asset, but this cannot be guaranteed – everything is possible in private equity.
- Some private assets fail and are written off.

It is possible that one realisation exceeds the amount that was invested in a private asset, so the definition of *invested capital* needs to make sure that the realisation does not result in a negative invested capital. This can only be achieved if we register which capital calls resulted in and which realisations related to which private assets. To do this, the look-through and the associated transaction logic are needed, but this information is rarely available.

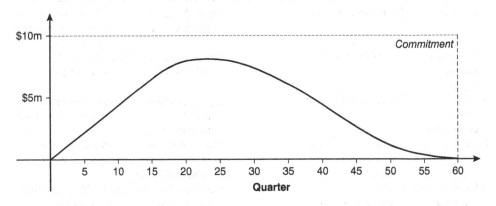

FIGURE 3.9 Repayment Age adjusted accumulated contributions to approximate invested capital

SUMMARY AND CONCLUSION

The exposure measures for funds discussed here and used by the industry have an often significantly varying impact during a fund's lifetime (see **Figure 3.10**). Investors arguably differentiate little between the LP's and the fund manager's perspectives on exposure; in practice, LPs tend to go along with the fund manager's focus on the NAV, mainly to assure compatibility across assets, quoted and private (see **Table 3.1**).

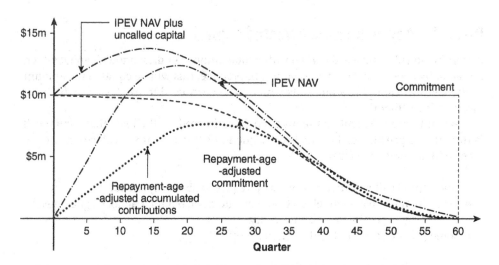

FIGURE 3.10   Summary (median exposure)

TABLE 3.1   Summary

Measurement		Reflecting uncalled capital?	Measuring capital invested	Comment
Commitment	Unambiguous	Yes	Upper bound for LP investment	Simple and one of the measures commonly used by LPs
Commitment minus capital repaid	Unambiguous	Yes	Upper bound for LP investment	Simple and often used by LPs
Repayment-age-adjusted commitment	Model based	Yes	Approximation for LP investment	Simple and robust but not commonly used
IPEV NAV	Valuation guidelines based	No	Can exceed capital invested by fund and by LP	Most widely used exposure measure
IPEV NAV plus uncalled commitments	Valuation guidelines based	Yes	Can exceed capital invested by fund and by LP	Most widely used basis for secondary market pricing
Repayment-age-adjusted accumulated contributions	Model based	No	Approximation for fund's invested capital	Simple and robust but not commonly used

The mismatch between definitions shrinks as the fund reaches maturity (unless exposure is measured by commitment), but during the time when exposures (and the associated risks) are largest, it can be significant and trigger LP investment decisions with adverse effects. To conclude, we view invested capital to be the most practical metric for pacing commitments and recommend to approximate this through the repayment-age-adjusted accumulated contributions.

An aspect we did not touch upon was environmental, social, and governance (ESG) factors. With increased scrutiny and interest in ESG, investors need to measure the exposure of investment also along these dimensions. However, the economics of exposure in this case are not straightforward. Here, a major complication is the question of reputational risk arising from an investor's exposure to ESG transgressions in her portfolio.[22] Here, and unlike the other risks that can be mitigated or diversified away, the risk of reputation-related damage grows as more investments are added to a portfolio. How to measure exposure in this context remains a question for future research.

While broad consensus on a single exposure metric is not practically achievable given the various ways to measure exposure, there still needs to be an alignment between the intended objective of a certain investment decision enacted by the LP based on any exposure metric and the actual effect of that decision. Therefore, a multifaceted view is important to take account of the relevant implications (see **Box 3.2**).

Box 3.2   Exposure efficiency

LPs manage their exposure to private assets through their commitment to funds, but for assessing diversification on the private asset level, LPs need to consider how efficiently the commitments on fund level over time turned into a real exposure to private assets.

EXPOSURE EFFICIENCY BASED ON THE EQUIVALENT NUMBER OF FUNDS

One of the first known approaches to tackle this question was a presentation by Rouvinez (2003) who discussed the concept of the equivalent number of funds (ENF).

Rouvinez argued that for seasoned funds of fund portfolios, the real diversification is often smaller than the number of funds suggested. Due to their different drawdown speed and development of their NAVs, funds have different weights in a portfolio. His approach derives from the *total exposure per fund* (TEXP) being defined as undrawn commitments + NAV.

To help managing diversification, the ENF aims to give the number of funds a homogenous portfolio would have to contain to show the same volatility of return as the original heterogeneous portfolio. According to Rouvinez, a reasonable approximation for a portfolio's ENF is

$$ENF = \frac{\left(\sum_{i=1}^{n} TEXP_i\right)^2}{\sum_{i=1}^{n} TEXP_i^2}$$

with n being the number of active funds in the portfolio. As an example, for a portfolio of three funds with TEXP equal to 1, 1, and 4, respectively, the formula suggests that a portfolio of two funds with equal exposure show the same volatility in returns:

$$\frac{(1+1+4)^2}{1^2+1^2+4^2} = \frac{36}{18} = 2.$$

The mathematics behind this approach was not disclosed in the presentation. However, intuitively, the approximation makes sense: if we have n funds with equal TEXP, the formula gives as ENF n, whereas in a situation where there is one fund with very large TEXP and $n-1$ funds of zero TEXP, the ENF is one. The ENF idea apparently was not picked up and developed further. To the best of the author's knowledge, no other papers were published that discuss the ENF.

One motivation of the ENF (as it reflects undrawn commitments) was to assess whether an LP really needs to commit to that many funds and, therefore, could be rather interpreted as shedding a light on costs; this measure could be extended by an LP cost model, as presented in Meyer and Mathonet (2005) (see **Chapter 9**).

EXPOSURE EFFICIENCY BASED ON INVESTED CAPITAL

We can approximate the LP's exposure $LP\_EXP_{n;t}$ to a fund n at time t by looking at the fund's percentage (measured against accumulated repayments $RP_{n;t}$ until time t) of total commitment that is still tied up in the fund at time t:

$$LP\_EXP_{n,t} = Commitment_n * \left(1 - \frac{\sum_{j=0}^{t} RP_{n;j}}{NAV_{n;t} + \sum_{j=0}^{t} RP_{n;j}}\right).$$

Moreover, we can approximate the invested capital $IVT\_CAP_{n;t}$ for a fund n at time t by looking at the percentage (measured against accumulated repayments $RP_{n;t}$ until time t) of the accumulated capital called $CC_{n;t}$ that is still tied up in private assets with value $NAV_{n;t}$ at time t:

$$IVT\_CAP_{n;t} = \left(\sum_{j=0}^{t} CC_{n;j}\right) * \left(1 - \frac{\sum_{j=0}^{t} RP_{n;j}}{NAV_{n;t} + \sum_{j=0}^{t} RP_{n;j}}\right).$$

Note that

$$LP\_EXP_{n,t} \geq IVT_{CAPn;t}.$$

Let us define the exposure efficiency XE_t at time t for a portfolio of n funds as

$$XE_t = \sum_{i=1}^{n} \frac{IVT\_CAP_{i;t}}{LP\_EXP_{i;t}}.$$

This ratio measures how much of the LP's committed capital is really turned into invested capital: $0 \leq XE_t \leq 1$. As in this ratio the second terms with NAVs and repayments are cancelling out, the XE only depends on commitments and capital calls.

Practically, LP's exposure can be managed mainly through primary commitments, as buying and selling are more constrained for illiquid private assets than they are for liquid public assets. For this purpose, LPs rely on commitment pacing, requiring cash-flow forecasting.

NOTES

1. See, for example, Anson (2013) or Belev and DiBartolomeo (2021).
2. See https://dictionary.cambridge.org/dictionary/english/exposure, [accessed 3 January 2022]
3. LPs, for instance, through over-commitments
4. For example, Chingono and Rasmussen (2015). See https://www.businesswire.com/news/home/20220110005016/en/PEO-Partners-Launched-by-Industry-Veterans-as-New-Private-Equity-Liquid-Alternatives-Firm, [accessed 2 May 2022]: 'PEO Partners' strategy selects Russell 3000 public equities that mirror the industries that traditional leveraged buyout firms invest in and the company characteristics that these LBO firms target, namely, high profitability, high payout ratio, and low multiples' or https://www.mackenzieinvestments.com/en/products/mutual-funds/mackenzie-private-equity-replication-fund, [accessed 2 May 2022].
5. See https://www.investopedia.com/terms/f/financial-exposure.asp, [accessed 1 December 2021] and https://www.ig.com/en/glossary-trading-terms/exposure-definition, [accessed 10 December 2021]: 'Financial exposure is the amount of capital that you stand to lose when you invest in an asset, otherwise known as *risk*.'
6. See https://wirtschaftslexikon.gabler.de/definition/exposure-36562, [accessed 3 January 2022]: 'Exposure bezeichnet grundsätzlich die Tatsache, einem Risiko ausgesetzt zu sein'
7. See https://capital.com/exposure-definition, [accessed 1 December 2021]: 'Exposure is an umbrella concept beneath which sit three distinct meanings. The first is the current market value of someone's open trading positions, including, of course, the impact on exposure of any leverage by way of derivatives. The second refers to the total amount of risk at any given moment, while the third refers to the percentage of an investment fund or trust that is invested in a particular market or asset. In all three cases, what is being discussed is the extent of someone's commitment to one or more assets.'
8. This is also in line with this definition of *financial exposure*: 'When investing, financial exposure is limited to the amount that you spend on opening a position – for example, if you invest in shares which become completely worthless, you would only lose the amount you paid. But, if you trade with leverage, your exposure increases because your capital is amplified beyond the initial outlay, known as your margin (deposit). In these cases, your profit and losses can be magnified.' See https://www.ig.com/en/glossary-trading-terms/exposure-definition#:~:text=Financial%20exposure%20explained&text=When%20investing%2C%20financial%20exposure%20is,lose%20the%20amount%20you%20paid, [accessed 19 February 2021]
9. The price the LP has to pay for this loan is the delta between the carried interest going to the fund managers that just takes the fund's invested capital into account and a hypothetical carried interest that takes the fund's committed capital as calculation basis. See Meyer (2020) for an in-depth discussion.
10. See Meyer (2014).

11. Note that this definition of commitment risk does not take the undrawn commitments into consideration.
12. Funds are initially blind pools, and at closing date, its manager's declared investment strategy is the best guess for the future strategy and its associated exposure.
13. Some LPs do a 'classification override' based on the look-through, reconstituting a fund's taxonomy after analysing the underlying portfolio, and if the majority of private assets are, say, in another geography than originally presented to the fund's investors, the fund will be relabelled accordingly. Arguably, this is an apple-to-oranges comparison: what the fund manager is originally declaring is related to the strategy applied over the fund's lifetime, whereas the classification override relates to a 'point-in-time' assessment of the underlying portfolio's composition.
14. See https://masteringprivateequity.com/glossary/, [accessed 3 January 2022]. See also Metrick and Yasuda (2010).
15. See de Zwart (2012): 'The key concept in our recommitment strategies is the investment degree, which measures the actual exposure of a private equity fund investment. Specifically, we defined the investment degree as the fraction of total capital that is actually invested in private equity.'
16. See Takahashi and Alexander (2002).
17. Another aspect of this exposure measure is that it is assumed to provide the right incentives to fund managers. In many cases, management fees are based on the full amount of committed capital, whether drawn down or not, minus capital that has been returned to investors from investments that have been exited. Basing management fees on the fair value of the private assets under management as reflected by the fund's NAV is often viewed as more attractive by fund managers. During the investment period, they tend to be fixed based on the commitment size, so not put pressure to engage in hasty deal-making.
18. The contrarian argument is that at time zero, the value of the fund is equal to total committed capital. Meyer (2020) argues that exposure needs to be looked at from the viewpoint of how the LP's investment is financed: the LP has bought the stake in the fund at time zero for its value, i.e. the commitment, and then is borrowing the proceeds as they are not needed yet. So, at time zero, from the LP's perspective, the exposure is: commitments (proceeds to buy LP stake) – commitments (borrowing from GP) = 0, thus aligning the two perspectives.
19. 50% men and 50% women may be OK, but it is definitely not a healthy balance if the population only comprises women over the age of 90 and men under the age of 10. It is not possible to change the composition of an age group later, except through immigration (secondary buys may be the equivalent from the LP's perspective) or over the very long term where the previous population is eventually replaced entirely.
20. Rouvinez (2003) defines the exposure to a fund as undrawn commitments + NAV.
21. See Meyer (2020).
22. Reputational risk increases if investors have specific responsibility; slightly sarcastically, if everybody is doing it, reputational risk is low.

CHAPTER 4

Forecasting Models

For investors in private capital funds, the Takahashi–Alexander model (TAM[1]), also often called the 'Yale model', is the cash-flow forecasting work horse. The TAM models a fund's contributions, distributions, as well as the net asset value (NAV)'s development over the fund's lifetime deterministically. Therefore, in contrast to a stochastic model, a single run of this model creates just one result for one set of input parameters and not a range of outcomes. Stochastic models that describe the dynamics of private capital funds probabilistically have been proposed, but analysts often prefer deterministic models. Simple as it appears, the TAM is difficult to beat; in many practical settings, it has better fitting properties and is viewed as more robust than its stochastic competitors. The TAM is computationally cheap, and it is precisely its simplicity that makes it easier for an analyst to identify causal relationships between input parameters and outcomes.

In this chapter, we will take a closer look at various approaches to forecasting and, in a later chapter, follow-on with a solution that combines their respective strengths and weaknesses: a stochastic model that is a probabilistic augmentation of the TAM and is compatible with it.

BOOTSTRAPPING

Around the time the TAM was conceived, cash-flow forecasting for private equity funds was tackled in the context of securitisations, i.e. collateralised private equity fund obligations. In 1999, the first securitisation of interests in a portfolio of funds took place when Partners Group closed the Princess Private Equity Holding Limited (Princess) deal.[2] To assess such securitisations, analysts followed a bootstrapping approach, sampling directly from historical funds' cash-flow data sets, also known as 'cash-flow libraries'.[3] Each sampled cash flow is then scaled to the size of the fund being modelled. This approach combines simplicity and robustness with the ability to capture variations in scenarios. The essential advantage of the bootstrap is that it is agnostic about probability density functions (PDFs) and can capture all kind of 'nasty' behaviours such as fat tails and jumps. Bootstrapping is particularly useful when there is little knowledge of the underlying process to be modelled and thus is often viewed as the 'gold standard' for modelling cash flows. **(see Box 4.1)**

The core belief is that the better we understand the past, the better we are at forecasting, with historic cash flows being able to capture the true dynamics of private capital funds. The underlying assumptions are that the pattern, i.e. the timing and amounts of cash flows, is the same regardless of the fund's quality, that a scaling can reflect the market's conditions, and that future funds will show the same dynamics.

Since the early 2000s, rating agencies, such as Fitch,[4] Moody's,[5] Standard & Poor's,[6] and DBRS,[7] have been relying on data from publicly available sources for cash-flow data, from Venture Economics (now defunct) and in recent years mainly from Burgiss and Cambridge Associates. The rating methodologies are very conservative, and apparently the available data are biased towards the universe of institutional quality funds. Kalra et al. (2006) saw limitations to this methodology; it only works if the data sets are comprehensive, reliable, and unbiased or, alternatively, conservatively adjusted. Moreover, the history needs to span a minimum of 10 vintage years to be able to model a realistically diversified portfolio.

Box 4.1   Black box and white box models

Simplistically, we can follow two antithetic methodologies for modelling. 'Black box' models deduce the relationship between a system's inputs and outputs based on the evidence gathered during an initial training phase. Such data-driven black models can be too complex to be straightforwardly interpretable to humans, which can undermine trust in the forecasts and limit their application, notably for risk-management purposes. Moreover, this approach depends on the availability of significant amounts of high-quality and up-to-date data, something that in private markets is difficult to get by.

'White box' models, on the other hand, are process-based, i.e. they take the knowledge of a system's internal logic into account and capture the relationship between its inputs and outputs by analytical approaches. While such models are often viewed as too simplistic, they are more transparent, and their results are easier to understand and explain. This categorisation is simplistic, but for cash-flow forecasting, the so-called 'bootstrapping' and 'machine learning' are black box models, whereas the TAM and stochastic models are largely white boxes.

Collecting a comprehensive and up-to-date data set is a cumbersome and expensive process.[8] Larger fund-of-funds players tout and enviously protect the rich histories in their data warehouses – with several thousand mature fund cash flows – that allow them to credibly simulate future cash flows of portfolios of funds.[9]

MACHINE LEARNING

A variation of bootstrapping is machine learning (ML), which in recent years has also been applied to forecasting cash flows for private equity funds. Here, in an approach similar to bootstrapping, ML-based models are trained based on historical funds' cash-flow data sets.

Based on their preliminary results, Karatas et al. (2021) claimed that the cash flows predicted in this way were aligned well with the actual cash flows. For the study, they used a set of quarterly fund performance data of 606 North American buyout funds reported by Preqin with a vintage year between 2000 and 2013. Removing funds with insufficiently complete cash flows reduced the data set to 371. The researchers found an improvement at capturing future cash-flow patterns compared to the quarterly adjusted (i.e. the annual cash flow divided by four) TAM, but were not able to provide more thorough comparative and back-testing results yet, which were announced to be added later as a future extension.

It is questionable whether the TAM is a meaningful reference: an ML approach should at least pick up the cyclicality of management fee payments, whereas the TAM does not go down to this level of detail.

The promise of ML lies in recognising things that humans are unable to do, such as detecting patterns in rich data sets that capture more context, notably macroeconomic data, stock market indices, and foreign exchange (FX) rates. However, the combination of small sample sizes with a lot of descriptive but probably irrelevant data is likely to result in overfitting, i.e. a model that has learned the noise instead of the signal and finds meaningless regularity (see **Box 4.2**). ML algorithms are 'lazy' and can quickly learn to 'cheat'. If not well designed, they effectively look for hints that boost probabilities but have nothing to do with the problem and, therefore, have no predictive value.[10]

The issues are essentially the same as for bootstrapping, i.e. the data required for training the model are difficult and expensive to get. For long-term projections, ML is essentially a different means for memorising the cash flow's 'standard curve'.[11] Due to the high costs for accessing, collecting, and maintaining the necessary data, the confidentiality issue associated with proprietary data and notably the black box nature of these techniques make these not viable options for most LPs.

Box 4.2 Machine learning limitations

Intuitively, we assume that 'more' is always better, whether computational power or amount of data. Artinger et al. (2015) researched the importance of heuristics, i.e. simple strategies that require little information but can be powerful, often outperforming artificial intelligence (AI) that makes use of Big Data. Simplicity can also help when a prediction is out of reach because we are faced with uncertainty, i.e. situations where not all alternatives, consequences, and probabilities are known. The authors, however, point out that it is often a challenge to discover powerful simple strategies.

It comes down to the argument made by Artinger that the hype surrounding AI is based on the claim that complex ML algorithms allow us to effectively address a complex world. Contrary to this belief, simpler and more robust models show similar promise, with the important advantage of being less susceptible to overfitting. The benchmark remains the performance of traditional techniques, which in most cases are difficult to beat and do not justify the additional cost and complexity that comes with ML.

TAKAHASHI-ALEXANDER MODEL

Justifiably, due to its wide adoption and its impact, the TAM has been called the 'mother of all cash-flow models'.[12] The TAM can be applied to private equity, private debt, and real asset funds, such as natural resources and infrastructure. It mirrors the limited partnership's actual investment cycle, distinguishing contributions as cash inflows, distributions as cash outflows, and the NAV, representing the fund's underlying assets. How the fund managers invest and divest drives the contribution and distribution characteristics from the LP's point of view. The TAM has an annual granularity, i.e. models cash flows year-by-year and portfolios are modelled fund-by-fund.

Model dynamics

The TAM describes a fund's development through a set of mathematical equations without any variables to give a random behaviour. For a given set of inputs, a unique set of outputs is produced.

The input parameters are the fund's capital commitment, its lifetime in years, its yearly rates of contributions, and the NAV's annual growth rate in per cent. A 'yield' and a so-called 'bow factor' together describe changes in the rate of distribution over time. For income-generating asset types such as real estate, the yield sets the minimum distribution level. As output, the model projects the fund's expected capital contributions, expected distributions, and expected NAVs (see **Figure 4.1**).

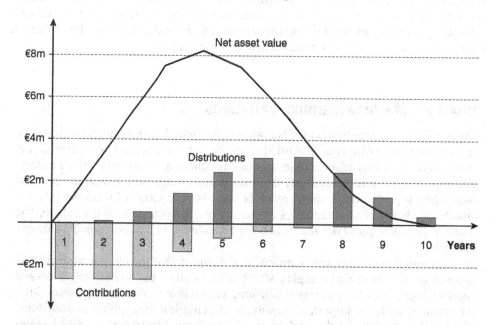

FIGURE 4.1 Forecast generated by the TAM under the following assumptions: commitment size €10.000.000, fund's lifetime of 10 years, NAV's annual growth rate is 10%, contribution rates 25% for year 1, 33.33% for year 2, and 50% for all following years, a bow factor of 2, and a yield of zero. By construction, the IRR of the contributions and distributions is 10%, consistent with the annual growth rate, and the fund generates a TVPI of 1,42.

Investing in a fund starts with committing capital. Staying with the notation used by Takahashi and Alexander (2002), the committed capital CC is not invested immediately and in full, but is called by the fund managers 'just in time', i.e. whenever there is an investment opportunity. The paid-in capital in year t $PIC_{(t)}$ consists of the total of capital contributions $C_{(t)}$ in previous years t:

$$PIC_{(t)} = \sum_{0}^{t-1} C_{(t)}.$$

The undrawn commitment is CC minus the total of contributions in previous years. The net contribution for the year is determined by the rate of contribution in year $0\% \le RC_{(t)} \le 100\%$ that varies with the current age of the fund and defines what percentage of the remaining capital commitment is called. The contributions for year t depend on the initial amount of committed capital, the amount of capital that is already paid-in and on $RC_{(t)}$:

$$C_{(t)} = RC_{(t)} * \left(CC - PIC_{(t)}\right).$$

Takahashi and Alexander (2002) define $RC_{(t)}$ in an annual schedule, which theoretically could be customised for each fund, but in practice this is rather done per sub-asset class or vintage year. In situations where the undrawn commitment is zero, there obviously will not be any contribution. However, a schedule based on contribution rates implies that the commitment will never be fully funded – this is representative of reality where funds often underinvest and do not call all the capital pledged.[13]

Every year a portion of the fund's NAV is distributed. The distributions $D_{(t)}$ in year t depend on the rate of distribution RD, the $NAV_{(t)}$ as the valuation of the portfolio held by the fund, and the fund's fixed growth rate $G \ge -100\%$:

$$D_{(t)} = RD * NAV_{(t-1)} * \left(1+G\right).$$

The NAV increases with positive G and/or new contributions. It decreases with the distributions and/or negative G:

$$NAV_{(t)} = NAV_{(t-1)} * \left(1+G\right) + C_{(t)} - D_{(t)}.$$

G combines both realised and unrealised returns. While the rate of contributions is set according to a schedule for each year, the TAM assumes the rate of distributions to be dependent on the fund's lifetime L and the greater of the fixed yield Y or a rate proportional to the age of the fund and a bow factor B:

$$RD = MAX\left[Y, \left(\frac{t}{L}\right)^{B}\right].$$

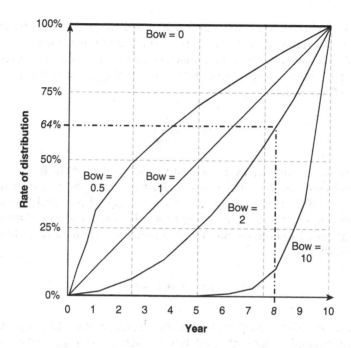

FIGURE 4.2   Bow factor

Essentially, this function describes whether the rate of distribution increases or decreases during the fund's life. Depending on B, the rate of distribution is larger either in the beginning or in the end of the fund's lifetime. Plotting the relationship between a fund's age and its distribution rates for various B (between 0 and 20; according to Burgiss, 2021) shows that for $B = 1$ it is a straight line, whereas for $B \neq 1$, it follows a curve, hence the term 'bow factor' (see **Figure 4.2**).

For $B = 1$, the rate of distribution does not change from year to year (see **Figure 4.3**). For example, for a fund with lifetime $L = 10$, each year 10% of the $NAV_{(t)}$ at this time would be distributed. For $B > 1$, the rate of distribution increases with the age of the fund, while for $B < 1$, it is larger in the fund's early years. The higher the bow factor, the longer it takes for significant distributions to set in before accelerating as the fund matures. So, for example, if $B = 2$ and the fund with an assumed lifetime of 10 years is in its eighth year, then the rate proportional to the age of the fund is

$$\left(\frac{8}{10}\right)^2 = 64\%.$$

This rate appears to be quite large, but for this maturing fund, there are just two years to fully liquidate.

For $B < 1$, the curve is concave. $B = 0$ describes the extreme where the entire $NAV_{(t)}$ for the year is always paid out immediately (see **Figure 4.4**).[14]

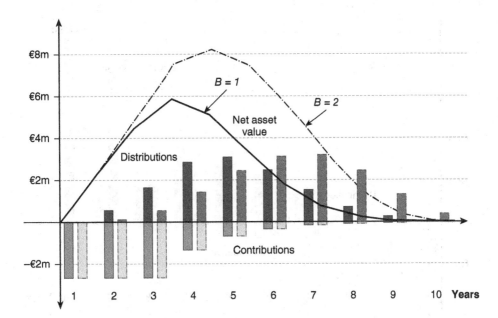

FIGURE 4.3 Forecast generated by the TAM, with a bow factor of 1 but otherwise the same assumptions as in **Figure 4.1**. Note, that the fund's IRR is still 10% but that its TVPI has come down to 1,25. This is caused by the fact that a lower bow factor implies that exiting the portfolio is accelerated and therefore the investment in private assets reflected in the NAV has less time to grow (for a negative growth rate the effect, however, would be reversed).

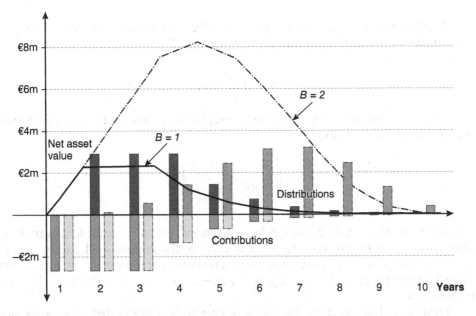

FIGURE 4.4 Impact of reducing the bow factor to zero. Again, the fund's IRR is 10% but now whatever has been contributed and invested is exited immediately after one year (reflecting that the TAM's granularity is annual). Consistent with a 10% annual growth of the capital called, the fund's TVPI is 1,1 – under the TAM's logic the lowest possible for an IRR of 10%.

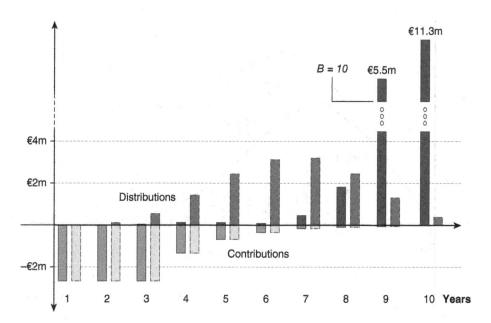

FIGURE 4.5 Impact of setting a high bow factor, in this case 10. Distributions are pushed back toward the fund's end of lifetime. By construction, the fund's IRR is always the same as the assumed growth rate, here 10%, but because the investments reflected in the NAV have a longer time to grow (reaching a maximum NAV of €14.5m), the high bow factor implies also a larger TVPI, i.e. 1,91.

For $B > 1$, the curve is convex, with $B \to \infty$ the extreme where the entire $NAV_{(t)}$ is paid out at the very end (see **Figure 4.5**), i.e. when $t = L$ and

$$RD = \left(\frac{L}{L}\right)^{B} = 1.$$

The rate of distribution can, of course, never be larger than 1; otherwise, more than the NAV would be distributed:

$$RD = MIN\left[1, \left(\frac{t}{L}\right)^{B}\right].$$

The yield $0\% \leq Y \leq 100\%$ is introduced to make the TAM useful for a variety of asset classes (see **Figure 4.6**). It sets a minimum distribution level and is used to model income-generating asset types, such as real estate or infrastructure. Funds with assets like venture capital may not generate a yearly income. In such cases, the yield is set to zero.

Yield can be interest, rental payments, but it can also describe depleting assets such as oil and gas. The higher the yield, the more accelerated the capital is distributed to the LP (see **Figure 4.7**).

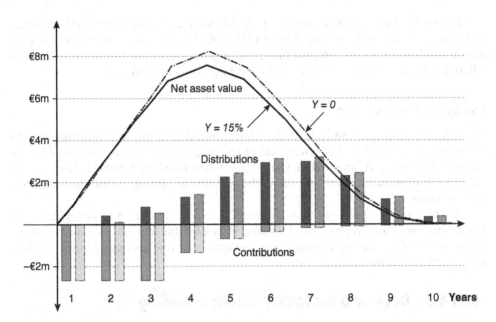

FIGURE 4.6 Forecast generated by the TAM, with a yield of 15% but otherwise the same assumptions as in Figure 1. The fund's IRR remains at 10% but the TVPI is now lower: 1,39. This is because also here the yield implies an accelerated distribution, thus giving the private assets reflected in the NAV less time to grow.

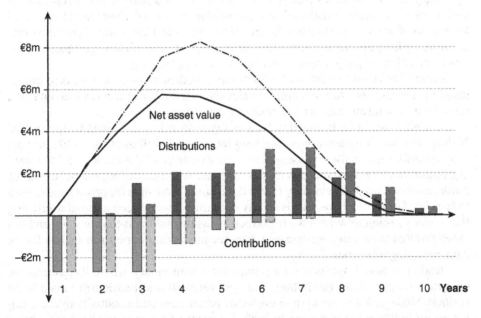

FIGURE 4.7 Impact of increasing the yield to 30% (compared to **Figure 4.6**). This reinforces the effect described before and results in an even lower TVPI of 1,31.

By construction, and irrespective of all the other parameters, the TAM generates cash flows with an internal rate of return (IRR) that is equal to G. Note that the TAM does not differentiate between cash flow types and does not show how much of the distributed amount is generated by the yield and how much by realisations.[15]

Strengths and weaknesses

According to Takahashi and Alexander (2002), and despite the TAM's simplicity, the projections generated fit historical data surprisingly well. This is supported by the arguments made in Artinger et al. (2015) that when faced with extreme uncertainty, complex problems are often best solved with a simple strategy where few variables are sufficient.

As the TAM is a parameter-driven model, it can be used even in novel situations where there are no or insignificant historical data available and rely on expert opinion. Per se the TAM has no forecasting value, the quality of the forecasts depends on how well the model's parameters are set.

Box 4.3   Data- and parameter-driven modelling

A data-driven approach uses historical cash flows from comparable funds to forecast. The alternative is a parameter-driven approach where the behaviour of the fund is modelled by inputs based on historical experience or provided by experts. This is essentially following the model classification proposed by Cox (1981), i.e. observation- and parameter-driven specifications (also see Koopman et al., 2012).

The TAM is a parameter-driven model with its information being represented within its parameters. Takahashi and Alexander developed their model based on known facts about closed-ended funds, taking historical data and experience into account. In fact, the delineation is not as clearly cut; one could argue that a data-driven model is simply just using historical data as parameters.

Researchers tend to work with observations as their priority usually is to understand the process, its structure, and the relevant factors. Whether historical data sets, the direction of future data is of secondary consideration.

Applying this in an investment forecasting context is constrained by the lack of high-quality and long-term data. For long-term-oriented illiquid assets like private capital funds, we can also not assume that the dynamics of the market and the asset class has remained constant; this may be the case when modelling the behaviour of public markets based on relatively recent data, but reliable data for private assets tend to be several years old; here, past is clearly not future and we need to avoid overfitting the model's parameter where we introduce a bias by making it too complex and too closely related to an outdated data set where the model cannot perform against future data, defeating its purpose.

Testing is more important for a parameter-driven model, where its assumption on structure, parameter estimation, and past versus future relationship need to be verified. Model risk related to the number of parameters and sensitivity to changing behaviour in illiquid markets can be high. Parameter-driven models have the advantage that they are flexible and can easily be applied in new settings. Where no reliable data are available, parameters can be set by experts or can be stressed.

While the TAM appears to explain the dynamics of illiquid funds quite nicely, one should not overly rely on this depiction being accurate. The NAV figure is determined by the model's inner logic. It must not be confused with the real accounting figures for the NAV reported by the fund manager and will rarely be reconcilable with them. The annual growth rate is assumed to be constant, i.e. identical to the fund's IRR on realisation. To address these weaknesses, several researchers and practitioners have been looking at how to improve on the TAM.

Variations and extensions

Tolkamp (2007) created an extension where one performance index drives the returns of all individual vintage years of a portfolio of funds. This index can then be related to the macroeconomic environment that facilitates the funds' performance. It consists of growth rates $G_{(t)}$ the funds were able to generate in that specific year. Tolkamp's model does not assume fixed yearly NAV growth rates, but a specific growth rate affects every vintage year. It is pooling cash flows and related performance numbers and models entire vintage years of funds. This modification of the TAM is used to fit projected performance data to actual performance data for the purpose of deriving an index.

The TAM assumes that distribution rates generally accelerate, driven by a bow factor larger than one, as the fund advances in maturity. Aspequity's 'Bow-Speed Time Option Normalised' (BOSTON) model is structurally similar to the TAM but accounts for the fact that the manager has less of an option to delay exits as the fund is approaching the end of its lifetime.[16]

Hoek (2007) presented another version of the TAM using aggregate data from Venture Economics for US venture capital and buyouts for estimates. A group of investment experts were consulted to critically evaluate whether the dynamics generated by the model are sufficiently in accordance with the behaviour of private equity in real life. Like Tolkamp (2007), Hoek (2007) also assumes that both the rate of return $G_{(t)}$ and the distribution rate $RD_{(t)}$ are stochastic with $G_{(t)}$ depending on the return on public equity but with 'marking-to-market' valuations taking place with some delay. The author discusses further extensions with a stochastic model (see **Box 4.4**) also for the contribution rate. While Hoek describes his model as 'stochastically extended', it nevertheless also creates just one result for one set of input parameters and not a range of outcomes.

Box 4.4 Deterministic versus stochastic models

A major shortcoming of the simple TAM is that it does not offer an intuitive link to market dynamics and uncertainty. Deterministic models do not reproduce the erratic nature of real-world-fund cash flows, and ignoring the underlying process's randomness can mislead: the forecast only represents the average and, as we only consider one scenario, is essentially always wrong.

This may still work well for the Yale endowment with its highly diversified portfolio of funds where the aggregated cash-flow pattern looks smooth and stable, but investors with relatively concentrated portfolios should be aware that individual fund cash flows may vary widely, and therefore, returns are substantially dispersed. Under these circumstances, any deterministic model does not sufficiently address risk measurement concerns, especially those related to the LP's funding risk. Notably, deterministic models do not capture the extremes and the volatility in regard to timing and amounts of cash flows.

Stochastic models reflect a system's random behaviour and forecast various outcomes and their probabilities. In principle, stochastic models are preferable as they capture uncertainty in the form of PDFs and, therefore, can provide a much richer set of key performance indicators (KPIs) than a deterministic model. On the other hand, users typically find deterministic models more tractable.

Of course, the differentiation is not as clear-cut as is comes across here, and many models in practical use are rather semi-deterministic, i.e. they are a hybrid between a one-dimensional deterministic model and some components with unpredictable behaviour.

A semi-deterministic model can show a range of different behaviours and can be used to investigate features that are not well described by a pure deterministic model, for instance, by looking at several set of input parameters that represent an optimistic, base, and pessimistic scenario. Where (semi-)deterministic models excel is the execution time that tends to be a magnitude faster than that of a stochastic simulation, and which allows using such models interactively.

Kocis et al. (2009) proposed a deterministic model too, but in contrast to the TAM assumed contributions, distributions, and NAVs to be independent. Further variations and extensions of the TAM were presented by Murphy (2007), Black et al. (2018), and Corvino (2020). Corvino altered the TAM by introducing cr as ratio of total contributions during the fund's life over the committed capital CC and the fund's investment period ip as additional parameters. The model assumes that during the investment period, annual contributions are constant, and after it, the contributions are assumed to become zero, so that

$$C_{(t)} = \begin{cases} cr\dfrac{CC}{ip}; \text{if } t \le ip \\ 0; \text{ otherwise.} \end{cases}$$

With $cr = 95\%$ and $ip = 5$, only 95% of CC is expected to be actually called over five years with the rest being held in reserve, giving

$$C_{(t)} = \frac{95\% * CC}{5}; \text{ for } t = 1, ..., 5.$$

Corvino motivates this change by the observation that for funds the investment periods are defined ex ante and should be reflected in the forecast.

Also, specialised consulting companies that provide private capital funds cash-flow forecasting services predominantly build on the TAM or comparable deterministic models. Examples are AssetMetrix,[17] FRG,[18] Novus,[19] and StepStone.[20]

STOCHASTIC MODELS

The result of a risk model should be a distribution and not just an expected value, a clear weakness of the deterministic TAM. While the TAM is a discrete-time model, de Malherbe (2004) and Buchner et al. (2010) proposed continuous-time stochastic models (see **Box 4.5**) for reflecting the dynamics of private equity funds and the erratic nature of their cash flows.

Stochastic modelling of contributions, distributions, and NAVs

A fund forecast model needs to reflect the dynamics of the rates of drawdowns and repayments over time. The fund's commitment size imposes constraints on how much capital can be drawn in total. This can be modelled through a mean-reverting process applied to the rate at which capital is drawn over time. Another question is how to model the fund's NAVs or how to take them into consideration.

de Malherbe (2004) uses Squared Bessel processes to model the dynamics of the rates of drawdowns and repayments over time, whereas the NAV's development is described as a log-normal process. One criticism of his model is that it relies on this specification of the NAV's dynamics, but the NAV, reflecting the unobservable value of the fund's assets over time, is essentially the fund management's estimate.

Buchner et al. (2010) look at two independent components, i.e. one for contributions and one for distributions, but do not forecast the fund's NAV development (also see Buchner, 2017). Comparable to de Malherbe (2004), Buchner et al. (2010) describe the rate at which capital is drawn over time through a mean-reverting square-root process. The fund's capital distributions are modelled as an arithmetic Brownian motion with a time-dependent drift component that reflects the typical fund's time pattern of realisations.[21] Building on this, Harte and Buchner (2017) proposed the 'PE Package' to model private equity.

Box 4.5   Discrete-time versus continuous-time models

Discrete-time models describe systems where states change only at specific points rather than continuously through time. The intervals between these points in time are usually assumed to be equal, in the case of the TAM one year. This quite large discretisation step length may have been chosen because of the funds' long lifetimes but also to keep the model tractable, as for shorter step lengths, it may be too difficult for an analyst to understand the link between the various parameters and the model's dynamics. The drawback here is that input data, depending on the choice of the discretisation step length, tend to be outdated, and therefore, the model's results may be imprecise. Another, from a practical perspective significant, disadvantage of discrete-time models is that switching from, say, annual time steps to quarterly ones is not simple.

Continuous-time models, on the other hand, generally yield more accurate results, because not only input data are nearer to the events they relate to but also the models can take the timing of the inputs into account.

Whether to build a continuous-time model and, if going for a discrete-time model, what discretisation step length to select are decisions that also need to consider how often data are made available in private markets. Standard industry reporting of fund valuations, as basis for tracking exposure, is done on a quarterly basis, which favours a discrete-time model. Capital calls and repayments from funds can happen at any point in time and, therefore, suggest a continuous-time model.

Finally, if the liquidity risks associated with the fund's cash flows are measured by cash-flow-at-risk measures, we need to set a time interval within which the cash flows can take place. To conclude, for fund forecasts, neither discrete-time nor continuous-time models have clear advantages.

Both models make more accurate predictions for contributions than for distributions. This should not surprise as contributions are less dependent on a specific fund's performance and the capital needs to be called within a contractually defined investment period. Variations in distributions, on the other hand, are driven by the funds' wide range of performance outcomes and lifetimes.

Like the TAM, such stochastic models can be fitted and calibrated to historic fund data and are said to provide a good approximation of the empirical distribution of a fund's cash flows over its lifetime.

Comparison

Several studies evaluated these stochastic models. Furenstam and Forsell (2018) compared Buchner et al. (2010) against the TAM: 'To summarize the comparison of the analysis, the Yale model performs better than the stochastic model on the tests we have conducted.' Black et al. (2018) conducted a comparable study for de Malherbe's model: 'Our analysis shows there is hardly any convincing performance improvement of the stochastic model in terms of calibration and robustness compared with the deterministic model.' Black et al. (2018) provide no information on where the data underlying their study were provided from. Furenstam and Forsell (2018) used data on 195 funds provided by an undisclosed Nordic financial institution.

Virtanen (2019) looked at the applicability of the TAM and Buchner et al. (2010) to private debt funds. He used data on 62 funds provided by an undisclosed financial institution in Northern Europe. The author found that the TAM seemed to do better for cumulated contributions of the subsample of mature funds, but he concluded that the stochastic model overall provides more accurate results. Ungsgård (2020), too, focused on Buchner et al. (2010), using data on 20 funds by an undisclosed large Swedish bank. Also, here, the sparse amount of data was identified as the biggest cause of potential errors in the analysis.

One may question whether forecast of average cash flows generated by the deterministic TAM and those generated by stochastic models that reflect the volatility of cash flows is a meaningful comparison, but these various analyses suggest that the TAM remains a good starting point.

CONCLUSION

Deterministic models like the TAM look overly simplistic, whereas, from a theoretical point of view, stochastic models look more satisfying. Indeed, according to Harte and Buchner (2017): 'We want this framework [i.e. Buchner et al. (2010)] to become the standard model used by investors for their PE positions'. On the other hand, the TAM is a classical practitioners' tool, and it is precisely its simplicity that made this model gain wide adoption and create the impact it had over the past few decades.

Approaches competing against the TAM come with more complexity, which here has several aspects: modelling and tractability. Bootstrapping is simple, too, as a model but relies on data that are expensive and difficult to compile and maintain. Stochastic models may not cause implementation problems, but their results are more complex to understand. The TAM is viewed as more tractable as it has a simpler underlying model structure, leading to a better understanding of the funds' behaviour.[22]

Certainly, as the late Dutch computer scientist Edsger Dijkstra observed, 'complexity sells better', but simplicity has important advantages.[23] The TAM's results are easy to understand and use, which makes it more likely that analysts rely on it. In conversations with cash-flow forecasting practitioners, it was repeatedly commented that it is better to run a less detailed model and to analyse its results frequently than interrogate a complicated model rarely.

NOTES

1. See Takahashi and Alexander (2002).
2. The stochastic model proposed by de Malherbe (2004) (see below), also aimed to address the forecasting needs for such collateralised private equity fund obligations.
3. Also see Beutler et al. (2023). These authors described a simulation approach that leverages historical cash flow data to address the TAM's limitations and generate ranges of portfolio outcomes without requiring input assumptions.
4. See Kalra et al. (2006).
5. See Perrin et el. (2006).
6. See Cheung et al. (2003).
7. See Chen et al. (2018).
8. Apparently, it is very difficult to turn this into a profitable operation, and over recent years, the market has witnessed not only increasing consolidation but also teaming up with stronger asset management players: Bison became Cobalt and a part of Hamilton Lane. eFront (Pevara) is now owned by BlackRock and Burgiss is now partially owned by MSCI.
9. See, for example, Hickman (2019).
10. Chollet (2018) sums this up quite nicely: 'Markets have very different statistical characteristics than natural phenomena and as weather patterns. Trying to use machine learning to beat markets [. . .] is a difficult endeavour, and you are likely to waste your time and resources with nothing to show for it.'
11. At the time of this writing, there are various attempts to address the uncertainty regarding the timing and the size of private equity funds' cash flows through ML. Results suggest that an ML algorithm provides significantly better predictions (out-of-sample) than a simple cash-flow model. However, 'longer term predictions tend to be worse with the ML algorithm compared

to the simple cash-flow [sic] model. This is because for longer term predictions the ML algorithm basically "stacks" short-term predictions (using idiosyncratic features) to get to a long-term prediction, while the simple cash-flow [sic] model makes use of averages (Law of Large Numbers) and does not rely on idiosyncratic features. As a result, the simple cash-flow [sic] model provides better predictions for long-term horizons.' (Communication with John Renkema and Rawy Segit, 5 August 2022).

12. See Aalberts et al. (2019). Just between 2001 and 2005, Dean Takahashi's and Seth Alexander's preliminary paper 'Illiquid Alternative Asset Fund Modelling' had been downloaded more than 10,000 times from Yale School of Management International Center for Finance's website. See http://icf.som.yale.edu/research/

13. However, in reality, funds also 'overinvest' by reinvesting (i.e. recycling) capital, a characteristic that is not directly captured by the model.

14. As there still can be contributions for the fund, it is still possible that it has a non-zero NAV in the following years.

15. I know of no further publication on the TAM that explores the yield parameter. Probably, more traditional techniques for modelling debt instruments are better suited for such a case.

16. See https://aspequity.com/boston, [accessed 8 November 2022]

17. See https://www.asset-metrix.com/media/1807-Whitepaper_Portfolio-Analytics-Einf%C3%BChrung-in-die-LP-Prognostik.pdf, [accessed 8 November 2022]

18. See Lenz et al. (2018).

19. See https://www.novus.com/articles/balancing-liquidity-constraints-in-a-private-investment-program, [accessed 8 November 2022]

20. See https://www.stepstonegroup.com/news-insights/cracking-the-illiquidity-code/, [accessed 8 November 2022]

21. See also Ungsgård (2020), building on Buchner (2017).

22. See Black et al. (2018).

23. See Yan (2022).

CHAPTER 5

Private Market Data

Data are the lifeblood of the investment industry. However, players in private markets, regardless whether they are fund management firms or the limited partners (LPs) that invest in funds, are reluctant to disclose data on their holdings. Fund management firms gain no commercial advantage from transparency and even have a strong motivation to keep as much information confidential as possible. In fact, the raison d'être of investing in private markets is to legitimately exploit opportunities associated with intransparency – it is called 'private' for a reason.

The resulting difficulty of obtaining high-quality data for cash-flow forecasting purposes creates problems: what conclusions can we draw from outdated and incomplete information and how much confidence can decision-makers put into their findings? No data set may exist on the entire universe of private capital funds, but to some degree, the industry has learned to live with this situation. To paraphrase the late Donald Rumsfeld, as an investor in private assets, you need to work with the data you have, not the data you might want or wish to have at a later time.

FUND PEER GROUPS

For our approach to cash-flow forecasting, we require benchmarking data that reflect a risk profile similar to the fund to be modelled. For private capital funds (see **Box 5.1**), it is common practice to use as a classical benchmark a vintage, geographic, and fund-type-specific benchmark, often referred to as 'peer group cohort' (e.g. 1995 European buyout funds) and to express the results of a benchmarking in terms of quartile relative to its benchmark.

Organisation of benchmarking data

The peer group is defined by its cohort characteristics, and its data are always organised by vintage year and, depending on the provider, also by size of fund, strategy (e.g. venture, buyout, real estate, infrastructure, secondary, and fund-of-funds), and geography (typically on a regional level, like Africa, Asia/Pacific, Europe, Middle East, Latin America, the US).

The industry practice is to arrange the data by quartiles, from smallest to largest and by reporting the quartile breakpoints for key metrics like internal rate of return (IRR), total value to paid-in capital (TVPI), distributions to paid-in capital (DPI), residual value to paid-in capital (RVPI), and distributed to committed capital (DCC):

- First quartile: the highest 25% of numbers.
- Second quartile: >50% to 75% (above the median).
- Third quartile: between >25% and 50% (up to the median).
- Fourth quartile: the lowest 25% of numbers.

Typically, for the ranges of these metrics for the first quartile, the 95% breakpoint is taken as a lower bound. This means that for the 5% funds for which a higher, say, IRR is reported, these IRR figures are ignored in the statistics. This is to cope with outliers that would distort results and reduce their usefulness and interpretability. The same approach is taken for the fourth quartile, where the 5% worst performing funds are ignored as such extreme figures are often flukes.

Box 5.1   Company-level benchmarks

Private market data providers also offer benchmarking data on company fundamentals.[1] These benchmarks capture the performance of investments in private companies made by buyout and growth equity funds mainly.

Key performance indicators (KPIs) like gross IRR, gross TVPI, annual revenue growth, EBITDA growth, EBITDA multiple, net debt multiple, and net debt/total enterprise value are published essentially in the same quartile structure like funds, but in this case, it is the privately held companies that are organised in peer groups by vintage years, geography, and industry.

These investment-level benchmarks are useful for assessing the performance of co-investments and direct investments and as a means to model their risks. IRR and TVPI are reported as gross figures, i.e. before management fees, expenses, and carried interest.

With this, a data analyst can compare a fund's net and gross returns, to get a better understanding of the fund's costs. This could also be used to model the impact of different incentives schemes.[2]

Reported fund-level returns are always 'net to LP', i.e. returns after all fees, expenses, and carried interest had been deducted.

Bailey criteria

Bailey et al. (1990) defined the so-called *Bailey criteria* as characteristics for appropriate investment benchmarks:

- **Unambiguous/knowable**. The names and weights of assets that comprise the benchmark should be clearly identifiable. Private capital benchmarks often only provide aggregate data and do not give a complete representation of the available opportunity set.

- **Investable**. The option is available to forgo active management and simply hold the benchmark. In an investment context, a benchmark represents the return to a passive investment strategy. It allows active investment decisions to be judged relative to the benchmark. In private capital, a passive strategy does not exist – LPs can only maintain their allocations by continuing to look for new funds to commit. It is notably this fundamental difference that explains why private capital portfolios exhibit widely diverging results.
- **Measurable**. It is possible to frequently calculate the benchmark performance. Private capital funds do not provide data that allow measuring accurately their risk and return characteristics.

Private capital benchmarks suffer deficiencies in nearly all of these dimensions. This raises the question whether private market data services can provide us with representative and significant data that we can use for modelling purposes?

DATA PROVIDERS

Most LPs will not have had the time and IT resources to collect and maintain a rich pool of private asset data and, for this reason, need to rely entirely on commercial databases. Such databases are created and maintained by mainly four well-established commercial firms[3]: Burgiss, Cambridge Associates, PitchBook, and Preqin, who offer valid data dating back to the 1980s, with the earliest relating to US private equity firms.

Business model

Having said this, this is a dynamic field, with a number of new entrants and leavers. For a long time, Thomson Venture Economics arguably was the most relevant data provider, with its VentureXpert survey and database covering the entire spectrum of private equity firms.[4] In 2014, however, and as Kaplan and Lerner (2017) suspect, for reasons likely related to poor-quality data, Thomson decided to discontinue its database and, instead, make Cambridge Associate available on its platform.

At the time of writing this book and without claiming completeness, examples for competing services that emerged in previous years are Bloomberg,[5] Cobalt LP,[6] eFront,[7] State Street Bank,[8] and Private Equity International. It is worth noting that these data providers operate in a difficult market and actually follow different business models to source the data that they can sell on to their subscribers. This has a significant impact on what universe they cover, in which level of detail, and the quality of their data.

Public route

Preqin and PitchBook obtain most of their data from public investors (such as state and local government employee pension funds, public university endowments, etc.) under the Freedom of Information Act (FOIA), and outside the US where comparable laws apply.[9]

In addition, both providers make direct requests to LPs as well as general partners (GPs) for submission. Confidentiality is less of an issue for data of public LPs, and therefore, in Preqin and PitchBook, individual funds can be identified. On the other hand, fund data harvested from FOIA disclosures or being provided voluntarily tend not to be checked in detail and only cover a sub-space of private markets that is not necessarily representative.

Voluntary provision

As their core business, Burgiss and Cambridge Associates provide fund administration services and thus are able to provide timely data, with verified accuracy, and arguably less subject to sample biases. Burgiss sources data exclusively from LPs, whereas Cambridge Associates utilises financial statements provided by the fund managers in the course of their regular reporting to their LPs. However, for confidentiality reasons, their LP clients only allow fund cash flows being made available in an aggregate format. Without cash-flow data for individual funds, there are limits to certain analyses, for instance those related to cash-flow forecasting.

Problem areas

As this is a private industry, it is nearly impossible to collect complete, accurate, and reliable data and build a representative benchmark.

Data are also expected to be error-prone, as, in fact, compared to public assets, relatively few parties work with the data: funds and portfolio companies are usually not accessible for investment purposes for a long time, and therefore, there is only a limited degree of peer review as a check and balance. Moreover, reporting of financial statements can be delayed, often significantly. Data tend to be stale, as they are often only updated after significant events. As some databases also cover funds of funds, their data could result in double counting. It is a general characteristic of an ever-changing alternative market space that innovations and emerging market spaces are initially not recognised as such, and this information is either not properly categorised or simply ignored entirely. As a consequence, all databases will cover high-quality as well as low-quality data.

Private capital data have significant gaps, as many market participants are not even known. Not all firms contribute data and underperforming fund managers often withhold negative information and drop out. Therefore, it is difficult to assess how complete a picture of the market is provided.

All four providers have similar sample sizes for North American buyout funds, but for venture funds in this region, this varies substantially. Regarding venture funds outside North America, the coverage differs, sometimes dramatically, depending on the provider. In line with the historical development of the private capital markets, notably for the 'rest of the world' (Europe, Asia, emerging markets), data are patchy. Also, for this reason, these databases do not necessarily capture the same data sets and can show differences of several percentage points for some peer groups.

It is not just the privacy of the data that causes issues. There is also significant innovation in terms of strategies and structures. For instance, according to Inderst (2018), infrastructure emerged as a dedicated asset classes in the 1990s in Australia, the spread to Canada and Europe in the early 2000s, followed by the US and other regions. Only in recent years, infrastructure funds have moved from exception to own category with data tracked for funds structured as limited partnership.

BIASES

A major concern regarding of the accessible private market data are biases that distort their representativeness and comprehensiveness. Various biases are documented or assumed:

- Regardless of whether commercial data providers go the public (i.e. FOIA) or the voluntary provision route for collecting data, the data from any one provider are certain to be incomplete.
- Where data are sourced directly from GPs their quality may suffer from deliberate distortions of valuations.
- Kaplan and Lerner (2016) point to a potential backfill bias, where databases report positive past returns for funds that are newly added to the database. This bias is caused by the fact that only successful firms will raise new funds. Their first-time funds, however, often do not have those institutional LPs that provide data to the data providers.

Voluntary submission, especially by GPs, may introduce selection and survivorship biases. As Preqin and PitchBook reveal the names of the funds, these data providers, according to Kaplan and Lerner (2016), have a potential selection bias.

Survivorship bias

In fact, the major concern regarding the representativeness and comprehensiveness is the survivorship bias, which refers to the fact that managers or funds that perform poorly tend to go out of business and, therefore, drop out of the peer universe. As a result, statistical data will mainly cover the currently existing and predominantly well-performing funds. As failed funds are not properly captured, this presents an average historical performance that is probably biased on the high side and gives an overly optimistic picture.

This bias is well-documented for stock and mutual fund indexes. Mutual funds are registered securities, with regulation requiring that results are reported. Indexes will cover active funds, so their average always includes members that have not failed so far. Failed, i.e. 'deceased', funds are excluded in these indexes, thereby skewing the average and overstating performance.

Certainly survivorship bias matters for stock and mutual fund indexes. Here, positive performers cannot and do not have reasons to report their results. Reporting is mandatory, so the index represents the full universe of accessible securities.

Survivorship bias in private markets

However, and as pointed out by Easterling (2004), in the academic discussion on survivorship bias, this issue has been expropriated from the public realm and misapplied to the world of private assets and their indexes.

Direct sourcing from LPs, thus covering their entire investment history, can eliminate certain aspects of selection and survivorship bias. As O'Hare (2008) argued, Preqin data 'come overwhelmingly from LPs, so we are collecting data on each LP's entire portfolio – the good, the bad and the ugly. No selection or survivorship bias here.'

Brown et al. (2015) referred to the comments by Cambridge Associates on their methodology: 'Whereas an underperforming stock manager may simply close up shop or drop out of databases as clients liquidate their positions and fire the manager, private investment partnerships owning illiquid assets continue to exist and require reporting to the limited partners, even if the original manager ceases to exist.'

However, it is not only the dropping out of poorly performing funds that distorts the picture. Another factor is that some firms have no problem raising money and, therefore, at a certain point see no need to report to the private market data providers.[10] Brown et al. (2015) quote Cambridge Associates' experience with active funds that stopped providing financial statements before they were mature and fully liquidated. Their analysis found that the performance of such funds 'has been spread almost evenly across all quartiles and has not been concentrated consistently in the poorer performing quartiles'.

Impact

How material is the impact of selection and survivorship biases? Smith and Smith (2021) investigated the performance reporting behaviours of GPs and LPs of VC funds. As GPs are self-reporting, there may be a bias, as discussed, either due to selective reporting for the most successful funds or from overstated performance.

Results indicated that selective reporting is the more important concern. In other words, GPs are more likely to report where funds show good performance. Smith and Smith (2021) used a subsample of LPs subject to FOIA to ascertain the extent of selective reporting by GPs and compare to aggregate performance measures for estimating the bias resulting from selective reporting. They found that mean and median IRRs and TVPIs reported by LPs are materially lower than those reported by GPs. The average IRR difference was found to be 2.2%, and the average impact on the TVPI to be 0.0635.

According to Spliid (2015), outliers could be a problem when measuring averages because these extremes can move the mean to a level that is unrepresentative of the sample. One way of addressing this problem is using the median instead of the mean to identify where values are more likely to occur. Additionally and as mentioned before, in many of the private market databases, the upper and lower quartiles are cut off at 95% and 5%, respectively, to mitigate the impact of outliers.

CONCLUSION

Survivorship bias can affect all investment manager databases, but for private assets, most of the time practitioners can live with these shortcomings or see them as irrelevant. Swensen (2000) argued that survivorship bias may be less of a problem for long-term-oriented illiquid investments, as this population is not changing rapidly. Indeed, managers of private capital funds enter and exit the benchmark statistics with considerably less frequency than their counterparts focusing on traditional marketable securities, as the limited partnership structure precludes easy departure from the industry.

According to Geltner and Ling (2000), it is not necessary to have a fixed and constant set of funds in the benchmark. Databases represent only a general proxy for the industry rather than being comprehensive. Classical financial service caveat is that 'past performance is not indicative of future returns'. But there is wide consensus among investors that there is a link between prior private capital fund returns and those in the future. What evidence there is seems to support such a link, although with a growing and maturing industry, the claim that first-quartile performance is repeatable is becoming weaker.[11]

There are many factors that have more impact than the biases discussed here. The trend emerging over the past few years shows a downward movement in absolute returns.[12] This, to a large degree, appears to be function of the large inflows into the private asset class, increased competition for deals, investors, and exit routes. The main conclusion is that we in many cases cannot rely too heavily on past returns, but we need to apply stresses. To this, we will turn in a later chapter.

NOTES

1. For example, Cambridge Associates' Investment-Level Benchmarks and Burgiss Company Fundamentals Review; available at https://www.burgiss.com/company-fundamentals-review-an-essential-component-of-buyout-analysis-october-2022, [accessed 26 October 2023].
2. Based on cash-flow forecast for the funds, we can also apply a 'reverse waterfall' calculation and, assuming a standard waterfall structure, calculate a fund's gross return based on its net benchmarking figures.
3. See Brown et al. (2015).
4. Kaplan and Lerner (2017) reported on the firm that initiated the data collection on venture deals, which Thomson Reuters eventually acquired, began operations in 1961.
5. See https://www.bloomberg.com/professional/expertise/private-equity/, [accessed 15 April 2023]
6. See https://www.cobalt.pe/benchmarking-data/, [accessed 15 April 2023]
7. See https://www.efront.com/fr/alternative-investment-software/efront-pevara-benchmarking, [accessed 15 April 2023]
8. See https://globalmarkets.statestreet.com/portal/peindex/, [accessed 15 April 2023]
9. In the UK, FOIA rules allow any organisation or member of the public to request information held by or on behalf of a UK 'public authority'. This can include pension funds that invest as LPs for central and local government and authorities, the National Health Service, the police and many other bodies discharging public functions.

10. According to Easterling (2004), this appears to happen at least in the context of hedge funds. His analyses found that 'hedge funds more often stop reporting returns following periods of positive performance, not when they are likely dying off [. . .] Both studies indicate that survivorship bias in hedge funds is skewed heavily toward "closings" (to new investors) rather than "closures" (going out of business). Given the lack of reporting requirements and the potential for both positive and negative drivers within the hedge fund industry, survivorship bias may actually cause an understatement of returns available from hedge fund investing.'
11. See Meyer (2014).
12. See Spliid (2015).

CHAPTER 6

Augmented TAM – Outcome Model

Experimenting with a pacing plans enables the analyst to see more detail, ask the right questions, and create new insights. Forecasted expected cash flows are easy to understand and explain, making the Takahashi–Alexander model (TAM) the model of choice for commitment pacing. However, the TAM cannot reflect the volatility and frequency of cash flows and, therefore, is of little use for assessing the limited partner (LP)'s funding risks that stem from the funds' illiquidity.

FROM TAM TO STOCHASTIC FORECASTS

Commitment pacing is an interactive planning process. Analysts compare different pacing plans and versions of these plans against each other. Pacing plans are continuously changed based on feedback and inputs from investment research and monitoring, new opportunities, changes in risks and budgets, and alternative uses of capital. Commitment pacing is essentially a negotiation around resources involving various stakeholders, where assumptions get challenged and need to be revised. Events that affect the pacing plan are unpredictable, and analysts will have to explore a range of scenarios to cope with this uncertainty.

Stochastic models allow deriving important risk measures for private capital fund investments. From a practical perspective, when using stochastic models for generating cash-flow scenarios, we rely on Monte Carlo simulations (MCS) that take significant computer resources and time to run and, therefore, are too cumbersome to work with interactively for step-wise refining a commitment plan.

Rather than giving up on the TAM and switching to a stochastic model or a cash-flow library-based approach, let us combine the advantages of these different approaches through an augmented, i.e. stochastically extended 'augmented TAM'.[1] This allows us to produce the stochastic cash-flow scenarios that are required for the assessment of risks but that can be reconciled with the simple to understand expected values forecasted by the TAM.

We approach this in two steps: first, we introduce in this chapter a semi-deterministic, the so-called 'A1*TAM', where the TAM remains unchanged, but its parameters are drawn randomly to quickly produce a set of scenarios of average cash-flow forecasts. In **Chapter 7** we extend this to a full stochastic model, the A2*TAM, that provides random cash flows and higher granularity: forecasts are not just on an annual basis, but can support discrete time steps, such as quarterly and monthly periods. Contributions are broken down into their components capital calls for investments and management fees, and distributions into repayments after realisations of investments and fixed return components.

USE CASES FOR STOCHASTIC CASH-FLOW FORECASTS

Due to the illiquidity of the private markets, commitment pacing is the main tool to manage a portfolio's risk/return profile. For this, the LP needs to consider the main sources of risk[2]: funding risk, market risk, liquidity risk, and capital risk.

Funding risk

LPs have committed to funds and have to provide the capital called for investments on short notice. The unpredictable timing of the funds' cash flows creates funding risk, i.e. where the LP's liquid resources are insufficient at the time when the capital is called (see **Box 6.1**).

The cash-flow-at-risk (CFaR) is one indicator for funding risk. The CFaR is the maximum cash flow for a portfolio of funds within a given time period for a given confidence level. PitchBook proposed the capital-call-at-risk (CCaR) as additional indicator.[3] The CCaR is the most capital a portfolio of funds will call within a given time period for a given confidence level (see **Figure 6.1**). For example, a CCaR of $700,000 at 95% implies

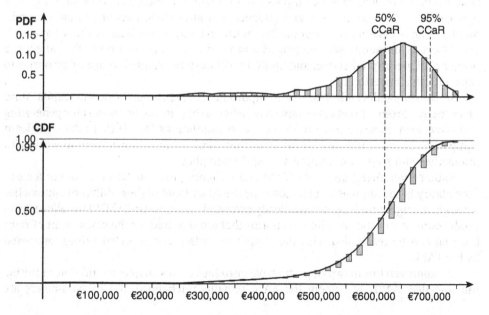

FIGURE 6.1   Quarterly Capital-Call-at-Risk Probability Density Function (top) and Cumulative Distribution Function (bottom), for sample portfolio of funds

that there is a 5% probability that the fund will call $700,000 or more in a given period'.[4] The CCaR reflects the constraint an LP is facing that has only a limited amount of capital available at a given point in time to honour a capital call.

CFaR is netting the portfolio's positive and negative cash flows, whereas the CCaR is reflecting the funds' contributions (referred to as 'capital calls' by PitchBook) only. For younger portfolios of funds and the short- to medium-term planning, CCaR is the more reliable figure to work with.

Box 6.1   Tiering liquidity for cash management

Stochastic models help to determine the probability distributions for deriving the CCaR and CFaR metrics. This allows us to improve on the cash management for the undrawn and uncommitted capital of the portfolio. The capital needs to be invested in liquid assets; the lower return generated on this cash is the price LPs are paying for being able to harvest the private assets' outsized returns.

How much of this capital will be called over, say, the next quarter? In the extreme, all undrawn commitments, but this will be very unlikely (see **Figure 6.1**). The major part of this amount will not be used for a long time, if at all. Schneider et al. (2022) analysed the capital call rates for private debt, private equity, and real estate funds between 1992 and 2020 and found that, on average, LPs waited two years before 50% of the commitments had been invested by the funds and 10% of the committed capital was not called at all. Specifically, for private equity funds, even less capital was put at work: after two years, only about a third of the commitments were invested and 20% was not called at all.

One approach how LPs address this so-called 'cash drag' is through 'over-committing', i.e. making capital commitments in excess of resources available for investments and relying on distributions from maturing funds to meet capital calls as they come in (see also **Chapter 15**). Over-commitments offer a high return as they are essentially invested in private assets, which in theory give the highest returns, but without the LP incurring opportunity costs.

Depending on the period (e.g. where management fees need to be paid) and the portfolio's maturity, where older funds will not call any capital, there is an extremely wide range for the portfolio's cash flows. As a consequence, one number for next period's expected (or another confidence level, such as 80%) contributions will be of limited use for cash management purposes.

Instead, Schneider et al. (2022) suggested a 'liquidity tiering' to provide investors with additional returns relative to cash but with less risk of falling short on liquidity. The LP's resources waiting to be called are allocated to three tiers of assets with decreasing liquidity but increasing return potential, with their durations also matching the likely contribution schedule:

- Cash needed for the next year's contributions are held in active ultrashort assets (primarily investment-grade US fixed-income issues with durations of less than one year).

- The next tier covers the contributions that are expected over the medium term, e.g. three years, and are held in assets with a slightly higher risk/return profile (primarily in corporate and other investment-grade fixed-income issues with durations of 1–3.5 years).
- All remaining contributions are held in public market equivalent assets. These assets depend on the type of fund to be matched, i.e. undrawn commitments for private equity funds may be invested in public equities, whereas those for private debt rather in high-yield bonds.

Shen et al. (2021) discussed a similar approach within the context of an asset–liability framework. They suggested a 'liquidity waterfall' comprising two liquid and one illiquid layer:

- The highest liquidity would be assured by 'passive public assets', i.e. investments in equity and fixed-income assets that are not expected to earn an alpha (e.g. an ETF on a broad-based index fund).
- The next, slightly less liquid, layer is 'active public assets' that are actively managed to earn an alpha over passive indices (e.g. an actively managed fund or a liquid hedge fund strategy).
- The 'illiquid asset' layer represents all investments in private assets that are, however, unavailable for liquidity. Shen et al. (2021) put the LP's funds themselves (net asset value (NAV) only) into this category.

The last point is in contrast to that followed by Schneider et al. (2022) who do not see the portfolio of funds as available for sale. Also, Shen et al. (2021) do not match the maturity of these layers with the portfolio's contribution schedule. In case of capital calls, assets are realised in sequence of the liquidity waterfall, starting with the most liquid ones.

Over-commitments could be seen as another layer in this liquidity waterfall, before hitting the 'illiquid assets' layer. They share important commonalities with leverage strategies, essentially 'leveraging over time', and show similar rewards and risks, notably that of becoming a defaulting LP. In this case, LPs need to scramble for financing, for instance by taking on debt on short notice and therefore under unfavourable terms, or, in the worst case, by selling off fund stakes at a loss. In this situation, over-commitments become the most expensive form of 'funding' capital calls.

With the probability distribution function shown in **Figure 6.1**, we can dimension the liquidity waterfall and how much to over-commit for assuring sufficient liquidity while minimising the opportunity costs of the undrawn and uncommitted capital.

CFaR is becoming more useful for mature portfolios and managing resources over longer time horizons, for example, for over-commitments and recommitment strategies, or to plan for alternative uses of repaid capital. CFaR as well as CCaR can be calculated for individual funds, but because of the wide ranges for the forecasts, this is not mean-ingful. Only for diversified portfolios, this figure can be determined so that it is useful for planning purposes.

Another aspect of funding risk is the exposure to counterparties, i.e. the inability to obtain necessary funding for the illiquid asset positions on the expected terms and when required, notably due to defaulting or reneging of pledges by the other LPs that have committed to a fund. This counterparty risk can be measured along the lines of credit risk, i.e. by ratings.

Market risk

The fluctuation of the market has an impact on the value of the private assets held by a fund. Market risk relates to factors like foreign exchange rate movements, interest rate movements, country risk, industry/sector risk, credit spreads, commodity and equity prices, and recessions.

As with other forms of risk, the potential loss amount due to market risk may be measured in a number of ways. Traditionally, one convention is to use the value-at-risk (VaR) as a well-established and accepted practice for short-term risk management. The VaR is the maximum mark-to-market loss a given portfolio can suffer for a given time horizon and a given confidence level. For an illiquid asset class, the treatment of market risk poses conceptual challenges. For private equity funds, the VaR measure proposed in Buchner (2017) is based on the implicit assumption that the LP can sell the position in a fund at any time at its current NAV.[5]

While in the case of tradable assets, VaR is usually computed for very short time periods (days or weeks), CFaR relates to longer periods, typically quarters and some-times even years. Marked-to-market portfolios are convertible into cash at short notice, and therefore, their VaR is also their CFaR. However, this argument does not apply to illiquid assets.[6]

Liquidity risk

LPs can sell their positions in private capital partnerships, for example, to finance their outstanding commitments. The illiquidity of these positions exposes the LP to liquidity risk associated with selling in the secondary markets at a discount on the reported NAV. To measure this risk, Buchner (2017) suggested the so-called 'liquidity-adjusted-value-at-risk' (LVaR). The LVaR models the worst transaction price that could be obtained for a fund on the secondary markets for a given level of confidence. Here, the main idea is to include secondary market discounts in the VaR calculation. For his analysis, Buchner obtained such discounts from the Preqin Secondary Market Monitor for the period rang-ing from March 2003 to March 2013. He found a wide range of discounts, depending on the type of asset and the market environment. Moreover, liquidity in the secondary mar-kets tends to dry up precisely when sellers need it most, for instance, during the Global Financial Crisis 2008 to 2009. Instead of using a complex model for secondary market prices, a simpler and probably more robust approach for LPs would be applying stress scenarios to the funds' valuations and cash flows.

Capital risk

LPs face the long-term risk of not recovering the value of their invested capital at realisation. This capital risk can be affected by a number of factors, but the quality of the fund managers stands out.[7] A fund rating methodology, as described in the following chapters, can help us to model the impact of low-quality fund management.

MODEL ARCHITECTURE

Based on these use cases, what are the characteristics of the desired forecasting model for funds?

- It should be based on an accepted model that has proven its usefulness in practical applications such as the TAM.
- The model should not be too complex so that its dynamics can be analysed, explained, and understood.
- Processing the model should be fast in order to give a good user experience and allow quickly assessing various what-if scenarios.
- The model should not depend on proprietary data and work with the poor quality and often incomplete data that characterise private markets.
- As commitment pacing also applies to already existing portfolios, the model should self-calibrate based on the fund's and the market's latest available data without the user needing to update and correct assumptions and parameters.
- The model should be able to capture fund-specific details such as management fee schedules.
- As far as the limited partnership structure itself permits, the model should allow us to capture changes in fund features and the associated dynamics.
- Finally, the forecasting model should support a MCS to put users into the position to analyse ranges for expected returns, risks, and dependencies within portfolios of funds.

While the TAM's mechanics are simple and allow going through various scenarios by adjusting input parameters, the need to estimate these parameters reduces the usefulness of this deterministic model. Particularly, the inability to project widening ranges clearly puts limits to the use of the TAM and its application to risk-management purposes.

The major input driving the TAM's projections is the fund's assumed growth rate, which by construction is its internal rate of return (IRR) on realisation. This growth rate is usually set based on a limited sample of funds or on expert opinion.[8] The mathematical formula for calculating the IRR with several alternating positive and negative cash flows is non-linear, and expert-based estimates for IRRs are not always reasonable and rational. Also, the adjustment to new information such as changes in a fund's expected lifetime is not straightforward. As the IRR implicitly is a function of total value to paid-in capital (TVPI) and lifetime, changing the lifetime of the fund and adjusting the various

TAM parameters so that the growth rate is equal to the IRR with the original lifetime is conceptually problematic. For this reason, in the following we do not consider the IRR but use lifetime and TVPI[9] as inputs into a fund's model.

The model architecture comprises (1) an outcome model for the ranges of possible outcomes in terms of a fund's lifetime and its TVPI on realisation, (2) a pattern model that describes the behaviour of a fund's cash flows, and (3) a portfolio model that reflects dependencies in outcomes between different funds.

Outcome model

The outcome model defines the probability density functions (PDFs) for ranges for a fund's lifetime (i.e. after how many years it matures) and its TVPI on maturity. Usually, TVPIs as well as lifetimes are specific to strategy (e.g. venture capital, buyout, and infrastructure), geography (e.g. the US, EU, and Asia), industry (e.g. technology and life science), management company, and notably vintage year (in line with diversification dimensions and the structuring of performance data used by private market data services). Vintage years reflect the different economic environments. We can use private market data benchmarks to determine the PDFs for TVPIs.

Pattern model

The pattern model describes the structure of a fund's cash flows. Because the TAM is a deterministic model, it produces for a given one set of input parameters one forecast for expected contributions, one forecast for expected distributions, and one forecast for the expected NAVs. In reality, there is extreme uncertainty regarding the timing and amounts of cash flows that need to be taken into account to properly capture a fund's risks.

It is a fair assumption that given the same fund return outcome and lifetime, a rational investor should prefer a predictable smooth cash flow to a randomly distributed cash flow (in terms of volatility but notably of frequency). A predictable smooth cash flow allows a more reliable planning and thus a more efficient use of resources.

Cash flows are idiosyncratic to the fund in question or explained by its age and, therefore, are diversifiable.[10] However, LPs with concentrated portfolios with few funds need to take the variations in fund cash flows into consideration. For measuring a portfolio of fund's liquidity risk, we need a stochastic model that captures the random behaviour of the fund's cash flows. Outcome and pattern are model components that at the first glance seem to be independent. However, there are a number of factors, such as constraints imposed by the fund's commitment size or the management fees, that depend on the NAVs (and therefore on the fund's TVPI outcomes) that create dependencies between the frequency and the volatility of cash flows.

According to Burgiss (2021), a reasonable range for a fund lifetime is between 1 and 100 years. The TAM could thus also model open-ended funds, simply by setting their lifetimes to 100. The problem is rather that this does not reflect the cash-flow patterns properly – while there is one well-defined cash flow in the beginning (the initial investment), the distributions (dividends and final realisation of the fund stake) are few and unknown, making the TAM less suitable for such 'evergreen' funds.

TABLE 6.1   Relationship between model components

		Pattern model	
		Semi-deterministic (A1*TAM)	Stochastic (A2*TAM)
Outcome model	Private market data derived PDF for TVPI, triangular distribution for lifetimes	Main use case: commitment pacing	Main use case: risk and treasury management

Portfolio model

The impact of diversification among funds, or lack thereof, is a risk dimension not considered by Takahashi and Alexander (2002) or Buchner (2017). Most LPs assume that spreading portfolios over a large number of funds is sufficient and model the funds' cash flows as independent from each other. This simplification can be misleading as portfolios of funds often concentrate, for instance, in vintage years, geographies, and strategies. The portfolio model to manage diversification will be discussed in **Chapter 9**.

System considerations

Our forecast model is the basis for the MCS. While this technique is conceptually simple, the computational cost and the time needed for simulations can rapidly increase with the number of funds in a portfolio, the additional details the model captures, the complexity of the scenarios in question, and the desired precision of the analyses and the number of samples required to achieve this.

Writing a software that supports parallel processing and running it on a powerful hardware (e.g. cloud computing and GPU) are part of the answer. However, there is a trade-off between precision and stability of the results generated by the simulation, and the simulation's runtime. Therefore, the architecture aims for a strong functionality but also for robustness by allowing a fallback to an experience that, while weaker, still delivers essential results within an acceptable time. We achieve this through combining the outcome and two pattern models (see **Table 6.1**).

Building PDFs for TVPIs based on private market data is straightforward and will be discussed below. PDFs for fund lifetimes, however, are more difficult to construct and are therefore described through a simple triangular distribution.[11]

SEMI-DETERMINISTIC TAM

In the first step, the deterministic TAM is extended to a semi-deterministic model, referred to here as the A1*TAM, which can quickly produce a set of random scenarios of expected cash flows. This is giving us for an acceptable computing runtime a 'good enough' approximation for uncertainty that allows exploring the variety of scenarios, for instance, a base case, an optimistic case, and a pessimistic case.

The TAM expects as input the fund's estimated growth rate, which we are determining based on the fund's lifetime and its TVPI on maturity (see **Figure 6.2**):

$$TVPI = \frac{\sum_{i=0}^{t} D_{(t)} + NAV_{(t)}}{\sum_{i=0}^{t} C_{(t)}}.$$

For the purpose of this discussion, the interim TVPI refers to the situation where $NAV_{(t)} > 0$, and therefore, the fund has not reached its final TVPI on maturity.

The following algorithm allows us to calculate the fund's growth rate:

- Get the fund's targeted pair of lifetime and TVPI.
- Get the fund's commitment and its historical contributions and distributions up to the actual state date.
- We need to create a relation between lifetime, TVPI, and the TAM and set up the coefficients for the forecast polynomial.
- As a root-finding algorithm, we apply the Newton–Raphson method to estimate the annual growth rate (IRR) so that the cash flows projected by the TAM meet the targeted lifetime and TVPI.

This growth rate is inputted into the TAM that forecasts the fund's contributions, distributions, and NAVs.

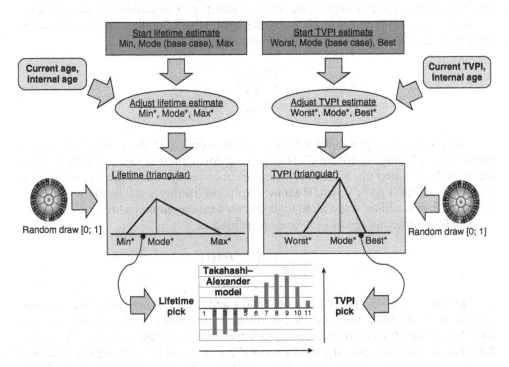

FIGURE 6.2   Outcome model

ADJUSTING RANGES FOR LIFETIME AND TVPI

Rather than aiming for the perfect forecast, the 'trick' is to update and correct the forecast as soon as new data on the fund and the market become available. The model is self-adjusting, adapting over time to the fund's development, and changing economic conditions.

This approach resembles a car navigation system that continuously updates the estimated time of arrival by taking live traffic information into account.[12] The amount of time a car will take to drive is simply the distance divided by the speed. In a similar way, we control this adaptation by the fund's internal age.

A fund's internal age[13] is modelling the uncertainty regarding its outcomes and reflects the fund's contribution age and its distribution age. The contribution age $CA(t)$ is the relationship between the sum of contributions until time t and the sum of contributions over its full lifetime, which cannot exceed the total commitment size CC:

$$0 \leq \frac{\sum_{i=0}^{t} C_{(i)}}{CC} \leq 1.$$

The maximum aggregated contribution over the full lifetime can be the commitment size. If the fund is allowed to recycle proceeds from realisations, the reinvested capital does not set the fund back in its contribution age. It is only the 'fresh' money, the undrawn and not yet used capital, that counts, assuring a monotonic increase of $CA(t)$.

A fund's distribution age $DA(t)$ is the relationship between the sum of distributions until time t and the sum of distributions over its full lifetime:

$$0 \leq \frac{\sum_{i=0}^{t} D_{(i)}}{\sum_{i=1}^{t} D_{(i)} + NAV_{(t)} + Undrawn_{t}} \leq 1.$$

The distribution age's development is not monotonic. If the portfolio of private assets' value is falling, i.e. the fund's NAV is going down, there is less to distribute in the future, so DA is going up. If the NAV going up, uncertainty regarding amount at exit is increasing, so DA is going down. Undrawn capital as liability is stable, but it is unclear how and when it will be invested, so high undrawn capital implies a low DA.

The fund's internal age $IA(t)$ at time t is defined as

$$IA(t) = \frac{CA(t) + DA(t)}{2}.$$

The internal age is a figure between 0 and 1 and measures how far a fund has progressed in its lifecycle, based on its contributions, distributions, and latest available NAV. In this way, the A1*TAM becomes sensitive to the ongoing cash-flow changes in the fund. At inception date, the fund's internal age is 0, and it is converging towards 1 the closer the fund is towards its maturity and the increasing amount of historical data makes its outcomes more predictable. As a simple outcome model, we use the triangular distribution function with initial parameters being set by experts, both for lifetimes and, for now, also for TVPIs.

Ranges for fund lifetimes

We first look at how to determine the ranges for a fund's lifetime. We need to differentiate between a fund's contractual lifetime (typically 10 years plus 1+1 extensions) and its real lifetime. Depending on whether the fund is operating in a boom period or during an economic crisis, the real lifetime can vary significantly. During the dot-com bubble, some funds, thanks to an exuberant IPO market, fully matured after four years. Other, more depressed, periods saw the emergence of zombie funds, vehicles that deployed investor's capital at peak valuations, often just before a recession, and then were forced to hang onto their assets much longer than the fund's contractual lifetime while searching for favourable exit opportunities. In such cases, fund lifetimes occasionally approached up to 15 years.[14] According to recent PitchBook data, the average lifespan of private equity funds has increased to around 13.1 years, with over 70% of funds having an age of between 10 and 15 years.[15]

Phalippou (2007) pointed out that, in practice, good funds have a shorter life than bad funds. The contractual lifetime is not fixed but rather should be seen as an upper limit that triggers a review of non-liquidated investments and whether to extend the fund's life. According to Murphy et al. (2022), there is evidence that general partners (GPs) tend to manage their investment towards a total value realisation, such as targeting a TVPI of 2, and, if needed, extend the duration of their investments accordingly. Treating a fund's lifetime and TVPI as independent random variables, therefore, appears to be a reasonable simplification.

For the forecast, we are only interested in the fund's real lifetime. Let us look at an example. At inception date with internal age of 0, the best guess for the fund's real lifetime would be its contractual lifetime but based on historical experience and not knowing how favourable or unfavourable private markets will perform over the next 10 years, a downward deviation, i.e. a shorter lifetime of three years and an upward deviation of five years looks realistic (see **Figure 6.3**).

Assume that the fund is now in its ninth year but only has an internal age of 0.83 (see **Figure 6.4**). One required adjustment is for 'speed' of the fund's development. To do this, we need to estimate the fund's lifetime. There are two interpretations of internal age: first, the fund is 83% through its lifetime, i.e. it is developing slower and, assuming that the speed of its development does not change, the fund should mature at a later date. The original estimate was the contractual lifetime set at 10 years. Factoring the fund's current 'speed', we project a lifetime of 10.91 years.

Another way of looking at it is that we are 83% certain about the fund's final outcome. For young funds, we need to give more weight to the estimates, but for older funds, there is more real data and those more weight needs to be given to these data. This weight is proportional to the internal age, and accordingly, the estimates for downward and upward deviation need to be adjusted for this increase in certainty.

At internal age 0, we know nothing specific about the fund in question and need to rely on initial estimates, typically based on historical data. As the fund matures, the

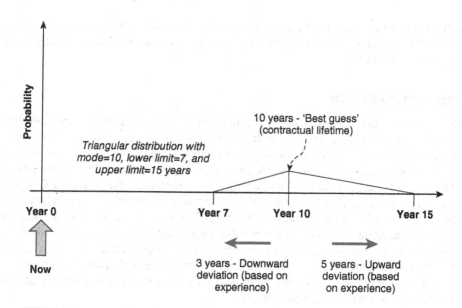

FIGURE 6.3 Initialize range for fund lifetime

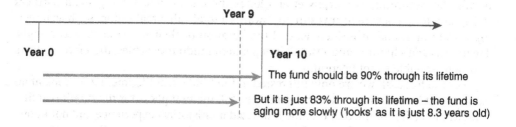

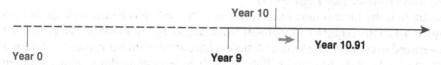

FIGURE 6.4 Adjust most likely lifetime for 'speed'

internal age becomes 1, and the forecast is the fund's real lifetime on maturity with downward and upward deviation equal to 0. We have all the facts, i.e. data for the fund and are completely certain. The initial estimates are irrelevant.

The 'speed' of ageing is less reliably measured during the fund's early years, where its history is too short, giving too few data points. For young funds, we therefore give more weight to the estimates, and for older funds, we give more weight to the measurements and the emerging trend line.

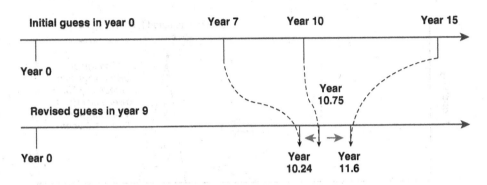

FIGURE 6.5   Adjust lifetime ranges for certainty

How certain are we that the fund will continue with this 'speed'? Reasonably certain, but not 100%. Instead, we take the average of the original and the current estimate, weighted by the internal age:

$$10\,\text{years} * (1 - 0.83) + 10.91\,\text{years} * 0.83 = 10.75\,\text{years}.$$

Then, we need to adjust the ranges of the fund's lifetime for certainty (see **Figure 6.5**). The downward deviation of three years at the outset is now, proportionately to the increasing internal age, reduced to

$$(1 - 0.83) * 3\,\text{years} = 0.51\,\text{years}.$$

Also the upward deviation shrinks:

$$(1 - 0.83) * 5\,\text{years} = 0.85\,\text{years}.$$

This is giving us the new parameters for the triangular distribution describing the fund's lifetime (see **Figure 6.6**).

Ranges for fund TVPIs

The same idea is applied to the fund's TVPI ranges. For simplicity and just to explain the principle, the triangular distribution is used again, before later looking at a way to get to a more realistic PDF. Based on historical data and after consulting an expert, let us assume that the best guess for the fund's TVPI on maturity would be 2. Some top-performing funds show multiples of 5, but it is also possible, albeit rare, that a fund is a complete failure, loses all the invested capital, and thus results in a TVPI of 0 (see **Figure 6.7**). These three estimates (the numbers are just for illustration) define the triangular distribution for the TVPI outcomes.

We look at the fund in its ninth year when it has an interim TVPI [i.e. distribution to paid-in capital (DPI)] of 1.35. Again, we determine the weighted average between the

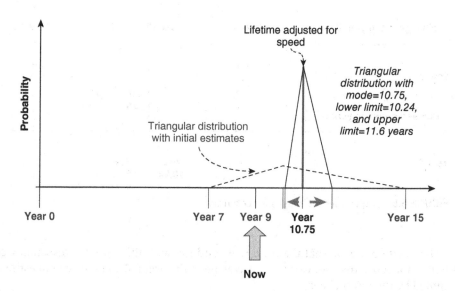

FIGURE 6.6   Update triangular distribution for fund's lifetime

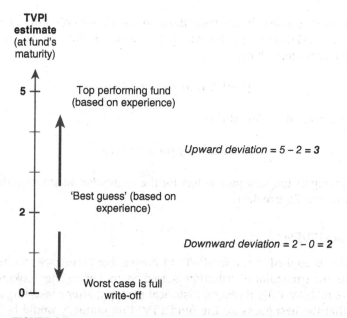

FIGURE 6.7   Initialize range for TVPI

currently measured TVPI and the originally estimated TVPI. This time, however, this is weighted by the distribution age (see **Figure 6.8**).

We could also use the fund's internal age for this weighting. However, the distribution age is a more reliable yardstick for how far the fund has advanced in liquidating its

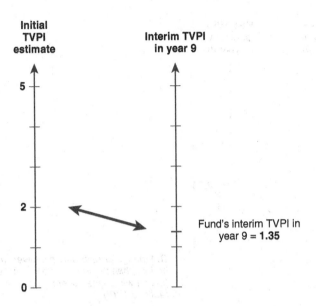

FIGURE 6.8 Adjust most likely TVPI for current trajectory

portfolio. As long as nothing is distributed, the distribution age is 0. Then, the original estimate is maintained, and there is 0 weight being given to the interim TVPI. When the fund starts distributing, we can take the interim TVPI as an increasingly reliable indicator for the fund's final TVPI.

For the distribution age of 0.5, we calculate the updated estimated TVPI as

$$1.35*0.5+2*(1-0.5)=1,68.$$

The internal age remains the overall indicator for certainty of outcomes. The higher the internal age, the smaller the error regarding the final estimated outcome. Thus, we need to adjust the estimates for the downward and upward deviation that determine the ranges within which the TVPI outcome is likely to fall (see **Figure 6.9**).

This adjustment is proportional to the internal age. The originally estimated upward deviation for the TVPI was 5 – 2 = 3 and the originally estimated downward deviation was 2 – 0 = 2. For the internal age of 0.73, we adjust the upward deviation:

$$3*(1-0.73)=0.81.$$

The downward deviation is

$$2*(1-0.73)=0.54.$$

So, the updated optimistic case becomes 1.68 + 0.81 = 2.50, and the updated pessimistic case becomes 1.68 – 0.54 = 1.13.

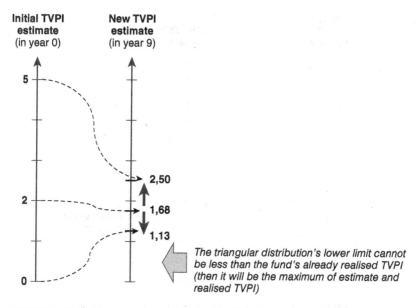

FIGURE 6.9 Adjust TVPI ranges for certainty

Note that the downward deviation cannot imply a worse outcome than the fund's already realised TVPI. In this way, the fund's individual history imposes constraints that further narrow the ranges of outcomes.

Picking samples

The ranges for a fund's lifetime and its TVPI essentially define a 'box' from which the MCS picks pairs of lifetime/TVPI samples (see **Figure 6.10**).

As described in the previous section, for each lifetime/TVPI sample, the fund's growth rate is calculated as input to the TAM, and based on this, its contributions, distributions, and NAVs are forecasted (see **Figure 6.11**).

Through the internal age mechanism, the 'box' from which the samples are picked is shrinking as the fund matures and is converging to a point defined by the fund's outcome in terms of lifetime and TVPI (see **Figure 6.12**).

At this point in time, all the fund's cash flows have become fact, and no further forecast needs to be produced.

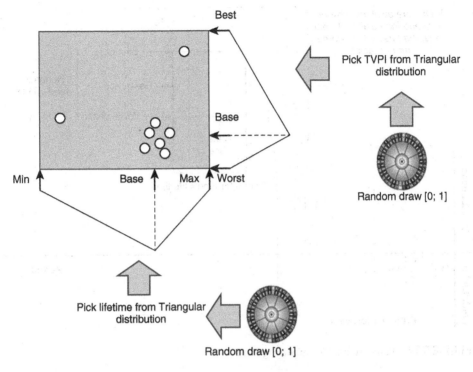

FIGURE 6.10 Pick samples of pairs (lifetime and TVPI)

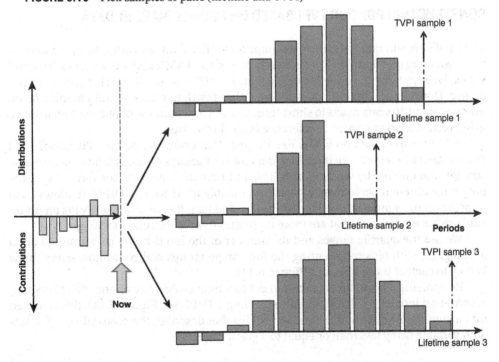

FIGURE 6.11 TAM forecasts scaled to lifetime and TVPI, three samples.

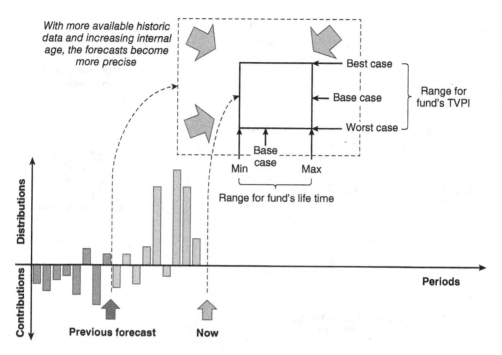

FIGURE 6.12   Forecast 'box' for maturing fund

CONSTRUCTING PDF FOR TVPI BASED ON PRIVATE MARKET DATA

The fund's growth rate is a critical assumption for the TAM, and often this parameter is set based on expert opinion. This is clearly one of the TAM's major drawbacks. To avoid subjective inputs for the growth rate, Tolkamp (2007) took public market returns as reference. However, it remains a question how the growth rate over a fund's lifetime of, on average, about 10 years reacts to short-term ups and downs in the public market. Instead, using private market returns as reference is an alternative.

Private market data providers like Burgiss, Cambridge Associates, PitchBook, and Preqin regularly report benchmarking data for peer groups of funds following the same strategy and ordered by vintage years. This information is given in the form of quartile ranges for different performance measures, notably for IRRs and TVPIs. It allows us to improve on the simple triangular distribution and base the sampling of TVPIs on up-to-date private market data that are more representative for the fund's strategy.

We use the quartile ranges and the number of the funds in the peer group to build a histogram with bins representing the four range groups and count how many funds belong to each of those bins (see **Figure 6.13**).

By applying a normalising factor to get to a total probability of one, this histogram is converted into a PDF. For randomly sampling a TVPI (see **Figure 6.14**), this is turned into a cumulative distribution function (CDF) that describes the probabilities of a random variable being less than or equal to a given value.

Date	Vintage	Strategy	Geography	Number of funds	TVPI 5%	TVPI 25%	TVPI 50%	TVPI 75%	TVPI 95%
03/2023	2013	Buyouts	European Union	55	0.66	1.03	1.48	1.62	2.68

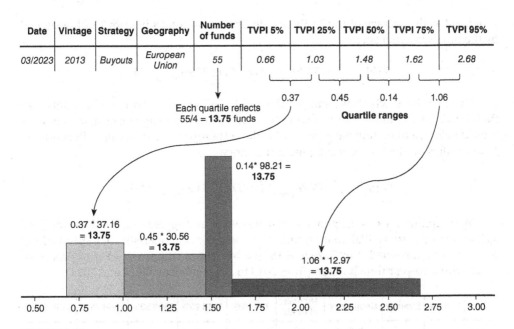

FIGURE 6.13 Building histogram for TVPI out of quartile ranges

random.**random**( )

Return the next random floating point number in the range [0, 1)

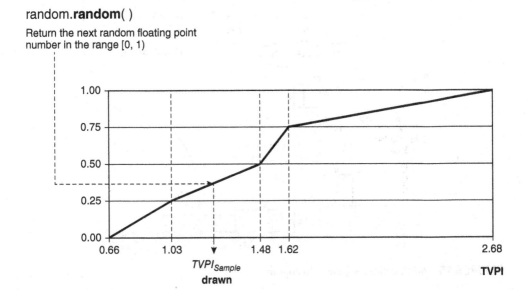

FIGURE 6.14 Sampling from Horizon TVPI CDF

Earlier, the internal age mechanism was applied to the triangular distribution to narrow the range for the forecasted TVPIs with increasing certainty regarding outcomes. Here, this is done differently but achieving the same effect. The forecasted TVPI is defined as the average of the TVPI sample drawn and fund's interim TVPI, weighted by the fund's internal age:

$$TVPI_{Forecast} = TVPI_{Sample} * (1 - IA) + TVPI_{Interim} * IA.$$

The PDF from which we sample the TVPIs defines the respective boundaries of their 'box'. A variation would be using the fund's distribution age instead, as this is, as argued before, a more reliable yardstick for the certainty of outcomes and filters out the J-curve effect on the fund's development trajectory:

$$TVPI_{Forecast} = TVPI_{Sample} * (1 - DA) + TVPI_{Interim} * DA.$$

By compiling various benchmark quartile ranges and aggregating for the same fund age, we can construct a PDF that captures the stochastic characteristics of a specific fund strategy to be modelled.[16] In **Figure 6.15**, the histogram compiles two peer groups of funds with a 10-year time horizon (from 2013 to 2023, and from 2014 and 2024).

Date	Vintage	Strategy	Geography	Number of funds	TVPI 5%	TVPI 25%	TVPI 50%	TVPI 75%	TVPI 95%
03/2023	2013	Buyouts	European Union	55	0.66	1.03	1.48	1.62	2.68
03/2024	2014	Buyouts	European Union	21	1.01	1.27	1.55	1.90	2.31

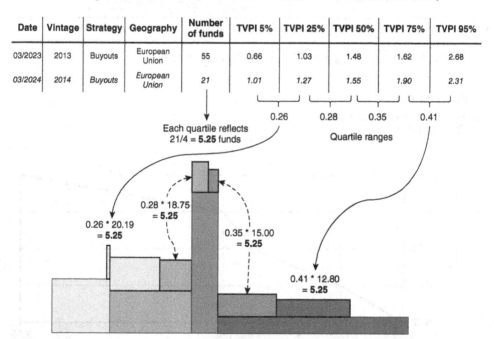

FIGURE 6.15   Adding vintage year to histogram

This process will be repeated for all the benchmark data representing vintages that are 10 years and older. In many situations, it can make sense to reduce this threshold and assume, say, eight-year-old vintage peer groups as sufficiently mature to build this 'horizon TVPI CDF'.

The same principle can be applied to other performance measures reported by the private market benchmark providers, for example, paid-in to capital committed (PICC), residual value to paid-in capital (RVPI), and DPI. PICC data allow us, for example, to

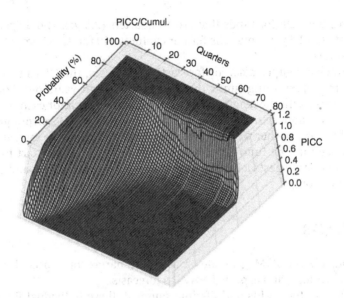

FIGURE 6.16 Cumulative distribution function PICC over time (capturing contributions)

reconstruct the average contribution rate for funds per time period. **Figure 6.16** shows the development for PICC over 80 quarters, i.e. 20 years, giving the CDF for each time horizon.

The longer the time horizon, the more the funds' portfolios are liquidated and the higher the number of the peer group's mature funds. Therefore, the longer the time horizon, the less a CDF will change. However, there are also fewer vintage year groups that are, say, 20 years old than that are 5 years old. So, with increasing time horizon, the number of funds per time period will go down. This is demonstrated by **Figure 6.17**

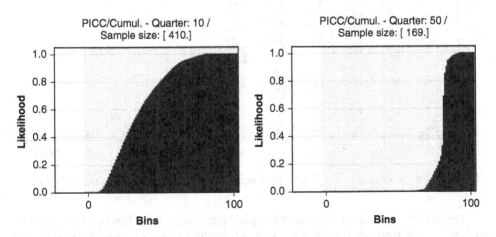

FIGURE 6.17 Sampling horizon and samples sizes

that compares the CDF for funds that are 10 quarters (2.5 years) old against the CDF for funds that are 12.5 years old. The former captures 410 funds, whereas the latter only reflects 169 funds.

As reasonable compromise, for forecasting purposes, the CDFs should be based on peer groups representing funds that are at least eight years old. Forecast errors generally increase with the length of the forecast horizon, but for cash flows, this relationship does not appear to have been looked at in detail. Do errors grow linearly, exponentially, or in another way with the time horizon? When we look at benchmarking data, we see that the fund's TVPIs and lifetime expectations start to flatten after some years, so this suggests a linear relationship between accuracy and the length of the forecast horizon.

A1*TAM RESULTS

For one fund, the A1*TAM generates a set of scenarios for expected contributions, expected distributions, and expected NAVs as forecasts.

Depending on the TVPIs and lifetime sampled, these individual forecasts can be categorised as optimistic, pessimistic, or as base cases. The combination of short lifetimes and low TVPIs leads to low (pessimistic) exposures (see **Figure 6.18**) where high multiples are consistent with high growth rates and over longer time frames lead to high (optimistic) exposures.

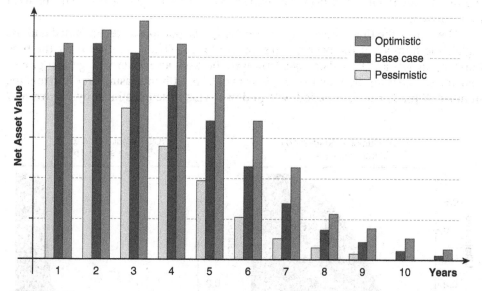

FIGURE 6.18   NAV exposure scenarios forecasted by A1*TAM (semi-deterministic TAM)

The A1*TAM allows us to determine plausible ranges for a fund's growth rate on realisation and through this also understanding the impact of investment risk. The model, however, does not fully reflect the LP's funding risk. The optimistic and pessimistic cash-flow forecasts do not mark the best and worst scenarios – they are only the 'best' and 'worst' expected cash flows and, therefore, do not capture the real extremes. For this, we need to model the random patterns of contributions and distributions.

NOTES

1. In a similar approach, Lenz et al. (2018) used the TAM as a 'base model' and included, among other factors, fund-specific, macroeconomic, and capital market variables. The authors claimed that this yielded significant improvements over the original TAM. In their enhancements, they additionally modelled the timing of capital calls, the magnitude of capital calls, the timing of investment distributions, and the magnitude of investment distributions. Like with the augmented TAM, this framework can be used in a simulation to allow investors to better understand the distribution of likely cash flows through time and to enable scenario analysis and stress testing.
2. See EVCA (2013) and Buchner (2014).
3. See Gelfer et al. (2020).
4. See PitchBook (2020).
5. Hickman (2019) approached the VaR calculation for private equity funds in this way, too, making the same assumption.
6. See discussion on this in Cornelius et al. (2011).
7. See EVCA (2013).
8. Palnitkar (2021) criticised the parameters proposed in Takahashi and Alexander (2002) as 'arbitrarily taken'. Furenstam and Forsell (2018) estimated the funds' growth rate as 12% per annum from one institution's historical data, and Virtanen (2019) drew on the help of another institution's experts to estimate the growth rate to be 8% per annum.
9. ILPA views the TVPI as the best available measure of performance before the end of a fund's life. See https://ilpa.org/glossary/total-value-to-paid-in-tvpi/, [accessed 3 July 2023]
10. See Robinson and Sensoy (2016).
11. The triangular distribution is often used in financial analysis; see, for example, Collan (2012). Wikipedia refers to the triangular distribution as 'lack of knowledge' distribution that is used when the only data on hand are the maximum and minimum values, and the most likely outcome (See https://en.wikipedia.org/wiki/Triangular_distribution, [accessed 3 September 2023]). Rudd (2016) challenged this, arguing that no random phenomenon commonly encountered in the real world actually has this distribution. Moreover, the maximally non-committal distribution would be the one with the biggest entropy. Therefore, for a random variable with hard upper and lower bounds, Rudd rather recommends the uniform distribution. While the triangular distribution was chosen not only for simplicity but also because it models the dynamics that drive the funds' lifetimes quite well, the approach described here does not critically rely on this assumption and also works with the uniform distribution.
12. See Maptrip (2021).
13. See Meyer and Mathonet (2005).
14. Harte and Buchner (2017) suggested fund lifetimes of between 10 and 14 years.
15. See Woodman (2023).
16. In fact, this is done dynamically, by first defining the strategy, accessing a sufficiently large set of matching quartile ranges from the benchmark, then randomly picking an entry (weighted by the number of funds represented in the peer group), and finally sampling from the selected entry (as described in **Figure 6.14**).

CHAPTER 7

Augmented TAM – Pattern Model

The Takahashi–Alexander model (TAM) clearly has stood test of time, as evidenced by its widespread use over decades and many papers building on it. As discussed before, alternative stochastic models have been proposed but at least so far have not really caught on and are not as often referred to as the paper by Takahashi and Alexander (2002).

With the A1*TAM, we randomly vary the TAM's input parameters, but the forecasted contributions and distributions remain expected values (see **Figure 7.1**).

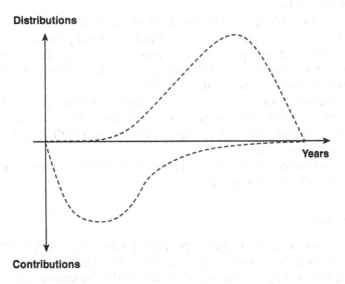

FIGURE 7.1 Expected contributions and distributions forecasted by the TAM

The A1*TAM with the original TAM at its core does not overcome the shortcomings of this deterministic model. The major weakness is that forecasts are only on an annual basis, whereas limited partners (LPs) often require more granularity, such as quarterly forecasts. The TAM can certainly be modified to meet this requirement, but this is not the end of the story. The expected cash flows forecasted by the TAM are unlikely to accurately reflect the level of liquidity risks of portfolios of funds, which only stochastic cash flows can capture.

In addition to the deterministic nature of the discrete-time TAM and the user-supplied parameterisation, a according to Harte and Buchner (2017) critically, limiting aspect of it is that it does not account for fees.

A2*TAM

The A2*TAM further generalises the TAM, building on the A1*TAM's results (target life-time, target total value to paid-in capital (TVPI), expected contributions, and expected distributions). The first important extension is by allowing for different periodicities, i.e. the typical annually, semi-annually, quarterly, and monthly granularities of cash flows.[1] Forecasts are often quarterly as this is also in line with the frequency of the investment reporting in the private industry. At least for short-term projections, LPs may even need monthly forecasts.

The A2*TAM is producing cash flows that are typical for funds. It describes the funds' typical behaviour unbiased by market so that in later stages of a Monte Carlo simulation (MCS), various stresses can be applied on the forecasted cash flows without double counting of risks.

To keep it compatible with TAM, the A2*TAM is designed as a discrete-time sto-chastic model. It projects randomly distributed cash flows and provides estimates for net asset values (NAVs) that are consistent with these cash flows. With increasing number of samples for cash flows, the A2*TAM's averaged results converge towards the TAM's expected contributions and expected distributions.

The real cash flows look more random (see **Figure 7.2**). There are long periods with-out any cash flows; notably, distributions from funds can be delayed by years. Moreover, while most cash flows are rather small, there can be extreme outliers that the TAM fails to model adequately (see **Figure 7.3**).

We require additional parameters for how often cash flows take place and how they are varying to describe this behaviour.

Reactiveness of model

The A1*TAM reacts to the fund's and its peer group's development. The changes in the fund's historical cash flows and its updated NAV affect the fund's internal age (IA). This is reflected in the trajectory along which the fund is forecasted to develop. The IA mechanism results in NAV changes having less of an impact, positive as well as nega-tive, for a young fund – where they 'heal' over the remaining lifetime – than for a fund close to maturity.

In this way, the A1*TAM uses the best available information for each step, e.g. contributions are projected based on the undrawn commitment for the year and the remaining distributions are based on, among other factors, the current valuation. The A2*TAM with a quarterly or even monthly granularity is likely to be more reactive to changes.

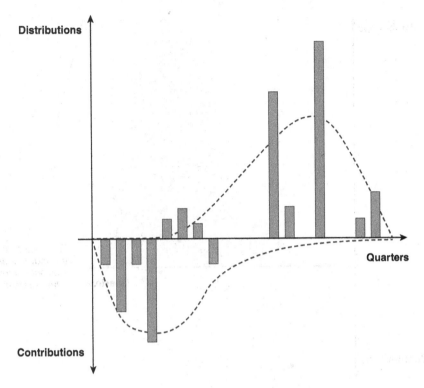

FIGURE 7.2 Stochastic cash-flow sample (simplified, schematic)

For the contribution side, the uncalled capital puts a constraint on the volatility and frequency of the capital calls. The forecasted management fees cannot exceed the uncalled capital and thus also react to the fund's development.

Model overview

This approach is implemented in several steps:

- As the outcome models are based on a fund's lifetime and TVPI, in the first step, the A1*TAM takes a fund's historical cash flows until the actual state date, its latest NAV at this date, its expected lifetime, and its TVPI on maturity to calculate the growth factor required for the TAM.
- The A1*TAM requires probability density functions (PDFs) and ranges for a fund's lifetime and TVPI. As with increasing maturity the uncertainty regarding the fund's outcome is decreasing, the ranges need to be adjusted based on the fund's history before the actual state date.
- For the outcome model, the horizon TVPI cumulative distribution function (CDF) depends on the fund's peer group and is derived from private market data.

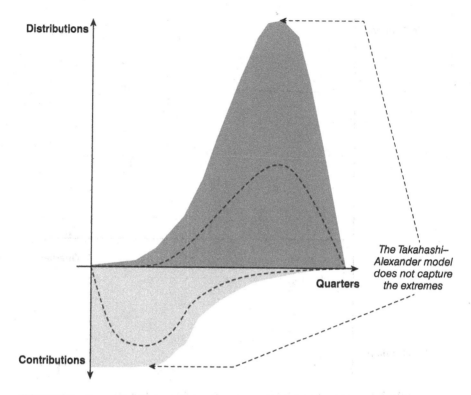

FIGURE 7.3   Towards a stochastic model

- Capturing liquidity risk requires a stochastic pattern model, which is termed here the 'A2*TAM'. While the TAM only produces annual forecasts, the A2*TAM supports higher granularities, such as semi-annual, quarterly, and monthly forecasts. Moreover, the A2*TAM produces randomly distributed cash flows that are in line with parameters set for the cash flows' frequencies and volatilities, and that form the basis for liquidity-risk-related analyses.
- The TAM produces one forecast for how a fund's NAVs develop over the years. Based on the A2*TAM's forecast, we determine the fund's cash-flow-consistent NAV PDF for each point in time that forms the basis for capital-risk-related analyses.
- When looking at stochastic cash flows, there are some components for which timing and amounts are actually well defined, notably the management fee schedule and the yield. Therefore, in a further refinement, contributions to funds are split into capital calls and management fees, and distributions from funds are split into realisations and their fixed return/yield component.

The funds' individual cash flows need to be assembled to a portfolio view that also takes dependencies between the funds into consideration.

CHANGING GRANULARITY

From a practical perspective, a significant disadvantage of discrete-time models is that switching from, say, an annual granularity to a quarterly one is not simple. To achieve this for the A2*TAM, the starting point is the fund forecast over the chosen time horizon of several years as generated by the TAM. The TAM provides yearly average contributions and yearly average distributions:

$$\overline{C_i}; i = 1, \dots, Y$$

$$\overline{D_i}; i = 1, \dots, Y.$$

Contributions and distributions are reaching a target multiple TVPI:

$$\frac{\sum_{i=1}^{Y} \overline{D_i}}{\sum_{i=1}^{Y} \overline{C_i}} = TVPI.$$

We need to determine quarterly distributions:

$$\widetilde{D_{i:j}}; i = 1, \dots, Y; j = 1, \dots, 4$$

so that

$$\forall i = 1, \dots, Y : \sum_{j=1}^{4} \widetilde{D_{i:j}} = \overline{D_i}.$$

The simplest way to spread a cash flow over four quarters is (see **Figure 7.4**) to divide the annual forecast by 4:[2]

$$\widetilde{D_{i:j}} = \overline{D_i} \Big/ 4 ; i = 1, \dots, Y; j = 1, \dots, 4.$$

The same approach is followed for the contributions. This is in line with previous research: Karatas et al. (2021) had to adjust the TAM's forecast, too, as they needed quarterly data and for this purpose also divided these annual forecasts by 4.

INJECTING RANDOMNESS

While the TAM forecasts expected contributions and distributions, in reality, the funds' cash flows look more 'random'. The simplest way of modelling this behaviour is through sampling directly from historical funds' cash-flow data sets that reflect the randomness. However, it is often not possible to acquire historic cash flows from comparable funds. Instead, using synthetic, i.e. artificially generated, fund cash flows can be an often more practical solution.

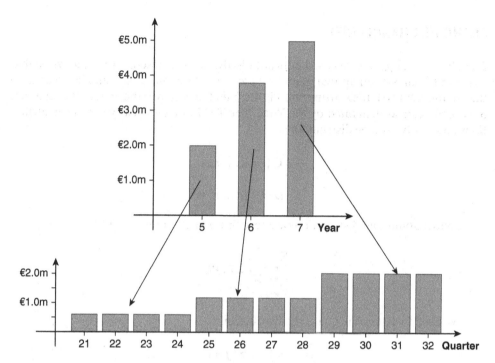

FIGURE 7.4   Splitting annual into quarterly cash-flows

The A2*TAM models this randomness through parameters for frequency *freq_ctrl* and volatility *vol_ctrl* of cash flows:

$$0 < freq\_ctrl \leq 1$$

$$0 \leq vol\_ctrl \leq 1.$$

freq_ctrl is defined as the probability of a cash flow taking place within a given period and obviously needs to be larger than zero as otherwise there would never be a cash flow. A *freq_ctrl* of one means that a cash flow is certain for the period.

With a *vol_ctrl* of zero, cash flows will not deviate from the TAM's expected cash flows, whereas a *vol_ctrl* of one means the maximum deviation possible for the period.

By funnelling data generated by the deterministic TAM through this noise-adding, a new data set of synthetic fund cash flows can be created. The resulting data set shows the statistical features and the useful patterns needed for capturing for the liquidity risks associated with the portfolio of funds.

Setting frequency of cash flows

The A2*TAM needs to capture the risk that there will be no positive cash flows with which an LP could fund other activities or that the LP will be called for amounts far higher than the average forecasts suggest. In reality, fund cash flows do not conform to the average projections suggested by the TAM, for example:

- There are many months where there are no cash flows at all.
- Usually, cash flows are small, but in rare cases there can also be very large cash flows.

This is modelled through a specific PDF for every step in the forecast's time line (i.e. there can be different PDFs):

$$\Pr_{i;j;k}[X]; i = 1, \ldots, Y; j = 1, \ldots, G; k = contributions \ and \ distributions.$$

This can be any PDF that generates only a positive cash flow X:

$$\Pr_{i;j;k}[X < 0] = 0; i = 1, \ldots, Y; j = 1, \ldots, G; k = contributions \ and \ distributions.$$

Also, as there can be periods without any contributions or distributions:

$$\Pr_{i;j;k}[X = 0] > 0; i = 1, \ldots, Y; j = 1, \ldots, G; k = contributions \ and \ distributions.$$

In addition, the expected values for the PDFs that model contributions are:

$$E_{i;j;contributions}[X] = \widetilde{C_{i;j}}; i = 1, \ldots, Y; j = 1, \ldots, G$$

and the expected values for the PDFs that model distributions are:

$$E_{i;j;distributions}[X] = \widetilde{D_{i;j}}; i = 1, \ldots, Y; j = 1, \ldots, G.$$

For the MCS, we need a number of N randomly drawn samples for stochastic cash flows that meet several conditions. The stochastic contributions for the nth sample are an array:

$$\left(C_{1;1;n}, \ldots, C_{Y;G;n}\right); i = 1, \ldots, Y; j = 1, \ldots, G.$$

The stochastic distributions for the nth sample are an array:

$$\left(D_{1;1;n}, \ldots, D_{Y;G;n}\right); i = 1, \ldots, Y; j = 1, \ldots, G.$$

The contribution samples need to be independently drawn from their respective PDF:

$$C_{i;j;n} = \Pr_{i;j;contributions}; i = 1, \ldots, Y; j = 1, \ldots, G.$$

Also, the accumulated contributions for sample n cannot exceed the amount the LP has committed to the fund:

$$\sum_{i=1}^{Y}\sum_{j=1}^{G} C_{i;j;n} \leq Commitment.$$

The distributions samples need to be independently drawn from their respective PDF:

$$D_{i;j;n} = \Pr_{i;j;distributions}; i = 1, \ldots, Y; j = 1, \ldots, G.$$

The cash flows need to reach the target multiple:

$$\frac{\sum_{i=1}^{Y}\sum_{j=1}^{G}D_{i;j;n}}{\sum_{i=1}^{Y}\sum_{j=1}^{G}C_{i;j;n}} = TVPI.$$

For large samples N of random cash flows, their average yearly cash-flow needs to be that generated by the TAM, i.e. for contributions:

$$\lim_{N\to\infty}\frac{\sum_{j=1}^{G}C_{i;j;n}}{N} = \overline{C_i}; i = 1, \ldots, Y.$$

Likewise, for distributions:

$$\lim_{N\to\infty}\frac{\sum_{j=1}^{G}D_{i;j;n}}{N} = \overline{D_i}; i = 1, \ldots, Y$$

$$\widetilde{D_{i;j}} = \overline{D_i}\Big/4 \; ; i = 1, \ldots, Y; j = 1, \ldots, 4.$$

For example, venture capital (VC) funds tend to follow a milestone approach for stepwise funding many portfolio companies of which, however, typically the majority fails, of the remaining most show mediocre performance, but in rare cases extreme winners emerge. During such funds' investment periods, we would expect a high frequency of smaller, rather regular contributions for the many initial investments and their follow-on financing, while for the divestment period, only few realisations of varying amounts would be typical.

Setting volatility for contributions

The A2*TAM's advantage is that the fund's individual history imposes constraints that narrow the ranges of probable and possible outcomes and cash-flow patterns, become more precise, and thus converge with new information towards the fund's real outcome at maturity. Contributions to funds are constrained in two ways: they cannot be smaller than zero and must not exceed the fund's uncalled capital at that time.

One way of controlling this randomness is through a beta distribution, i.e. a family of continuous probability distributions that are defined on the interval [0, 1] and determine how the contribution rates for a given period will be set (see **Figure 7.5**).

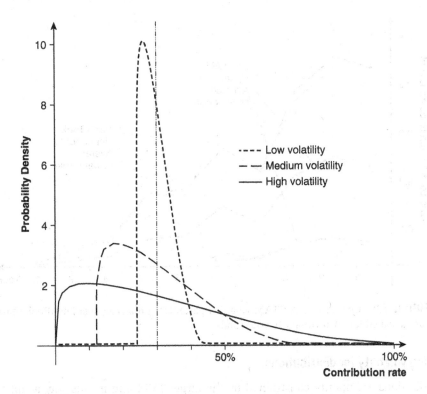

FIGURE 7.5 Controlling volatility of contributions through a beta distribution; here for expected contribution rate of 30%

While the A2*TAM produces randomly distributed cash flows, they cannot be independent between the different periods. *freq_ctrl* and *vol_ctrl* are best understood as dials between regular cash flows and noisy cash flows:

- A high *freq_ctrl* translates into a higher probability of capital calls, which due to the limited commit size increases the likelihood that in later periods, there is no commitment left and thus no cash flow is going to happen. The constraint on the total commitment size leads to situation, where *freq_ctrl* may not be the cash flow's frequency.
- A total paid-in close to the committed capital at termination date leads to an expected value of the PDFs summing up to be close to the committed capital, too. Hence, as the cash flows are randomised, we can end up with cases that we exceed the committed capital. The way we can avoid this issue is to imply less randomness to the contributions, i.e. either adjust *freq_ctrl* or *vol_ctrl*. High volatility also translates into lower commitments available at later periods, which also leads to less volatility then – a behaviour in line with the real world, as the comparison against PitchBook data (see **Figure 7.6**) demonstrates.[3]

Essentially, this is the behaviour stochastic models capture through a mean-reverting process applied to the rate at which capital is called.[4]

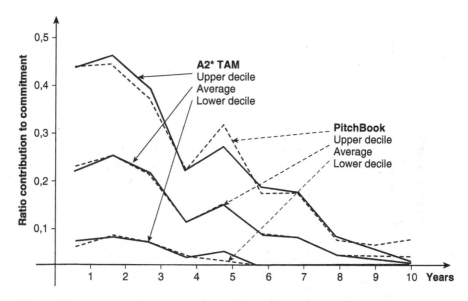

FIGURE 7.6   Comparison A2*TAM volatility parameter impact against PitchBook yearly capital called for 2006 vintage buyout funds

Setting volatility for distributions

Distributions are mainly constrained by the target TVPI and in this way adapt to the fund's historical development. They cannot be smaller than zero, but their maximum is undefined. For instance, VC funds often produce few extreme winners compared to buyout strategies that tend to show more but less spectacular realisations.

To capture this behaviour, we need a probability distribution that starts at zero but shows a heavy tail, i.e. a larger probability of getting very large values, to allow us to dial up from 'no' over 'mild' to 'wild' randomness. The log-normal distribution captures this behaviour quite well (see **Figure 7.7**).

To allow for $vol\_ctrl \leq 1$, we assume a maximum standard deviation of, for example, $\sigma = 5$ and normalise σ to a $[0, 1]$ range.

Scaling and re-picking cash-flow samples

While using the forecasts generated by the A1*TAM as template, cash-flow scenarios are generated separately for contributions and distributions and between periods. Therefore, in most cases, the $TVPI_{generated}$ will be different from $TVPI_{A1*TAM}$. If they are reasonably close, i.e. $\left| TVPI_{generated} - TVPI_{targeted} \right| \leq \varepsilon$, a simple rescaling of the distributions with a factor

$$\frac{TVPI_{A1*TAM}}{TVPI_{generated}}$$

will give a good approximation for cash flows that meet the stated conditions while assuring that $TVPI_{A2*TAM} = TVPI_{A1*TAM}$.

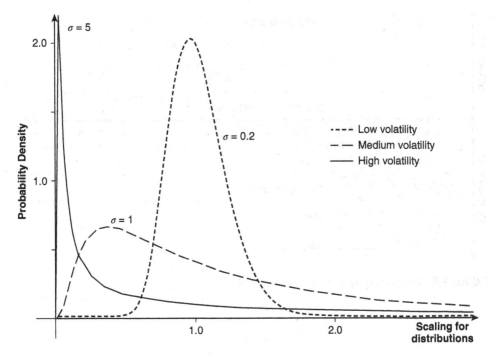

FIGURE 7.7   Controlling volatility of distributions through log-normal distribution

If $\left| TVPI_{generated} - TVPI_{targeted} \right| > \varepsilon$, we need to 're-pick' and generate a new cash-flow scenario. If after a maximum allowed number of re-picks, there is still no cash-flow scenario with a sufficiently close $TVPI_{generated}$, the model would simply continue with the closest one. If course, the likelihood of having to re-pick depends on how small or large ε is set. The smaller the ε, the more precise the fit of A1*TAM and A2*TAM will be.

CONVERGENCE A2*TAM TO TAM

Figure 7.8 shows how with an increasing number of samples generated by the A2*TAM results[5] converge to the cash flows forecasted by the TAM (within 5–95% confidence band). This example assumed a high *freq_ctrl* for quarterly cash flows and a low *vol_ctrl*. While the A2*TAM's average contributions quickly converge towards the TAM's expected contribution forecast, for the A2*TAM's distributions, this process typically takes longer.

Figure 7.9 shows the same TAM but assumes a high volatility and high frequency of cash flows for the A2*TAM. Here, the 'wild' randomness leads to a narrowing band for the contributions, as undrawn commitments are being used up more quickly.

Experience with the model suggests that for all practical purposes, the generated scenarios are 'good enough' to be considered as compatible with the TAM.

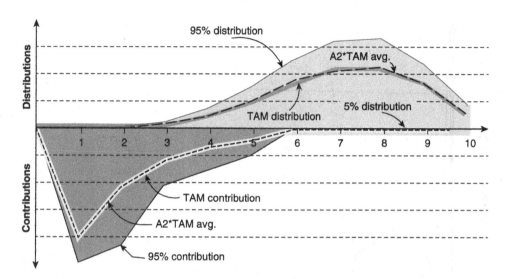

FIGURE 7.8 Impact *freq_ctrl*=0,7 and low *vol_ctrl*

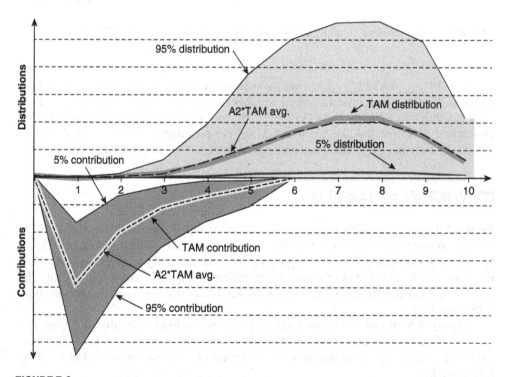

FIGURE 7.9 Impact high *vol_ctrl* and *freq_ctrl*=1,0

SPLIT CASH FLOWS IN COMPONENTS

For yearly deterministic forecasts, it makes sense just to consider two types of cash flows, i.e. contributions and distributions. Cash-flow data from private market data providers like PitchBook or Preqin do not provide the level of detail that would allow a model to identify further cash-flow types. Only internally built cash-flow libraries, drawn from own administration systems that capture different transaction types, would be able to do this.

For a stochastic model and other periodicities, we need to differentiate between cash flows that remain largely deterministic and cash flows that are more random in nature. Therefore, the A2*TAM forecasts four different types of cash flows: capital calls, management fees, realisations, and fixed returns with:

$$Contributions = capital\ calls + management\ fees$$

$$Distributions = realisations + fixed\ returns.$$

These additional details further improve the forecasts by incorporating prior knowledge of relatively certain cash flows. The A2*TAM requires additional parameters to model management fees and fixed returns:

- The usual <u>calculation basis</u> for management fees is either committed capital or invested capital.
- The <u>investment period</u> defines until when management fees are to be calculated based on the committed capital. Once the investment period expires, the vast majority of fund managers begin to receive a discounted management fee.
- Most commonly, after the <u>termination of the investment period</u>, the management fee rate will remain the same, but the calculation basis of the fee will change. Usually, the fee rate starts accruing on what the fund managers put to work, i.e. the acquisition costs of the unrealised investments (i.e. the invested capital). Occasionally, managers continue using the value of commitments, but the fees are discounted by tapering the charged amount annually by reference to the amounts charged in the immediately preceding year.
- The <u>fee schedule</u> is defined by the period (within a year) of the first payment and the frequency in which the management fees are paid. An example for an assumed monthly periodicity is: first fee payment in March, quarterly payments (i.e. every three months).
- The TAM's yield parameter is extended by being able to set its frequency and the first period of when the yield is generated (example for monthly periodicity: first payment in February, twice a year) as <u>yield schedule</u>.

Management fees are also one explanation of a fund's J-curve (see **Box 7.1**). They are not covered by the TAM, but can have a significant impact.[6] Management fees occur even during periods without capital calls or realisations. Their aggregated impact is too significant to be ignored for a capital-call-at-risk (CCaR) calculation.

Fees

Fund managers are compensated through fixed and variable fees. Variable fees comprise the carried interest, the performance-related incentive that is key to the fund structure, and fees charged to the portfolio companies, such as transaction and monitoring fees. For setting up the fund, usually a flat fee (up to 1% of the committed capital) is charged, and management fees are predominantly fixed.

According to Harte and Buchner (2017), management fee schedules tend to be 'plain vanilla' rather than exotic combinations. Fees are usually paid quarterly and range from 1% per annum to 3% per annum. Management fees result in cash flows from the LP to the fund manager, but LPs do not, at least not directly, see the variable fees as cash flows from the fund to the LP are net, i.e. after these fees have been deducted.

Box 7.1   Market practices management fees

For private credit funds, Doherty and Kolman (2018) observed more variability in management fees as well as carried interest terms. This reflects the very different risk-return profiles of various credit fund strategies. According to Norton (2020), management fees do not exceed 1.5%.

For primary funds of funds (FOFs), Auerbach and Shivananda (2017) assume a management fee of typically less than 1% and for secondary fund managers a management fee of roughly 1%.

Usually, no or reduced management fees are charged for co-investments, which theoretically allows LPs to significantly reduce their costs. However, that co-investments come 'for free', i.e. no management fees or carried interest need to be paid by the LP is over-simplistic. Investments made via co-investment funds are typically charged a 1% fee and 10% carried interest, and also fund managers are occasionally getting incentivised through a so-called 'promote' to strengthen the alignment of their interests with those of the co-investing LPs.[7]

Using net TVPI figures from private market benchmarks circumvents the problem of modelling the impact of carried interest.[8] This works at least in situations where the fund's style corresponds to the peer group's style represented by the private market database.[9] In case the fit is not too close, we need to apply stresses that are proportional to the degree of deviation (see **Chapter 12 and Chapter 16**).

The usual calculation basis for management fees is either committed capital or invested capital. The investment period defines until when management fees are to be calculated based on the committed capital. Once the investment period expires, the vast majority of fund managers begin to receive a discounted management fee.

Box 7.2   Credit lines to finance capital calls

The TAM as proposed by Takahashi and Alexander (2002) predates important developments in global private equity markets. It can be relatively easily applied to secondary investments and co-investments as increasingly important components of LP portfolios. But there has also been innovation in the form of credit lines (also called 'capital call lines' that come mainly in the form of subscription lines and NAV-based credit lines) that have an impact on how to model cash flows.

Subscription lines are short-term credit lines where the general partner (GP) takes out a loan that is secured by the capital that can be called from the fund's LPs. The lenders will assess the quality of the fund's LP base, with terms generally more favourable if the fund's LPs comprise large institutions with a track record in this type of investments.

NAV-based credit lines, which are secured against the overall fund's assets, are another approach to borrowing. Here, the lender needs to assess the quality of the fund's assets that form the collateral. In private markets, this requires specialist know--how, which explains why the subscription line market is still several times the size of that for NAV-based credit lines.[10]

MOTIVATION

GPs understand that LPs are not the only source of funding. They also exploit the fact that most LPs do not view undrawn commitments as part of an allocation to private capital and use these commitments as collateral for a line of credit. Instead of calling undrawn commitments from investors, fund managers use this loan to finance the acquisition.

LPs as well as GPs see advantages in the use of this financial engineering technique. LPs often need to wait several years for their committed capital to be deployed. Here, capital call lines can reduce the overall duration of a private capital portfolio.

Over its lifetime, the fund calls the same amount of capital, but capital calls are larger and their number is significantly lower. This is particularly relevant in the case of private debt funds that make a much larger number of investments than private equity funds.[11] The credit lines simplify the administration as fewer calls need to be processed. By bridging the time between a new investment and when the funding is received from the LPs, the fund managers do not need to call capital separately for each deal. Moreover, it is possible that deals fail to get closed. Credit lines have the advantage that there is no need to call capital in anticipation of a new investment, and therefore, also no capital needs to be returned to the LPs in case the deal falls through. From the LP's perspective, this, at least in theory, improves cash management.

The shorter time frame between cash contributions and distributions increases the fund's internal rate of return (IRR), and thus, also the carried interest fund managers can charge their LPs. LPs can reduce the money they have to pay upfront, which in theory gives them flexibility to invest the capital while it is uncalled. On the other hand, this is resulting in less capital being put to work and possibly a negative impact on the LP portfolio's exposure efficiency.

The shorter time frame between cash contributions and distributions increases the fund's IRR. Therefore, LPs may pay higher carried interest, although less of their capital is put to work and they continue paying fees for unused but committed capital. This magnifying effect, however, also can work against fund managers in situations where their investments are underperforming.

IMPACT

Capital call lines do not change the fund's committed or invested capital, but initially the fund's interim IRR gets a significant boost. This matters for LPs who try to mitigate their fund's performance J-curve and particularly for GPs marketing their subsequent funds and who want to show a strong performance. Over the fund's lifetime, this effect abates, but the fund's IRR on maturity will still be higher than without the credit line.

The costs of the facility have a negative impact on the fund's TVPI, but the benefits to the IRR typically outweigh this downside. For buyout funds, Murphy et al. (2022) assessed the extreme case of once-annual capital calls. Here, the use of a subscription line could increase the IRR at maturity by up to 1.2% while decreasing the TVPI by less than 0.05.

Ahlin and Granlund (2017) estimated that the IRR increase was on average 2.7% gross and 0.7% net. Credit lines can also be used for exits. Here, fund managers draw on commitment facilities to pay themselves and return LP money earlier. The proceeds from portfolio sales are then used to repay the borrowed money. Baker (2018) estimates that this can add 100 basis points to the IRR.

FINANCING CONDITIONS

Fees to set up these credit lines are generally small, and the short time frame and limited size of the loan imply a modest interest. According to Murphy et al. (2022), even when interest rates are rising and borrowing costs are going up, the dynamic does not change much. These authors found that increasing the base secured overnight financing rate by 1% may reduce IRR degradation by only 10 bps or less.

DISCOVERY

In the case of these credit lines, instead of calling for capital from LPs, the fund managers call for funding from their lenders. This, however, will not be directly noticeable by the LPs. They could discover this, for instance, by looking whether there are significant NAV changes without revaluations or capital calls.

Could we use private market benchmark data to discover specific uses of credit lines and what impact various practices have on fund cash flows? This would be very interesting in a situation where LPs are concerned about changes in the current environment, anticipating faster or slower capital call rates and the respective mitigations through credit lines. Practically, this is unlikely to work, at least over the short term. It will take years before this impact is significant and can be detected in the private market benchmarking data. Generally, if there is an effect, it will show up too late to matter. Instead, LPs would rather apply stresses to their forecasted contributions.

Private market data also do not differentiate between funds with and without credit lines and the associated market and lending practices. Even if fund cash-flow data are provided, to respect confidentiality, they are typically aggregated over at least five funds. There are funds in the peer group that use credit lines and some that do not. Funds in funds in the same vintage year will nevertheless start in different months, so cash flows across the funds are not synchronised. Both effects will blur any signal regarding credit lines.

The author communicated with one LP who tried to employ machine learning (ML) to her own high-quality historical fund cash-flow data but found even this methodology to be unable to pick up the presence or absence of credit lines.

MODELLING

The broad adoption of these capital call lines as short-term financing tool for portfolio investments has a strong impact on the fund's cash-flow pattern. Such credit lines do not change the fund structure but alter, from the LP's perspective, the profile of cash flows. These changes cannot be addressed through the TAM any longer, but they can be modelled using the A2*TAM.

Related to cash-flow forecasting, the promise of capital call lines is that they make the timing of investments more predictable. Fund managers could set a regular capital call schedule, such as semi-annually, to provide the LP with guidance on the upcoming drawdowns.

When generating a sample for a fund's cash flows, it cannot be ruled out that a cash-flow pattern is 'impossible' from a business perspective. The presence of credit lines makes it even possible that the fund repays capital without having called any before. Capital call lines for funds are, therefore, modelled in the following steps:

- The A2*TAM generates a scenario for the fund's capital calls, management fees, realisations, and fixed return under the assumption that no credit line is present.
- The fund's cash-flow-consistent NAV is calculated based on this scenario, as the NAV should not be affected by the credit line.
- For the credit line, a schedule is defined that covers the facility's initial set-up, the first month when the LP will eventually be called for capital, and the frequency under which capital is called subsequently.

The scenario's cash flows are the aggregated according to the schedule (see **Figure 7.10**).

$C_{t_{C;i}}$ is the contribution (i.e. capital call or management fee) the fund needs at times $t_{C;i}$, assuming no credit line. $t_{Cr;j}$ is the time set in the schedule for the jth credit line capital call, with $t_{Cr;0} := 0$. The amount $CR_{t_{Cr;j}}$ is requested from the LP at time $t_{CR;j}$ is:

$$CR_{t_{CR;j}} = \sum_{\forall i: t_{CR;j-1} < t_{C;i} \leq t_{CR;j}} C_{t_{C;i}}.$$

This schedule condenses the capital calls in line with what is to be expected under the credit line.

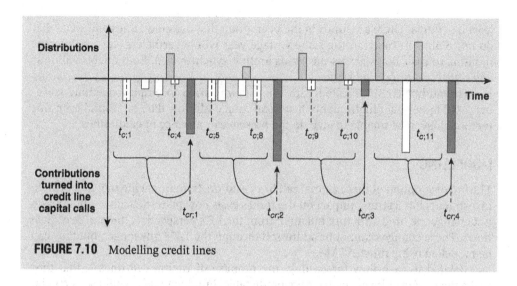

FIGURE 7.10   Modelling credit lines

There are different bases for calculating management fees, such as the NAV, but committed capital and the net invested capital being the most relevant ones. Also, management tend to be different during the investment period than during the divestment period. Typically, management fees are a percentage of commitments during the investment period and during the divestment period either taper or the basis for their calculation changes to net invested capital. According to Norton (2020), this is the standard approach for private equity and some private credit funds. However, other private credit funds only receive the fee on invested amounts, with disparity in how the *invested capital* is defined. (see **Box 7.2**)

Fixed returns

It is widely accepted that the TAM is applicable to private equity, but its yield parameter is rarely referred to by practitioners and academics. Yield is foreseen for real estate, debt, and infrastructure funds, but arguably is specific to a fund rather than to its strategy. Together with the bow factor, the yield just assigns weights to the yearly rate of distributions. The TAM does not differentiate between the part of the distributions stemming from the yield and the one from realisations.

In the A2*TAM, this differentiation is made and the cash flows implied by the yield are specifically modelled as 'fixed returns'. The fixed return calculation is controlled by a schedule comprising period base and period unit that set the frequency and the first period of when the fixed return is generated. The yield is the annual fixed return, which is recalculated into the quarterly, etc., fixed return, according to the period unit. If period base is 'yearly', then yield and fixed return are equivalent.

For the fixed return, there are two possible interpretations. The TAM calculates the yield based on the fund's NAV, thus reflecting depleting assets or rental payments and thus cannot result in the fund defaulting on its liabilities.

An extension is to apply the fixed returns to partially debt-funded fund vehicles. Here, the basis for calculating the fund's fixed returns is the debt-funded share of the invested capital instead, which, however, can put the fund into a default situation. In case the fund does not grow sufficiently, the NAV may fall below the invested capital and be insufficient to pay out the amount implied by the fixed return in full.

The first date where the amount becomes insufficient and the fund fails to pay back the debt in full becomes the time of default. Simulating the various cash-flow scenarios allows us to determine the fund's probability of default / loss given default (PD/LGD).

CASH-FLOW-CONSISTENT NAV

The TAM is setting a deterministic relationship between contributions, NAVs, and distributions. In this model, forecasting the fund's NAV at various points in time can be narrowed down to predicting its growth rate. Like in the TAM, it is assumed that the underlying portfolio, which is reflected in the NAV, is growing with the rate given by the fund's IRR.

The A2*TAM applies the TAM's logic to estimate a NAV that is reconcilable with the fund's cash flows.[12] However, this 'nice' relationship between cash flows and valuations does not hold any longer if contributions and distributions are randomly distributed. The main idea is inspired by the observation that funds tend to have mainly contributions in the beginning of their life and mainly distributions at the end of their lifetime.

Principal approach

Like in the TAM, we assume that the underlying portfolio's value that is represented by the NAV is growing with the rate given by the fund's IRR. As the fund's cash flows were modelled as random, there can be several problems, for example:

- A realisation can exceed the calculated NAV.
- There can be a realisation even if there was no capital call before – something that can even happen in reality, for instance, in the case of subscription lines. But a realisation requires that there is a NAV.
- At the end of the fund's lifetime, there is still a NAV, but all realisations have happened already.

Note that this is the NAV attributable to the LPs, as the A2*TAM, like the TAM, projects realisations on a net basis – which is consistent with the data provided by private market benchmarks.[13]

First contributions, then distributions

Funds tend to have mainly contributions in the beginning of the fund's life and only distributions at its end. There is some fuzziness during fund's midlife, where there are contributions as well as distributions within the same period. However, during this phase, the NAV tends to show its maximum, so that it is unlikely that distributions exceed the available NAV. This observation suggests a two-pronged approach, comprising a forward pass and a backward pass applying the same logic as in the TAM.

Forward pass

The forward pass is starting at the fund's last reported NAV. The capital called is added to the NAV, the capital repaid is subtracted from the NAV, and then the growth rate is applied until the next cash flow occurs. This forward pass typically works well during first years of fund's life, when there are no or just few realisations.

Backward pass

The backward pass is initiated at the end of the fund's life. The last capital repaid to the LP is added back to NAV, the capital called (initially none) is subtracted from NAV, and then the amount is discounted by the growth rate until the previous cash flow. This backward pass typically works well during the last years of fund's life, when there are no or just few capital calls.

As the backward pass moves closer to the fund's inception date, the backward pass tends to overstate NAV in case there have been capital calls. Therefore, it is possible that at the beginning of the fund's lifetime, the backward pass calculates a non-zero NAV.

Combination

In the last step, the results of the forward and the backward pass are merged, giving more weight to the forward pass during the early years of the fund and vice versa for the backward pass, and not allowing for a negative NAV.

As we can generate many cash-flow scenarios, the cash-flow-consistent NAV can give us important information. Instead of having just one expected NAV for a fund at a given point in time, we have as many different NAVs as scenarios generated. With this marked-to-model valuation, we can determine the PDF for the NAVs at a given point in time and thus are able to determine various capital risk figures for the portfolio, such as its value-at-risk (VaR) in the definition put forward by Buchner (2017).

Essentially, the cash-flow-consistent NAV is applying a discounted cash flow (DCF) model to valuing the private assets held by the fund. The DCF model's discount rate is assumed to reflect the aggregate riskiness of these private assets. Simulating cash flows using historical means and variances and then still discounting such flows using a risk-free rate would overstate the value, however. Therefore, the A2*TAM is used for an MCS that involves sampling cash flows under the risk-neutral probability measure to take account of the cash flows' risk properties. For each cash flow, the payoff is calculated and discounted at the risk-free interest rate. 'Risk-neutral' means that cash flows are assumed to be real, even though that is not, in fact, the actual scenario. Simulating cash flows and then still discounting such flows in addition to the risk-free rate would overstate the value.[14] The risk-free rate is the minimum rate of return investors would demand from an investment with zero risks.[15] As this rate is usually above 0%, changes in the timing of cash flows have an impact on the fund's PV.

The risk-free rate reflects the expected inflation in the respective currency and expected real interest rates from the LP's external perspective.

SUMMARY

The various enhancements to the TAM by the A2*TAM allow modelling the stochastic behaviour of a funds' cash flows and its NAVs over time and help to measure a portfolio's important key performance indicators (KPIs) like the portfolio's CCaR, its cash-flow-at-risk (CFaR), and exposure ranges for its NAV development.

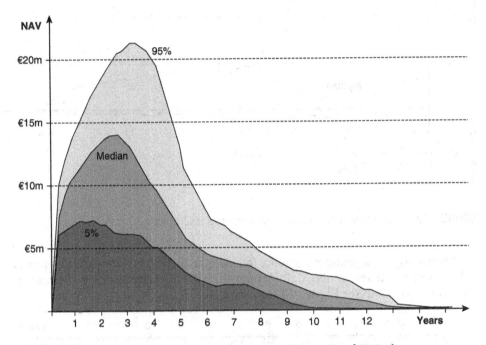

FIGURE 7.11   Cash-flow-consistent NAV (total commitment size of €100m)

Figure 7.11 shows the NAV development over time for a portfolio of funds with a total commitment size of €100 million (of which €30 million were added in year four). The different levels of confidence with which the NAV can be forecasted suggests a VaR-like measurement of the portfolio's risks, as proposed in Buchner (2017).

VaR has become an integral part of financial regulation ever since financial institutions were allowed to use VaR in regulated capital modelling in 1996, although applying it to portfolios of private capital funds, which are highly illiquid and for which market prices are not observable, is not yet widely accepted. Nevertheless, a VaR calculated in this way can provide important insights for a risk manager.

For managing the LP's risks, the VaR concept is difficult to apply as the funds' value mainly takes the form of investments in illiquid assets that cannot be monetised easily. In this situation, the CFaR can be another relevant measure for the LP's risk exposures. For the same portfolio, **Figure 7.12** shows the wide ranges for the portfolio's netted contributions and distributions, which are mainly caused by the high uncertainty in respect of the portfolio's distributions.

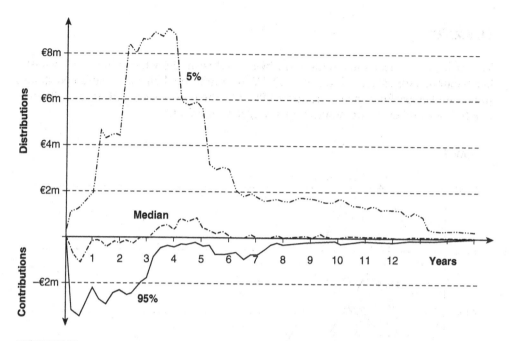

FIGURE 7.12   Cash-Flow-at-Risk (total commitment size of €100m)

Particularly for a younger portfolio, following a cash-flow J-curve, it therefore can make more sense to rely on its CCaR for improving the management of its undrawn and uncommitted capital (see **Figure 7.13**)

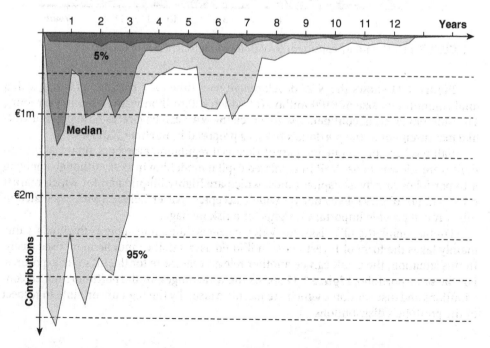

FIGURE 7.13   Capital-Call-at-Risk (total commitment size of €100m)

Compared to stochastic models proposed, for example, by de Maherbe, Buchner, and others, the A2*TAM provides a more granular view on the different types of cash flows, in particular management fees and fixed returns that are more predictable than capital calls and realisations. From a practical point of view, these enhancements assure an upward compatibility, where the A2*TAM as a discrete-time model can be reconciled with the TAM, that for simpler use cases, e.g. not related to liquidity risk, analysts prefer to work with. The modelling idea is simple in principle, but the implementation is more challenging compared to traditional stochastic models that need no reconciliation and fitting with the TAM.

NOTES

1. See Burgiss (2021).
2. Note that we cannot simply convert the TAM's internal logic to a quarterly granularity: if we divide annual contributions by 4, as a result, we are looking at four equal amounts that, however, grow over different periods – four quarters, three quarters, two quarters, and one quarter – and as a result, such quarterly forecasts cannot be reconciled with the annual TAM's forecast.
3. The deviations in year 5 between PitchBook and the A2*TAM are explainable by the fact that capital calls go up as funds approach the end of the investment period and fund managers want to maximize the capital put at work. As discussed in **Chapter 4**, Corvino (2020) proposed to reflect the investment period in an additional parameter. That could be done in the A2*TAM, too, and would additionally require setting an uptick in volatility during the last year of the investment period. Deviations closer to the end of the funds' contractual lifetime can be explained through extensions and the pick-up in management fees that LPs need to contribute for this purpose.
4. See de Malherbe (2004) and Buchner (2017).
5. A2*TAM's individual forecasts aggregated and averaged.
6. Kanabar (2021): 'I show that VaR approximately doubles when fees are introduced and dynamics change significantly when accounting for skews in private equity returns.'
7. See Kupec and Jason (2022) and Mathonet and Meyer (2007).
8. It is possible to quantify the carried interest through applying a reverse waterfall calculation to the cash-flow forecasts. If the catch-up is zero, the result is not unique during the catch-up period, but ranges can be determined.
9. For instance, according to Auerbach and Shivananda (2017), in the case of primary FOFs, the carried interest is 5%, and for secondary fund managers, it is about 12.5%. For special situations and distressed debt, Norton (2020) suggests a carried interest rate be closer to 17.5–20%. For private credit funds, the carried interest rate often ranges from 10% to 15%, which is attributable to the comparatively limited volatility of the underlying assets (see Doherty and Kolman, 2018, and Norton, 2020).
10. See Murphy et al. (2022).
11. See Norton (2020).
12. PitchBook (2022) describes a comparable approach that also turns to the TAM's logic for creating a fund's NAV profile.
13. We can use a reverse waterfall calculation to calculate the fund's gross cash flows and its gross NAV. With this information, we can also calculate the NAV attributable to the fund managers. Real NAVs tend to underestimate the true (unobservable) economic value, as they are appraisal-based valuations with a conservative bias.

14. See Cornelius et al. (2011).

15. In general, this would a well-developed country's government bonds (e.g. US treasury bonds, German government bonds). This hypothetical rate of return, in practice, does not exist because every investment has a certain amount of risk. See https://www.statista.com/statistics/885915/average-risk-free-rate-select-countries-europe/

CHAPTER 8

Modelling Avenues into Private Capital

This chapter deals, from the institutional investor's perspective, with the important avenues into private capital and how to model them. Usually, institutions seek intermediation through the limited partnership structure as few have the experience and especially the incentive structures that would allow them to invest directly in unquoted companies.

The limited partnership structure has long been described by the Takahashi–Alexander model (TAM), which could be seen as the simple Lego®-block for building portfolios of funds. The paper published by Takahashi and Alexander (2002) relates to primary commitments only. Since then, other approaches to investing in private capital have emerged. Notably, secondaries and co-investments have been gaining importance; the focus of this chapter is how to model these avenues within the context of commitment pacing.

The growth of private capital has been accompanied with proportional increases in size and liquidity in the secondary market, allowing investors to buy or sell existing interests in funds. Secondaries can allow investors to build exposure and achieve their allocation targets more quickly.

According to Aalberts et al. (2020), the fastest approach for investors for increasing their exposure to private capital involves co-investments. This refers to the situation where a limited partner (LP) invests directly into a private asset that is backed by the funds where she participates. Co-investments, however, require that the LP has already built a portfolio of funds with which she can co-invest.[1]

Both secondary transactions and co-investments have become a routine component of institutional allocations to private capital, but they remain largely opportunistic, and the availability of suitable investments is rather limited (see **Table 8.1**). A detailed discussion of the nuts-and-bolts of secondaries and co-investments goes beyond the scope of this book.

PRIMARY COMMITMENTS

Primary commitments are the 'plain vanilla' approach to private capital investing for which the TAM has been conceived. **Figure 4.1** in the chapter on forecasting models

TABLE 8.1   Avenues into private capital, LP perspective[1]

	Primary commitments	**Secondaries**	**Co-investments**
Approach	Planned	Opportunistic	Opportunistic
Availability	High	Cyclical	Medium
Size	Large	Medium	Small
Evaluation	Blind pool	Valuation	Valuation
IRR J-curve	Long	Inverted, short	Short
TVPI J-curve	Medium	Medium	Short

describes this situation. In this example, the fund's NAV peaks in year 5, which coincidentally is also the end of the typical fund's investment period. At this point in time, less than 7% of the original commitment remains to be called for management fees and follow-on investments. The fund really starts to distribute from year four onwards and is projected to become cash-flow positive in year 7 when cumulated distributions begin to exceed cumulated contributions.

Many investors are concerned about their portfolio of primary funds' J-curve and the associated accounting losses. In theory, secondaries and co-investments could eradicate or at least mitigate the J-curve and reduce the duration of the overall private equity portfolio. Differences between these routes into private capital show mainly in the cash-flow patterns and the value development.

MODELLING FUND STRATEGIES

The TAM is a parameter-driven model that has been used to describe various fund strategies and can be flexibly tailored and allows analysing the impact of changing market conditions. For example, Takahashi and Alexander (2002) suggest that an unfavourable exit environment could be reflected by extending the life of funds or by slowing down the distribution rate, an approach that we will revisit in the context of stress scenarios (see **Chapter 16**). Generally, cash-flow profiles vary across fund strategies and clearly the TAM's forecasts rely on the quality of the input parameters. **Table 8.2** shows parameters for the TAM suggested by various researchers and practitioners (in historical order).

Parameter as suggested by Takahashi and Alexander (2002)

Takahashi and Alexander (2002) fitted the Yale endowment's historical data with their model to derive these parameters for different periods in the venture capital (VC) market. The figures they put forward suggested that the 1984-to-1986 vintages reflect the early days of the industry, with a 'dismal' average growth rate of 7%, delayed distributions, and with 18 years very long average lifetimes.

Their other VC model assumes a whopping 20% annual growth rate combined with high early contribution rates. These parameters apparently reflect the dot-com bubble period where endowments in general were reporting high returns.[2] The extraordinarily

TABLE 8.2 TAM-strategy-specific parameters

Strategy	Contribution rate in year (%)					Bow	Yield (%)	Invt. prd. (years)	Lifetime (years)	Growth (%)	Source and comments
	1	2	3	4	5						
Venture Capital (1993 vintage)	25.00	33.33	50.00	cont.	cont.	2.50	0		12.00	13.0	Takahashi and Alexander (2002); used by Black et al. (2018) and Murphy (2007)
Venture Capital	29.00	30.00	30.00	cont.	cont.	1.20	0		20.00	20.0	Takahashi and Alexander (2002)
Venture Capital (1984 to 1986 vintages)	20.00	25.00	30.00	cont.	cont.	2.20	0		18.00	7.0	Takahashi and Alexander (2002)
Leveraged Buyouts	25.00	50.00	50.00	cont.	cont.	2.50	0		12.00	13.0	Takahashi and Alexander (2002)
Real Estate	40.00	40.00	40.00	cont.	cont.	5.00	5		12.00	8.0	Takahashi and Alexander (2002)
Oil & Gas	30.00	50.00	50.00	cont.	cont.	1.00	15		15.00	8.0	Takahashi and Alexander (2002)
Leveraged Buyouts	25.00	33.33	50.00	cont.	cont.	2.50	0		10.00		Tolkamp (2007); based on Takahashi and Alexander (2002)
Private Equity	39.00	31.15	35.71	37.04	41.18		0		12.00		de Zwart et al. (2009)
Buyout funds	18.67	18.90	24.84	27.82	31.65	1.26	0		12.50	12.0	Furenstam and Forsell (2018)
Global Buyout funds	24.51	32.00	31.91	cont.	cont.	1.81	0		11.98		Burgiss (2020); general parameters
Global Buyout funds	14.07	18.13	22.09	cont.	cont.	2.79	0		10.98		Burgiss (2020); recessionary parameters
US Buyouts	29.67	20.97	29.75	cont.	cont.	5.01			12.00	14.4	Shen et al. (2020); averaged over 2005 to 2014
US Buyouts	28.00	25.00	30.00	cont.	cont.	4.00	0		12.00		Jeet (2020)
Private Equity	19.00	23.00	31.00	44.00	79.00	3.50	0	5	12.00	15.0	Corvino (2020)
Private Debt	32.00	46.00	86.00	cont.	cont.	1.50	0	3	7.00	8.0	Corvino (2020)
Real Estate	24.00	31.00	45.00	83.00	0.00	1.50	0	4	9.00	13.0	Corvino (2020)
Infrastructure	19.00	23.00	31.00	44.00	79.00	3.00	5	5	15.00	10.0	Corvino (2020)
Private Debt – all						2.02		5	6.39	8.0	Virtanen (2021)
Private Debt – mature						1.29		5	7.17	8.0	Virtanen (2021)
Private Debt – liquidated						2.65		5	4.64	8.0	Virtanen (2021)

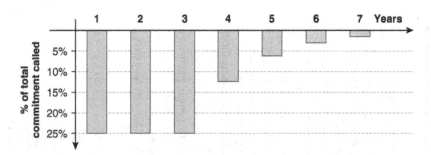

FIGURE 8.1   Based on contribution rates for venture capital according to Taka-hashi and Alexander (2002). Rate of contribution RC year 1: 25%; year 2: 33%, 50% for all following years

long 20 years' lifetime assumed in this case is inconsistent with a favourable exit envi-ronment. While the delayed distributions, also implied by a lower bow factor, were pessimistic from a liquidity risk perspective, from a return perspective, this is far too optimistic, as this implicitly assumes that this extraordinary average growth rate could be maintained over the following decades, thus leading to a fantastically high total value to paid-in capital (TVPI).

Instead, Takahashi and Alexander (2002) used the 1993 vintage year VC fund popu-lation for their base model, suggesting an average 13% growth rate and 12 years' lifetime. They saw this as more meaningful for a standard model. Compared to the other fund strategies, the contribution rate schedule is more spread over time (see **Figure 8.1**), in line with the several financing rounds in VC where providing additional future funding is contingent upon the portfolio company meeting certain milestones in executing their business plan.

This contrasts with the contribution rate schedules for leveraged buyouts, real estate, and oil and gas (see **Figure 8.2**), which suggest that the bulk of investment is done upfront with follow-on financing declining more quickly.

Takahashi and Alexander (2002) model oil and gas focused funds with a long life-time of 15 years, a bow factor of 1, and a yield of 15% to describe the depleting assets held by the fund.

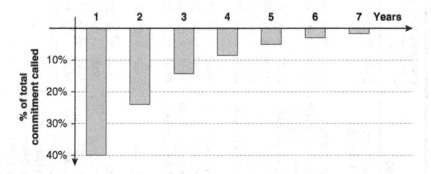

FIGURE 8.2   Based on contribution rates for real estate according to Takahashi and Alexander (2002). RC = 40% for all years

Further findings on parameters

Various authors have put forward parameters for buyouts. The wide differences are possibly reflecting variations in strategies, different time periods, geographies, economic environments, and notably differing proprietary data sets used to fit with the TAM. For leveraged buyouts, Tolkamp (2007) was assuming the same contribution rate schedule as Takahashi and Alexander (2002) did for VC, albeit with a shorter fund lifetime. de Zwart (2009) used private equity fund data obtained from Thomson Venture Economics (now defunct) from 1980 and 2005. This long time span explains the differences compared to other findings that were also based on proprietary data.

Burgiss (2020) presented different sets of parameters for global buyouts funds, one addressing the situation in general and the other one for the recessionary environment anticipated during the COVID-19 pandemic. As private markets are characterised by limited and imperfect data, it is difficult to see how the highly precise parameters recommended in Burgiss (2020) can hold over a long time. Jeet (2020), apparently working on the same or similar data set as Shen et al. (2020), proposes less precise, but in all likelihood more robust figures for the contribution and distribution rate (i.e. the bow factor) schedules.

Corvino (2020) modelled private debt with, compared to private equity, an accelerated contribution rate schedule and not differentiating between VC and buyouts. For private debt, a significantly shorter lifetime and growth rate compared to private equity were assumed. Virtanen (2021) fitted the TAM with data on private debt provided by a Northern European financial institution, which explains the precise figures. The quite varying bow factors and lifetimes suggest that high precision is not meaningful, and analysts rather use robust settings.

The capital call rates and lifetimes for real estate assumed in Corvino (2020) are significantly different compared to Takahashi and Alexander (2002), possibly reflecting different time periods and geographies. Note that Corvino (2020) sets no yield for real estate.

Infrastructure as a fund strategy is not covered in Takahashi and Alexander (2002), reflecting that this is a rather new asset class. Bitch et al. (2010) report that infrastructure assets have an extended lifespan but are typically done through private-equity-type funds with just 10–12 years' duration. This constrains the time horizon of the LP's investment, although the life of an infrastructure asset will continue after the exit of the fund. For infrastructure funds, Corvino (2020) assumed a relatively slow capital call rate schedule, a yield of 5%, and a 15-year lifetime.

Basing parameters on comparable situations

Infrastructure as a relatively recent fund strategy illustrates that in many situations, there will simply be no data to fit the TAM with any precision. Generally, many LPs will not have sufficient own historical data to calibrate the TAM, or comparable fund models, for different strategies and market environments. However, an understanding of the industry, backed by research and looking for comparable situations, allows making educated guesses for coming up with realistic parameters for fund lifetimes, their rate of contributions, and their bow factors.

For illustration, according to Doherty and Kolman (2018), distressed debt funds have a return profile with terms similar to that of buyout funds. They typically have investment periods as short as three years and have lifetimes of only six to eight years. They, therefore, invest at a quicker pace than private equity funds, requiring a faster contribution rate schedule.[3]

FUNDS OF FUNDS

For institutional investors, the most relevant approach to investing in private capital is through fund-of-funds (FOF) specialists as intermediaries or through similarly structured dedicated in-house private capital investment programmes.

FOFs can help to initiate and ramp up diversified allocations to private capital while getting access to high-quality funds. FOFs are also an effective way to create specific exposures, such as to secondaries and co-investments, geographies, like emerging markets, or industry sectors, like tech-investments through VC. FOFs became mainstream in the 1990s but were not dealt with in Takahashi and Alexander (2002). Nevertheless, the TAM has been applied to FOFs, either by looking through and applying the TAM individually to the funds that comprise the FOFs' portfolio or by modelling this as one commingled vehicle. In the latter case, the TAM requires different parameter settings:

- The FOFs take a longer time to deploy and return capital. The FOFs commit to underlying funds over a two- to three-year investment period.[4] The underlying funds then invest capital in private assets over their investment period of typically five years.
- Therefore, an FOF may call capital over a time frame of eight years and will be fully liquidated, depending on whether its focus is primary commitments or other strategies, after anywhere from 12 to 15 years – a significantly longer lifetime than that of a primary commitment. According to Auerbach and Shivananda (2017), private equity FOFs on average reach net-cash-flow breakeven after 11 years and longer.
- The TAM can capture this by assuming evenly distributed contributions over the extended investment period and a bow factor of 1, suggesting exits that are evenly spread as well.[5]

On top of the underlying funds' management fees and their carried interest, the FOFs charge an additional fee and may also participate in the investment success. Many FOFs have a generalist focus and also incorporate co-investments and secondaries into their investment strategies. The double fee layer and the higher degree of diversification of FOFs result in lower growth rates, but also in much lower risk.

SECONDARY BUYS

Through secondaries transactions, investors can acquire stakes in relatively mature funds where a significant share of capital has already been called and invested in private assets (typically 50–80%, according to Aalberts et al., 2020). This puts capital at work much faster and distributions tend to occur much earlier. Sells are irrelevant from a cash-flow forecasting perspective. In a secondary buy, an LP acquires a fund's future cash flows for given proceeds (see **Figure 8.3**).

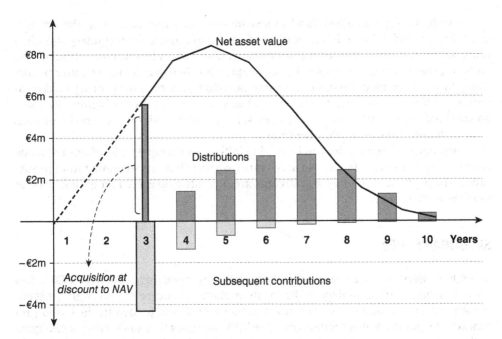

FIGURE 8.3 Secondary buy of interest in fund. For discount to NAV acquirer takes on liability for the fund's uncalled capital, and receives its NAV plus subsequent cash-flows (distributions from fund as well as contributions)

A positive performance level can be achieved more rapidly than in the case of a primary commitment. A secondary buy, if at a discount, typically shows an inverted J-curve, first showing a high internal rate of return (IRR) that, however, over time comes down again (see **Figure 8.4**). If the position is bought at a premium, it is the other way round, i.e., first showing a low, sometimes even negative IRR, that then climbs over time.

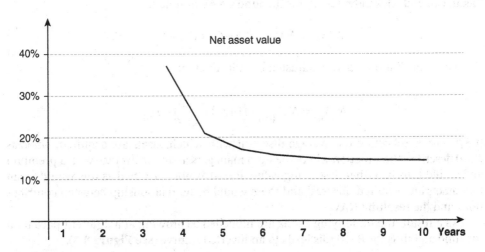

FIGURE 8.4 Inverted J-curve consistent with acquiring the NAV in year 4 at a 20% discount (primary fund's growth rate is 10%)

Essentially, the secondary fund model inherits its parameters from the primary commitment model. There is one outflow of capital to acquire the secondary stake in a fund, but there are also undrawn commitments that have to be taken on, although the amount to be drawn is usually smaller and capital is called over a much shorter period. Going forward, the model assumes the same cash-flow pattern as the primary fund commitment. Moreover, we need to assume a (at least effectively) shorter lifetime for a secondary fund, here assumed to be seven years. For a 12% growth rate, the model projects a net-cash-flow-breakeven after five years.

Theoretically, secondaries can be used to initiate and ramp up allocations to private assets, mitigate J-curve effects, and accelerate cash distributions stemming from private capital. In practice, secondary investments are difficult to execute and do not scale as much as often desired.

SECONDARY FOFs

Secondary investing is a specialist activity, typically involving secondary FOFs. LPs choose managers of secondary FOFs for their ability to source opportunities, negotiate attractive prices and transact on them, rather than trying to identify deals and gain exposure to specific funds themselves.[6] The TAM assumes that underlying assets grow in the same way as the fund and does not cater for the situation where assets are bought at a discount, and therefore, the TAM's NAV does reflect neither the resulting value add nor the fund's J-curve.

Particularly during economic crises, there are 'forced sellers' with need for liquidity and rebalancing – ironically a situation a proper commitment pacing aims to avoid. Secondaries as an investment strategy are exploiting this potential for buying assets at an, often significant, discount to fair valuations.

To model this situation, we introduce a new parameter P, which is the premium (in the sense of the value added by the managers of the secondary FOFs) resulting from the average discount on assets acquired. Reflecting this follows on from the calculation in Takahashi and Alexander (2002) for the fund's NAV at time t:

$$NAV_{(t)} = NAV_{(t-1)} * (1+G) + C_{(t)} - D_{(t)}.$$

The contribution rates are adjusted by P, leading to:

$$NAV_{(t)} = NAV_{(t-1)} * (1+G) + \frac{C_{(t)}}{1+P} - D_{(t)}$$

$0 > P > -1$ is reflecting the average discount with which assets are acquired, whereas $P > 0$ describes the situation where the fund managers assets on average with a premium and would thus be rather destroying value. $P = -1$ is not permitted as this would mean that assets are acquired 'for free' and there would be no relationship between contributions and the resulting NAV.

As a result, the underlying assets are modelled as growing at a different pace than the fund and thus for $P < 0$ this leads to an inverted J-curve (see **Figure 8.5**).

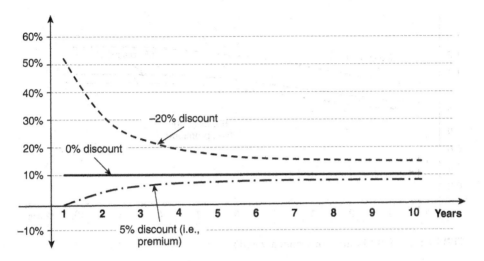

FIGURE 8.5 Inverted IRR J-curve for secondary FOFs

Note that the original TAM is not capturing the IRR J-curve as it assumes that the fund buys all assets at their fair value. Therefore, plotting the interim IRR over time only shows a flat line. $P < 0$ reflects the fund managers systematic ability to acquire assets at a discount to their fair value. Particularly for venture investing the IRR J-curve is widely assumed phenomenon; this would be consistent with a premium $P > 0$, implicitly caused by the fact that many start-ups are failing in their early years[7].

As discussed in **Chapter 4**, by construction the original TAM generates cash-flows with an IRR that is equal to G. The IRR could be seen as the fund's 'external growth', i.e., from the LP's perspective, whereas G reflects the fund's underlying portfolio's growth, i.e., the fund's 'internal growth'. In the original TAM they are identical, but with $P \neq 0$ the fund's IRR and G differ. P is also affecting the fund's final TVPI; therefore we need to account for this when generating this adjusted TAM's annual growth rate to meet the targeted TVPI. This is achieved by adjusting the polynomial coefficient calculation when applying the Newton–Raphson method for estimating the fund's growth rate.

Also the TVPI J-curve is in line with similar analyses based on empirical data (see **Figure 8.6**).

Aalberts et al. (2020) modelled a secondary FOF with a one-year investment period based on the expectation that 75% of the committed capital to be drawn in the first two years with close to the entire amount of commitments called before the end of year 4. This could be modelled in the TAM by assuming contribution rates of 50% for the first two years.

The secondary FOFs will need capital for the underlying funds' follow-on investments, but these requirements for capital are often offset by distributions from the portfolio; therefore, the model can assume no or very low rates of contributions afterwards. Due to the advanced maturity of the underlying funds, cash distributions set quite early and continue; this suggests a low bow factor and also a shorter lifetime for the secondary

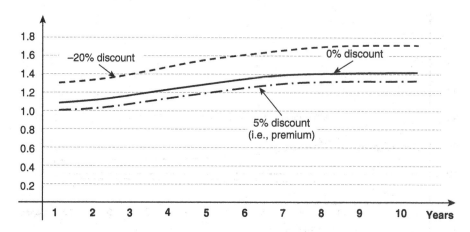

FIGURE 8.6   TVPI J-curve for secondary FOFs

FOFs. Secondary investments are not the only method to mitigate early losses and reach profitability faster, co-investments can also be used in a similar way.

CO-INVESTMENTS

Another important case is a co-investment strategy, where LPs invest directly into a private asset that is backed by the funds where they participate. Building on the fund manager's due diligence, LPs can enter into specific deals, usually expecting an outperformance compared to primary commitments in the long term. This makes sense, as LPs can select under reduced uncertainty and will pay significantly lower or even no fees. In the case where portfolio companies are exited through an initial public offering, the GPs and co-investing LPs often continue to hold shares in the publicly listed company to further benefit from increases in valuations and dividends.[8]

Basic approach

Like in the case of secondaries, co-investments put capital at work much faster and generate returns more rapidly. Co-investing could be seen as a hybrid between a direct and a fund investment and thus can also be modelled using the TAM.

Unlike stakes in primary or secondary funds, however, there is no commitment associated with a co-investment and thus no capital calls for follow-on investments the LP is obliged to pay out. Instead, commitment equals proceeds, combined with a 100% contribution rate at time of investment. There is one outflow of capital, resulting in the full amount being invested in a private asset alongside the fund.

The co-investment's TAM inherits several parameters from the primary commitment model of the fund it is co-investing with. The remaining lifetime of a fund serves as the 'best guess' for co-investment's lifetime. The TAM's yield can be used to describe the interest payments of the co-investment's debt part.

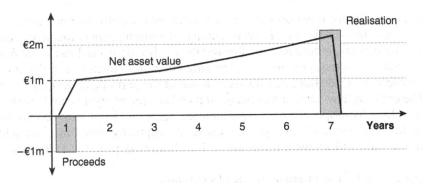

FIGURE 8.7 Co-investment profile, bow factor 100, growth rate 15%

The bow factor models the rate of distribution for the co-investment's equity part and the repayment of principal for debt. A high bow factor (>5) is consistent with an exit of the portfolio company close to fund's maturity (see **Figure 8.7**).

The challenge is to determine realistic ranges for the co-investment's TVPIs. Unless there is specific information, one approach would be to base this on the private market data providers' company-level benchmarks.

Co-investment funds

FOFs often leverage their co-investment capabilities and offer dedicated co-investment funds on a customised, as well as a co-mingled basis for investors. There are also specialised independently managed co-investment funds that pick up such opportunities from LPs. Co-investment funds tend to become net cash-flow positive faster and can be used to mitigate early losses. Their IRR J-curve follows that of primary commitments rather than that of secondaries.

Syndication

Some institutional investors bypass the traditional intermediation through funds and invest directly in private assets. The TAM is not well suited for capturing this situation. However, direct investments are often done in syndication with GPs and their funds, also with exits led by the fund managers. Provided that information on these funds, notably their remaining lifetime, is accessible, these syndicated direct investments can be modelled like co-investments.

SIDE FUNDS

Side funds (or annex funds or top-up funds) are investment vehicles designed to increase the follow-on investment capabilities of an original fund with whom the side fund will invest in parallel. Generally, side funds are launched some years after the creation of the original fund and are managed by the same fund manager but often under different terms and conditions. Investors joining a side fund are normally the original fund's LPs, but there can also be new ones. However, though the mechanism is apparently straightforward, there is no predefined structure and the motivation to establish a side fund can differ depending on the circumstances. The only common characteristic is that the investee companies of a side fund will always be a part of the portfolio of the original fund.

Theoretically, any LP that has negotiated co-investment rights could create a 'virtual' side fund by simply always exercising these rights and by proportionately topping up the fund's investments into private assets. Conceptually, side funds resemble co-investments, and indeed the lines are blurred, and can be depicted as a hierarchy:

- Investors only take a passive role as LPs in funds.
- In addition to being LPs in funds, investors use side funds.
- Investors selectively co-invest alongside funds in individual private assets.
- Investors directly source, invest in, and manage private assets.

Rather than cherry-picking companies – requiring that the LP has a direct investment capability – side funds could thus be interpreted as a further bet on a fund management team.

IMPACT ON PORTFOLIO

While secondaries and co-investments can be value creating in their own right, LPs try to combine them with their primary commitments to improve their liquidity and to mitigate the J-curve impact (see **Figure 8.8**).

Secondaries can initially show high IRRs but usually lead to low TVPIs. The typical co-investment's J-curve follows that of primary commitments, with initially low IRRs but eventually generating a higher TVPI.

Practically, there are limits to realising the potential benefits of combining these strategies. The secondary market is a fraction of what is covered by primary commitments

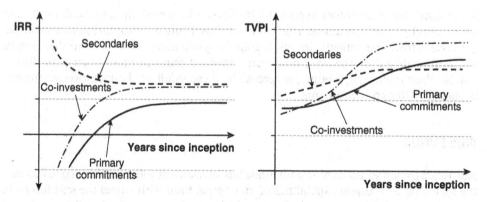

FIGURE 8.8 Comparison evolution of performance over time, schematic (based on Cornel and Wittlin, 2019)

and not well suited for managing a portfolio's diversification. Secondaries can create new exposures, but many may be unwanted. Also, co-investments are too much of a specialist activity to be scalable to the desired degree. Even when using side funds, the deal flow is driven by the fund managers and thus can only amplify existing exposures.

There are also limits to modelling these effects for the portfolio of primary commitments. The TAM does not capture management fees and regarding the valuations assumes a constant growth rate G. By construction, it therefore generates cash flows with an IRR equal to G and thus does not show an IRR J-curve. This is another important reason for the A2*TAM's improvements on the original TAM.

NOTES

1. Also see Cornel and Wittlin (2019).
2. See Lerner et al. (2005).
3. See Norton (2020) and Doherty and Kolman (2018).
4. See Auerbach and Shivananda (2017).
5. See Aalberts et al. (2020).
6. See Auerbach and Shivananda (2017).
7. Mulcahy et al. (2012) found in their portfolio the J-curve to be an unusual outcome and suggested that there be no consistent evidence of a J-curve in venture investing since 1997.
8. However, such holdings are then part of an allocation to liquid quoted assets.

CHAPTER 9

Modelling Diversification for Portfolios of Limited Partnership Funds

According to the quote attributed to Nobel Prize laureate Harry Markowitz, 'diversification is the only free lunch' in investing. Sophisticated institutions have long been incorporating funds investing in illiquid alternatives – private equity and real assets – into their portfolios to improve the diversification and performance.

This chapter focusses on the intra-asset diversification within these illiquid alternatives and how to aggregate the cash-flow forecasts for funds in a portfolio.[1] For modelling the diversification for their portfolios of funds, limited partners (LPs) should look at several key performance indicators (KPIs) related to the pacing of their commitments, how this is translated into exposure to private assets, and the risk/return profile of the resulting performance outcomes. The question of what are 'good' or 'bad' KPIs and how to manage them are, however, out of scope of the discussion.

THE LP DIVERSIFICATION MEASUREMENT PROBLEM

Markowitz's modern portfolio theory (MPT) suggests that correlation be one of the main building blocks of portfolio construction, along with expected returns and expected volatility. The correlation coefficient is a statistical measure of the strength of the relationship between the relative movements of two variables. Combining uncorrelated assets assures diversification: one asset's gains can be expected to at least partially mitigate another asset's losses and, consequently, reduce a portfolio's expected volatility.

LPs generally still approach diversification very simplistically, assuming that their portfolio being spread over a large number of funds is sufficient. A portfolio comprising 30 funds appears to be well diversified; however, if all funds were raised within the same vintage year, an LP should be worried. Not only are these funds exposed to the same economic conditions but also their contributions will coincide and thus create a significant strain on liquidity. Generally, stacking a portfolio with too many similar funds leads to concentration risk. Also, many portfolios are poorly diversified in the sense that a targeted level of protection could also be achieved with a smaller number of funds. Avoiding this uneconomical diversification would allow investors to be more selective and to save expenses for sourcing investment opportunities, due diligence, legal structuring, and monitoring.

Fund investments

Correlations are difficult to apply in the context of fund investments. Firstly, data on private assets are either not available or of too poor quality to measure correlations. Private capital's history as alternative asset class is not very long, but for long-term-oriented funds, correlations also change significantly over time. Correlations regularly break down during times of economic stress and are, therefore, practically not suitable for measuring dependencies over the time frames relevant for LPs investing in funds.

Secondly, LPs are committing to a fund, and then, the fund is investing in private assets. It is this double layer of investing in combination with the illiquidity of private markets that creates issues around diversification. To complicate matters, a fund at the beginning of its lifetime will have no portfolio and, therefore, has nothing invested yet. Funds are held over a long time, have a start date and a maturity date, and the holding period of private assets held by a fund matches this fund's lifetime. The cause of exposure (the commitment to a fund at one time) and the resulting effect (the amounts actually invested in private assets and then their performance on maturity) are separated by years.

Lastly, private capital is, after all, not bound by any labelling like geography or industry, which for such a long-term-oriented asset class can only be fuzzy anyway. On the other hand, practically, there are mobility barriers that effectively constrain a fund's style and form the basis for the more systematic approach to diversification management to be discussed here.

Diversification or skills?

By its very virtue diversification sacrifices on quality, as the pool of the 'proven performers' needs to be assumed as limited at any given point. Stanford Management Company, the university's endowment, is an example for an investment philosophy that sees over-diversification – investing with too many different fund managers – as an obstacle to driving superior returns. Consequently, until 2020, it nearly halved the number of about 300 external fund management firms it was working with originally, pursuing fewer but stronger relationships with chosen fund managers.[2]

For private assets, this is not the full story. Avoiding over-diversification is impractical for larger LPs like, for example, CalPERS with its allocation to private equity of $52.8 billion as of June 2022.[3] Here, scaling is an important factor that needs to be taken into consideration. Such LPs have no other option than to invest in many more funds than would be meaningful from the perspective of diversification solely for risk mitigation. They can concentrate in certain styles but for scaling reasons are forced to commit to many fund management firms.

TABLE 9.1 Relation between KPIs

	Commitment efficiency	Exposure efficiency	Outcome assessment (e.g. Sortino ratio)
Tells	How similar are funds, how does the portfolio cluster under market stress	How much is invested, when capital is called and repaid	Impact of diversification, resulting return range
Does not tell	How much capital will be drawn and invested, diversification of funds' underlying private assets, impact of diversification	Impact of diversification, diversification of funds' underlying private assets, success of investments	How much of the commitments were really invested, how much undrawn capital is remaining

ASPECTS OF DIVERSIFICATION

Diversification can be looked at from various angles. The KPIs considered here are related to the commitment efficiency (CE), the exposure efficiency (XE, see **Chapter 3**), and an outcome assessment (notably the Sortino ratio) (see **Table 9.1**).

To explain the different stories these KPIs tell us and how to interpret them, let us look at a medieval battle (see **Figure 9.1**), such as the one fought by Shakespeare's Henry V at Agincourt.

A (non-ESG-compliant) analogy

> *'All things are ready, if our mind be so'.*
>
> —— William Shakespeare, Henry V

The first question would be how the king should position his troops on the battlefield, say, his archers, for illustration?[4] This actually captures the idea of 'commitment' quite

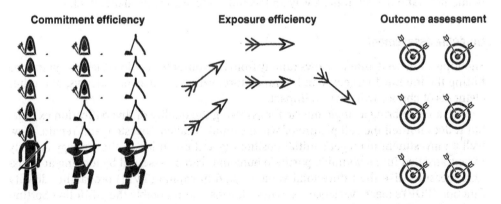

Commitment efficiency	Exposure efficiency	Outcome assessment

FIGURE 9.1 Diversification KPIs

well, as this term is applied to funds but, even more commonly, to the commitment of troops, too.[5]

The way how the archers are committed best – concentrated or spread out – depends on the situation. Some position taking is more suited to cope with a developing situation, while other ways of commitment basically doom an army from the outset.

Commitment efficiency

In the CE, we measure how efficiently the troops are spread, to stay with the analogy, over the battlefield. Replace 'troops' with 'funds' and 'battlefield' with 'financial markets' and you get the idea.

For portfolios of funds, the calculation of CE uses a cluster partitioning algorithm that takes the diversification dimensions relevant for an LP and the similarities within these dimensions into account. CE as KPI is based on the assumption that an evenly and widely committed portfolio offers the best diversification and, consequently, the best protection against unforeseen future developments in the portfolio. Having said this, the highest CE does not necessarily equate to best performance. Diversification is essentially protection against lack of knowledge, and investors who trust their superior research insights would rationally concentrate their portfolios in situations where they believe that some outcomes are more likely than others; very much like a military commander acting on new intelligence, or a better understanding of the terrain, would focus the majority of the forces available on the weakest spots of the opponent. This, however, does not mean that things will always go as intended.

Exposure efficiency

For an investment manager, the XE shows how the initial set-up will be translated into the real exposure to private assets.

Likewise, medieval troops starting from a position could engage in more or less effective ways. How many of the archers are active and really putting arrows into the air? Maybe they are too close, do not manage to find a rhythm, and shoot volleys at one time followed by longer breaks. Under these circumstances, a smaller number of archers would not stand in each other's way and would achieve an equivalent effect.

Outcome assessment

Shooting many well-aimed arrows rapidly from a favourable position does not guarantee hitting the intended targets. Wind, temperature, variations between arrows, and other elements of chance will have an impact.

CE aims to bring a single metric for assessing the quality of diversification ex ante, but it does not tell the full picture of when capital is called, invested, and repaid. How well an investment manager's initial positioning and execution of the strategy is likely to be translated into favourable portfolio outcomes can be assessed by looking at statistical measures like the future total value to paid-in capital (TVPI) probability density function (PDF)'s mean, variance, skewness, kurtosis, and notably the portfolio's Sortino ratio. While CE is exclusively controlled by the LP, XE is the result of the fund managers' activities. The Sortino ratio (see **Box 9.1**) reflects the LP's as well as the fund managers' decisions.

Box 9.1   Risk/return profile

For this discussion, risk-adjusted return is the return (or potential return) on a fund or a portfolio of funds compared to that of a risk-free asset. For an LP, one important way of managing the risk-adjusted return of her portfolio of funds, and therefore its risk/return profile, is through diversification. Relevant measures of risk-adjusted returns are the Sharpe ratio and the **Sortino ratio.**

For liquid assets, the Sharpe ratio (also called 'reward-to-variability ratio') is one of the most commonly used methods for measuring risk-adjusted returns. It is calculated as the ratio of expected performance minus the risk-free rate to the standard deviation.

The Sortino ratio is a variation of the Sharpe ratio. While the Sharpe ratio takes into account any volatility in return of an asset, the Sortino ratio differentiates volatility due to up and down movements. The up movements are considered desirable and not accounted for in the volatility. The Sortino ratio is the return in excess to the risk-free rate (or a certain threshold) over the downside semi-variance, so it compares the return to 'bad' volatility. The Sortino ratio allows assessing risk in an arguably better manner than simply looking at excess return to total volatility, since investors are primarily concerned about downside risk.

DIVERSIFYING COMMITMENTS

Given the high transaction cost of selling private fund interests in the secondary market, achieving and maintaining a targeted allocation is practically a matter of choosing commitments to new fund investments.[6]

To achieve good diversification benefits, the portfolio construction needs to assure a high degree of independence between funds comprising the portfolio. From a risk perspective, portfolios should be evenly diversified, i.e. it should not happen that all other diversification benefits are nullified because there was a concentration in one particular dimension, as often happens with vintage years. We approach the diversification of commitments in the following steps:

- Definition of the classification groups for the diversification dimensions;
- Definition of the classifications for each classification group;
- Definition of pairwise similarities[7] between these classifications (within one classification group);
- Adjusting the similarities for the vintage year intervals for all pairs of funds;
- Aggregating similarities over all classification groups, possibly weighted by the importance assigned to the classification group, to the pairwise similarity between funds;
- For all funds and their pairwise similarity as input, apply a clustering algorithm.

Assigning funds to clusters

In their simplest form, clusters are sets of data points that share similar attributes. A clustering algorithm is the method that groups these data points into different clusters based on their similarities. Good results were achieved by using agglomerative clustering with average linkage, but the approach to diversification management does not critically depend on which clustering algorithm is used. Members in the same cluster tend to react similarly to an external event and differently from members in another cluster. We model the pairwise similarity between funds across their various diversification dimensions and apply cluster analysis to the management of diversification.

DIVERSIFICATION DIMENSIONS

Some diversification dimensions are specific to private capital, such as the stage focus and the vintage year; others are also applicable for standard asset classes, such as the industry sector, the geography, the currency, or the agent concentration. Funds are either specialists or generalists. Specialist funds focus on an industry (e.g. biotech) or a country (say, India).

There are generalist funds that have no industry sector focus or funds that focus on several. There are also funds that focus on 'multiple' geographies. It is possible to extend the approach discussed here to situations where a fund is focusing on several geographies, industries etc. For example, for a fund that plans to invest in 60% information and communication technology (ICT) and 40% life sciences, the similarities can be aggregated weighted by these allocations.

Self-proclaimed definitions

The approach needs to work with the information at hand when investors commit to a fund. As funds are 'blind pools' (i.e. there is no portfolio yet), there are limits to the level of detail and the reliability of how the diversification dimensions can be classified. As practically LPs rely on primary commitments, they also need to base their diversification on a commitment basis and on the self-proclaimed strategy stated by the fund managers.

On the fund level, investors need to plan with the fund managers' declared focus for the entire fund, which will naturally be rather fuzzy. According to Lhabitant and Learne (2002),[8] relying on what the manager says is the only classification scheme that is effectively accessible to most investors. This is because at the beginning of the fund existence, the fund strategy and the resulting composition of the portfolio just exist as the stated intentions of the manager and only become apparent after the fund starts calling capital and its portfolio of private assets evolves.

Market practices

Analysis of nine institutional investors managing portfolios of private equity funds and one meta-study[9] on this subject suggests the following ranked importance of diversification dimensions:

1. Vintage year
2. Geography
3. Industry sector focus

4. Fund strategy (buyout, venture capital, infrastructure, etc.)
5. Fund management firm (fund manager)
6. Stage focus (early stage, pre-IPO, etc.)
7. Fund size

Why do LPs rely on these dimensions for managing diversification and why does this make sense?[10] One explanation is practicality: it is easy to classify funds accordingly. Private placement memoranda provide such information as fund manager aim to differentiate their proposal from others. Finally, private market data providers organise their statistics along these dimensions.

The other explanation is that they can be mapped on the different risk factors relevant for private markets: liquidity risk, operational risk, skill risk, market risk, country risk, currency risk, and innovation risk. The dimensions overlap to some degree, for instance, country and currency risk are difficult to separate.

The importance of diversification over vintage years

The consensus view is that diversification over vintages is the most powerful way to spread risk. Indeed, time separates all other dimensions. The institutional private capital market is organised around 'single-use', closed-end funds. The capital is used once, invested over the course of four, five, or six years, after which the harvesting of those investments begins. Within a 10- or 12-year period, capital goes in once, is invested once, and then is returned once.[11] The vintage year, or date on which a fund begins its investment activities,[12] is thus a critical determinant in the outcome. Investors should commit over the full course of the economic cycle and not be concentrated in any one year to reduce the risk of getting in or out at the wrong time.

Another key reason to diversify by vintage year is to manage liquidity risk by spreading the funds' cash-flow patterns (contributions followed by distributions) and duration profile. This, for instance, mitigates the risk that an LP is faced with a high number of capital calls taking place within short time windows. Diversification over vintage years is approached by making, for all other diversification dimensions, the similarities time dependent.

Other dimensions and their impact on risks

Geography can diversify various risks: operational risk exposure to natural catastrophes, political turmoil, and wars. Country risk is related to specific monetary policies, fiscal policies, regulation, and different stages in economic development. With different stock markets and exit environments geographies, geographies are related to market risk, too. There is some overlap with the strategy dimension. Diversifying over geographies is more feasible for later-stage investments than for venture capital (VC), which tends to be concentrated in few innovation hubs.

Industry sectors cover supply chains, alliances, competitive environment, and innovation, reflecting technology risk. Industry clusters are an exit market for M&A, so this is related to market risk. Likewise, certain industries are excluded under environmental, social, and governance (ESG) criteria. Geographies and industries can overlap; take Silicon Valley as example, but many industries operate worldwide.

Industry sector classes group companies that operate in a similar business sphere. The key assumption is that different industry sectors perform differently from each other at different periods of an economic cycle. For example, technology companies tend to perform above average during boom periods. Companies in the same class are exposed to similar market risks.

Fund strategy is reflecting financial risk as a consequence of access to finance, investor demand, availability of investment opportunities (restructuring, entrepreneur-ship, and innovation), and investment stage, where VC's early-stage investments carry a higher risk of failure.

Diversifying over various management firms addresses operational risk as well as skill risk, associated with key persons. This also diversifies the LP investor basis as the portfolio is supported by more deep-pocket investors. Strengths in terms of skills, experience, and networks need to be in line with the style of funds managed by the fund management firm.

Stage focus is a diversification dimension that captures financial risk and business risk and has a significant overlap with fund strategy. For example, VC investing is predominantly in companies in their early stages, whereas buyouts focus on later stages. It, therefore, makes more sense to avoid a double counting and reflect stage focus in the fund strategies.

Fund size at the first glance seems to be misplaced as a diversification dimension but has a significant impact on the fund's style. The lessons learned from various market crises have led management firms to seek reserves to become resilient against shocks in financial markets, and to reduce the risk that market stress will spread. In this respect, fund size reflects financial risk.

Fund sizes drive the accessible investee universe and are thus also related to market risk, with small companies not a meaningful target for mega-buyouts and small funds not being able to acquire and turnaround large companies. Only management firms with high reputation are able to raise large funds, so fund size can reflect a significant entry barrier.

Include currencies?

Note that currencies are not listed as diversification dimension here. Currency and geography often overlap strongly, like Great Britain (geography) and Pound Sterling, which would reduce the impact on the other important dimensions, such as vintage year and strategy.

In the context of securitisations for portfolios of private equity funds rating agencies such as Standard & Poor's also consider currencies as one of the main dimensions of diversification.[13] Other reasons for incorporating currencies in the diversification model are as follows:

- Currency is a characteristic of a fund as an instrument rather than the market it is operating.
- Notably in emerging economies, currencies like USD are in wide use. Also, the increasing use of crypto currencies would decouple currency from country.

- Overlap can also be an issue with other diversification dimensions. For instance, industries often also correspond to geography, e.g. Israel's private equity industry is dominated by investments in technology.
- If needed, we can use weightings to mitigate the bias towards geography.

Possible approaches to determine similarities between currencies are:

- Cross-volatility between currencies over long time periods;
- Differentiation between pegged currencies and non-pegged currencies;
- Comparing countries/trade blocks (as proxy for currencies) according to their relative economic strengths, maybe taking country rating into consideration.

DEFINITIONS

The ability to precisely assign funds to classes is extremely valuable for portfolio management. A minimal similarity leads to a higher classification accuracy and little or no overlaps. The fewer classes, the easier they are to separate, but there are also disadvantages. Often a fund needs to be assigned to a class where it does not really fit or only share few characteristics with the other class members. In the CE calculation, relying on too few classes lead to premature clustering, although in reality funds would be still dissimilar. On the other hand, the more classes are considered, and the narrower they are therefore defined, the higher the likelihood that, in practice, these classes represent an empty set or have too few members to be relevant and provide a significant sample. Practically, most classes and their definitions are subject to some degree of change over time – take technology investments as example, which nowadays look markedly different than, say, during the dot-com period or during the 1980s.

Styles

A fund's style is defined by a combination of diversification dimensions and the classes within these dimensions. The style reflects the fund's specialisation related to investment targets and method for value creation. Therefore, its style is indicative for how the fund will perform in different economic conditions. Classes according to private market data providers are indicative for a specific style's relevance, a sufficiently large sample size represented, and a different assumed risk/return profile of the target companies invested in.

Styles reflect the fund manager's expertise regarding geography, industry networks, and strategies as their approach to value added. Implicitly, these styles are assumed to represent different risk/return relationships. Clusters reflect concentrations of fund styles. LPs aim to compose a specific mix of assets, although assigning classes is to some degree judgemental and subjective. In an environment of uncertainty, change, and long investment horizons, the gap between the originally declared style and the one that is implemented will be wide, which is a reason why fund managers need flexibility and can only adhere to broad styles.

Classification groups

In line with the diversification dimensions, we define n classification groups

$$G_i; i = 1, \ldots, n.$$

Classification group i has m_i classifications

$$C_{G_i;j}; j = 1, \ldots, m_i.$$

Diversification aims to maximise returns for a set level of minimum acceptable risk by investing in different positions that can be assumed to react differently under the same market conditions. We use the pairwise similarity between funds under a given classification scheme as a proxy for their dependency. A dimension's similarity matrix defines the similarity between each pair of classes as a number within an interval [0, 1], with 0 being completely dissimilar and 1 being identical.

For each classification group, there is an $m_i \times m_i$ similarity matrix:

$$S_i = \begin{bmatrix} s_{i;1;1} & \cdots & \cdots \\ \cdots & \cdots & \cdots \\ \cdots & \cdots & s_{i;m_i;m_i} \end{bmatrix}; 0 \leq s_{i;k,l} \leq 1; k, l = 1, \ldots, m_i$$

with $s_{i;k,l}$ being the similarity between the two classifications k and l for classification group i. For practicality, from a user's perspective, we assume that these similarities are scored based on expert judgement.

For illustration, the classification group 'geography' could comprise the classes 'Austria', 'Germany', 'Belgium', etc. An example for a fund's style could be 'US VC fund with biotech focus'.

The pairwise similarities are symmetric, i.e.

$$s_{i;k,l} = s_{i;l;k}; i = 1, \ldots n.$$

The ranking above suggests that vintage year is generally viewed to be the most important diversification dimension, but how this compares to the other dimensions is uncertain. Diversification dimensions may not of equal importance, and classification groups can therefore be weighted:

$$0 \leq w_i \leq 1; i = 1, \ldots, n.$$

Weights for all the diversification dimensions need to sum up to 1:

$$\sum_{i=1}^{n} w_i = 1.$$

However, under the high uncertainty that characterises the alternative investment markets, in most cases, we will be unable to determine the strongest diversifier. Here, in most cases, it is best to assume equal weight:[14]

$$w_i = \frac{1}{n}, \forall i.$$

Style drifts

The classes reflect the LP's diversification objectives the fund managers need to adhere to within a set degree of flexibility. The flipside of such flexibility is the so-called 'style drift'. For hedge fund world, style drift is one of the areas that worry investors as it is seen as one of the major causes of investment failures. A too close parallel to hedge funds, however, is misguided as investors in closed-ended funds need to follow a different modus operandi. In the hedge fund world, the concern regarding style drifts, where investors aim to control and regularly rebalance their portfolios of funds, is justified, but in private capital, a rebalancing of a portfolio of funds is clearly impractical. Here, in fact, flexibility assures resilience and needs to be encouraged as long as it does not involve straying away from a firm's core competencies.[15]

Robustness of classification schemes

Generally, the higher the number of classes within a dimension, the more they overlap, the more difficult they are to separate. There is a trade-off: the higher the number of classes, the more nuances can be captured by the model. On the other hand, the fewer classes are considered, the lower the scope for the fund being assigned a wrong classification.

In principle, for each dimension, the higher the resolution, the more we will be able to differentiate funds, but in private markets, definitions can only be very fuzzy. Incorporating too many diversification dimensions carries the risk of reversion to the mean, i.e. where the average of the similarities between the individual funds does not allow a clear separation and assigning them to clusters. Classifications should represent sets of comparable resolution. For instance, it makes little sense to combine a geographical zone like 'North America' with a small region such as 'Cornwall'.

Also, introducing new classifications does not make them independent. For instance, Germany and Austria may be different countries, but their economies are tightly interwoven, suggesting a high degree of similarity. The more classification groups and classifications therein we look at, the more difficult it becomes to properly separate them and the less explainable and robust the resulting clusters are. There may be a high number of samples representing a fund's peer group, but many may not fully similar to the fund in question. Alternatively, the peer group may be very similar, but there may not be enough samples to capture the full range of potential outcomes.

Therefore, it is better not to become overly sophisticated and only consider 'strong' diversification dimensions. Better keep the scheme simple, with clear-cut classification groups and few but clearly dissimilar classifications.

Despite industry sector focus generally being perceived as the third most important diversification dimension, it is doubtful whether this provides LPs with meaningful information. Kshetrapal (2016) investigated the industry exposure of buyout funds with the objective of developing classifications, concluding that only four are sufficiently different from each other:[16] 'Technology', 'Health', 'Financial Services', and 'Diversified', with 'Diversified' (funds that are opportunistic in their pursuits of investment targets and do not have a sector focus approach) being the most frequently used classification. Industry sector focus is more relevant for private assets directly held by an investor or for an LP's co-investments.

Based on these considerations, LPs should manage their portfolio's diversification over the dimensions vintage year, geography, fund strategy, and fund management firm.

MODELLING VINTAGE YEAR IMPACT

As discussed before, the most important source of diversification is by vintage year. This is modelled by making the measure for similarity time dependent. As the funds are spread over time, the impact of diversification over time becomes stronger and the similarities start to decrease. Even if the management firm is the same, the similarity between two funds managed by this firm is time dependent. Blackstone today is not Blackstone 10 years ago, and therefore, the funds will not necessarily fall into the same cluster. Two sub-portfolios having exactly the same composition cannot form a cluster if they are separated by 20 years.

Let y be the year impact parameter that defines the time interval during which there can be a similarity between funds. **Figure 9.2(i)** looks at two funds A and B, which start their operations at the same time and which have classifications that are fully similar.

For classification group G_i, let $\bar{s}_{G_i;A;B}$ be the vintage-year-adjusted similarity between fund A with classification $Cl_{G_i;A}$ and fund B with classification $Cl_{G_i;B}$. If the similarity is $s_{A;B}$, the vintage year for fund A is vy_A, and the vintage year for fund B is vy_B, then the vintage-year-adjusted similarity is

$$\bar{s}_{A;B} = s_{A;B}\left\{1 - \frac{\min\left(\left|vy_A - vy_B\right|; y\right)}{y}\right\}.$$

Figure 9.2(ii) shows the situation where fund B starts its operations later than fund A. The time interval between the start times is 75% of the year impact parameter Y:

$$\frac{\left|vy_A - vy_B\right|}{y} = 0.75.$$

This results in a vintage-year-adjusted similarity $= 0,25$. **Figure 9.2(iii)** shows the situation where the time interval between the start times of funds A and B exceeds y:

$$\left|vy_A - vy_B\right| > y.$$

(i) **Similarity matrix - same vintage year**

	Fund A	Fund B
Fund A	1	1
Fund B	1	1

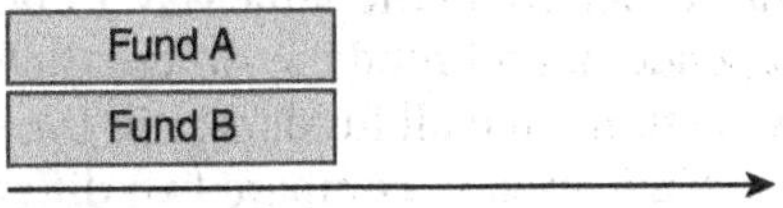

(ii) **Similarity matrix - spread over vintages**

	Fund A	Fund B
Fund A	1	0.25
Fund B	0.25	1

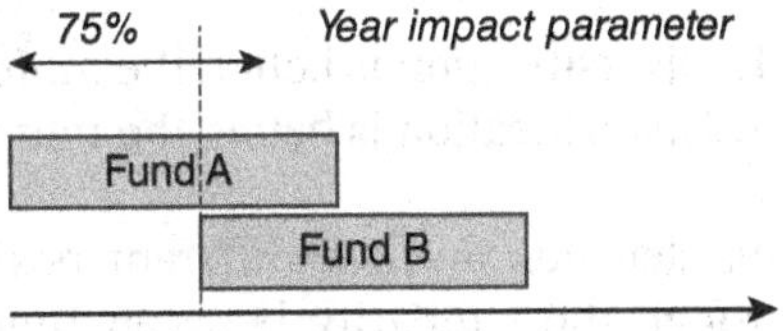

(iii) **Similarity matrix - independent vintages**

	Fund A	Fund B
Fund A	1	0
Fund B	0	1

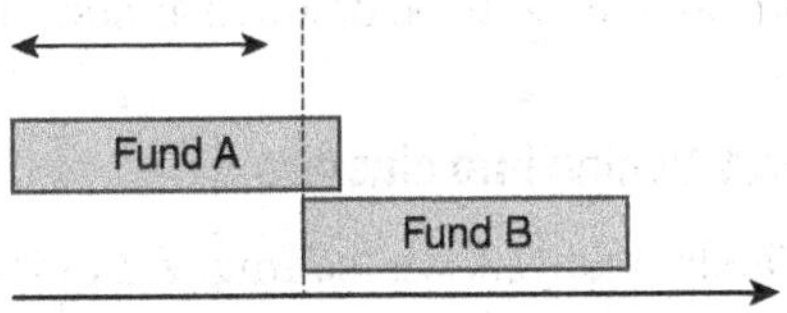

FIGURE 9.2 Vintage year impact on similarity

This results in a vintage-year-adjusted similarity $\bar{s}_{G_i;A;B} = 0$ for classification group G_i and funds A and B.

COMMITMENT EFFICIENCY

The CE measures how efficiently funds are spread over various diversification dimensions.

Importance of clusters

Generally, stresses in the market, such as economic crises and market booms, will result in situations where assets are becoming increasingly correlated as market participants need to adapt in order to survive or exploit opportunities. This is modelled by making similarities between funds dependent on a parameter that describes the market's stress level. Under an increasing stress level, the minimum similarity between two funds required to consider them as independent (i.e. being members of different clusters) is going up – the proposed method therefore looks at the tendency of a portfolio to form clusters under increasing level of market stresses.

Under increasing market stress, portfolios form clusters of funds that essentially start to behave in the same way. Funds in the same cluster are expected to be completely dependent, and funds in different clusters are expected to be completely independent. We assume that all funds within the same cluster perform in the same direction.[17]

CE is used to compare two different portfolios for determining which one is better diversified and therefore better able to withstand stresses (adverse changes) in the market environment. This KPI is based on two key assumptions:

1. Diversification is better, the more funds/clusters form the portfolio.
2. Diversification is better, the more evenly the funds/clusters are sized.

This depends on how different positions actually are, a question we are addressing through the similarity between funds. Practically, there are diminishing benefits of diversification.[18] How many funds we can add to a portfolio depends on the classification scheme: the fewer diversification dimensions exist, the faster the funds within a portfolio need to be deemed as similar and form clusters.

Partitioning into clusters

Cluster analysis is a technique that is used to classify objects into relatively homogenous groups that share some common trait. The basis for clustering is a similarity measure.

We can express the similarity between two funds by first summing up the time-adjusted similarities over all classification groups, weighted by their importance and then deducting this sum from 1:

$$D_{A;B} = 1 - \sum_{i=1}^{n} w_i \overline{s}_{G_i;A;B}.$$

This measure should be small for very similar funds and large for very different funds. It has to fulfil four properties:

$$Identity : d(i,i) = 0, \forall i$$

$$Non\ negativity : d(i, j) \geq 0, \forall i, j$$

$$Symmetry : d(i, j) = d(j, i), \forall i, j$$

$$Triangle\ inequality : d(i, j) \leq d(i, k) + d(k, j), \forall i, j, k.$$

Depending on their similarity and the overall stress level set for the portfolio, two funds are either in different clusters or in the same cluster.

To classify funds, we use a so-called 'agglomerative clustering algorithm'[19] as a simple and effective way to classify data: the algorithm starts with every fund being its own cluster, finds the 'most similar' pair of clusters, and then merges smaller clusters into bigger clusters incrementally until all funds end up in the same cluster. An in-depth discussion of the various algorithms for clustering goes beyond the scope of this book.

Measurement approach

Figure 9.3 shows a portfolio of 10 funds; under a stress level of 0, these funds are assumed to be fully independent (i.e. belong to its own cluster). With increasing stress level, they get into each other's 'reach' and several funds then form one cluster. The gradual increase of stress leads to new clusters only at specific points, when a new fund gets in reach of a cluster. Therefore, the portfolio clusters in discrete cluster steps. In this case, after eight cluster steps,[20] one single cluster forms (in the figure, each newly formed cluster is depicted in a different grey shade).

We look at the portfolio composition for a given cluster step. Based on the assumptions, the best case is a perfectly balanced portfolio, i.e. for each fund in the portfolio one cluster of equal size only. The CE measure implicitly assumes naïve diversification (i.e. same commitment size for all funds in the portfolio).[21] This is a realistic assumption, as a large body of empirical work exists that confirms that naïve diversification works best under extreme uncertainty (and in practice even better than Markowitz's MPT[22]).

Let N be the number of clusters occurring for different stress levels and $j \varepsilon \mathbb{N}$ be the number of cluster steps, where $j \leq N - 1$. $j = 1$ indicates the first step, where all funds can

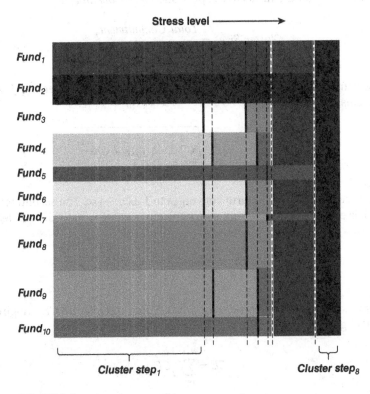

FIGURE 9.3 Increasing portfolio concentration

still be considered as independent. At step j, the smallest distance between two cluster steps is denoted as d_j. Cluster step C_j is defined as follows:

$$C_1 = d_1$$

$$C_j = d_j - d_{j-1}, \ 2 \leq j \leq N-1$$

$$C_N = 1 - d_{N-1}.$$

Hence, it can be seen that

$$0 \leq C_j \leq 1$$

and

$$\sum_{j=1}^{N-1} C_j = 1.$$

Now, for each cluster step j, the cluster size of cluster i is defined as the total commitment size of the funds in cluster i at step j, *Total Commitment*$_{ji}$, relative to the total commitment size of all the funds in the portfolio *Total Commitment*:

$$Cluster\ Size_{ji} = \frac{Total\ Commitment_{ji}}{Total\ Commitment}.$$

We measure the commitment efficiency CE_j for one given cluster step j, with n_j the number of clusters at step j:

$$CE_j = \frac{n_j - 1}{n_j} - \frac{1}{n_j} \sqrt{\sum_i \left| \frac{1}{n_j} - Cluster\ Size_{ji} \right|^2}.$$

It can be seen that the first term converges to 1 as $n_j \rightarrow \infty$. The second term, on the other hand, is equal to zero, if within step j, the clusters are equally distributed, i.e.

$$Cluster\ Size_{ji} = \frac{1}{n_j} \text{ for all } i.$$

Therefore, CE_j is at most 1 and 0 for $n_j = 1$. Summing over all CE_j weighted by the cluster step C_j gives the CE for the portfolio (see **Figure 9.4**):

$$CE = \sum_{j=1}^{N-1} C_j CE_j.$$

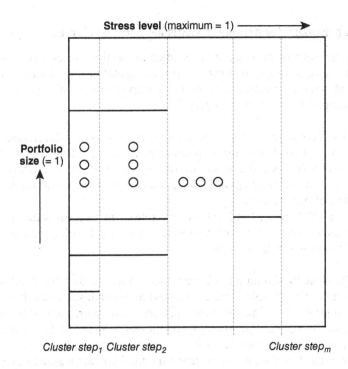

FIGURE 9.4 Commitment efficiency over portfolio

Remarks

We can show that CE is monotonically decreasing with j, as we are using the l_2-norm. CE goes up with the number of funds in the portfolio but goes down as similarities between the funds are increasing. The theoretical case of CE of one requires an infinitely high number of entirely independent funds. Neither does this number of funds exist nor does any classification scheme support this, as at a certain point, we are running out of classifications that are completely dissimilar from all others. However, for a realistic number of, say, 100 funds in a portfolio, the highest CE achievable would be 0.99 and thus sufficiently close to one for all practical purposes.

MOBILITY BARRIERS

The assumption behind the CE is that fund managers are essentially attached to their style. Barriers restrict the fund manager's mobility to switch from one style to another. Such barriers arise, for example, from fund managers needing sector specific knowledge and networks within industries and geographies.

When splitting a portfolio of funds, the clusters reflect a group's membership stability due to high mobility barriers (i.e. to entry and exit) that prevent easily switching back and forth.[23]

Similarity is a measure for barriers to switching between classes

Mobility barriers impede movement between groups as this comes with substantial costs and uncertainty regarding outcomes. For funds, regulation like the Alternative Investment Fund Managers Directive (AIFMD) in Europe forms an obstacle to geographical mobility. Examples for high barriers are:

- During its lifetime, a VC fund cannot switch to become a leveraged buyout fund (and vice versa), as this requires an entirely different skillset. For VC, the ability to evaluate technologies and to grow companies is critical, whereas a leveraged buyout fund creates value through its ability to get access to debt finance and to the financial structuring of transactions;
- Likewise, a US-focused fund will not be able to pursue investments in emerging markets, as this would require an entirely different network of sourcing opportunities and creating profitable exits.

Typically, in such situations, a fund's LPs are aware that the fund management team's skills are not applicable in other settings and prevent such switches. Barriers also define the contestability of the peer group cluster within which a fund is operating – for instance caused by strong reputations or relationships between LPs and management firms. If barriers are low, clusters become less well separated.

The classes used by the private market data providers are assumed to have different risk/return characteristics, cover sufficiently many samples to be relevant, and are sufficiently clearly defined to be separable. They also reflect the fund's style based on which the management firm is competing in the market.[24] Also, in narrow sub-markets, fund managers will confront established fund management competitors going for the same target companies. LPs are well aware of such difficulties and also want to control their own diversification over styles; therefore, they more often than not will not allow a fund manager to style drift by switching from one significantly different sector to the other.

Similarity is not correlation

Similarities are defined in a form of a matrix, which could be confused with correlations and associated covariance matrixes. This calls for some clarifications.

In complex systems, such as financial systems, correlations are not constant but vary in time. Over time horizons relevant for private markets 'Black Swans' are the rule rather the exception. Here correlations between assets can differ substantially and the relationships observed in quieter market regularly break down entirely.[25] Additionally, investors with apparently well-diversified portfolios should be concerned with 'contagion', i.e. the spread of economic crises from one market or region to another, as virtually all markets are connected through monetary and financial systems.

The CE assumes that sooner or later a crisis will spread and measures how resilient a portfolio is to contagion. This is done by scanning through the full range of stress levels and look at how quickly clusters of potential 'infections' are forming and how large such clusters would be at each stress level. This idea is inconsistent with the concept of correlations that measure a linear and stable relationship.

IS THERE AN OPTIMUM DIVERSIFICATION?

Conceptually, CE is an enhanced and managed naïve diversification, based on the assumption that an evenly balanced portfolio of independent assets works best. DeMiguel et al. (2009) investigated the performance of a number of portfolio selection strategies and compared them against the simple heuristic where all stocks in the portfolio receive an equal share of investment. This so-called '1/N heuristics' consistently outperformed more sophisticated techniques.

How many funds?

How many funds are needed to achieve a good diversification or, in other words, how large is N? A widely accepted rule of thumb is that it takes around 20–30 different positions to adequately diversify a portfolio. Various studies, mainly related to publicly quoted funds, come to different results, ranging from 10 to several hundred positions.

For private capital, the answer depends, among other factors, on the funds' strategy-specific risk/return profile and how this changes when putting together portfolios of funds. One of the first studies on the impact of diversification on the risk profile of portfolios of private equity funds was undertaken by Weidig and Mathonet (2004). They and similar studies that followed concluded that diversification would only be beneficial, as expressed by HarbourVest (2018): 'Investors should not be overly concerned with over-diversification'.

However, these studies did not take into consideration how much the diversification is costing the LP. Moreover, these simulated risk/return profiles did not really reflect potential dependency between funds. This dependency is likely to increase as the portfolio is 'packed' with more and more funds.

Costs of diversification

An LP cost model would reflect fixed (e.g. infrastructure; staff, such as investment managers and back-office, to operate investment programmes; overheads, such as general administration and IT systems) and variable costs related to managing a portfolio of funds. In alternative assets, in general, the variable costs comprise by expenses for due diligence, legal structuring, and business travel related to the monitoring of individual funds. They are far higher than, for example, the management fees an investor would have to spend on regulated ETFs. Diversification clearly drives the variable costs but incrementally also leads to an increase of fixed costs caused by, for instance, hiring new staff and additional office space.

Faced with this cost structure, LPs question whether there could be an optimum level of diversification and, despite previous findings, whether there might even be an over-diversification effect? This was looked at in Meyer and Mathonet (2005) by investigating the relationship between the Sharpe ratio/Sortino ratio and the number of funds.

While the Sharpe ratio suggested that for smaller portfolios of funds, like €100 million available for commitments, there be an optimum somewhere around 30 funds, the effect was barely recognisable and vanished for larger portfolios above €200 million (see **Figure 9.5**).

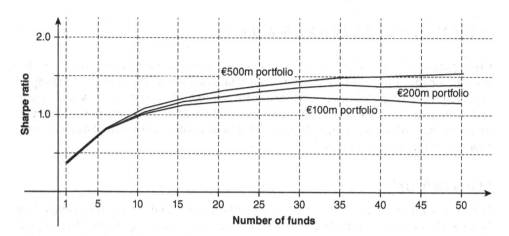

FIGURE 9.5 Sharpe ratio versus number of funds per portfolio

However, when looking at the Sortino ratio, there was a clear optimum around 15 funds for the smaller portfolio, but once the portfolio size goes up to €500 million and beyond, the diseconomies will only set in for a very large number of funds (see **Figure 9.6**).

This is explainable: if we, say, diversify €100 million over 10 funds, the average commitment size is €10 million, whereas if we diversify €500 million over the same number of funds, this average commitment size goes up to €50 million, with the costs having much less impact on what the LP gets out of the fund's overall performance. In other words, for the typical institutional investors with allocations to private capital of significantly more than €1 billion, the number of funds in the portfolio will have no relevant impact on the risk/return profile. The diseconomies of average fund sizes going down to a level where the costs start to have an impact on the Sortino ratio will come at such a late point that other adverse effects become more relevant.

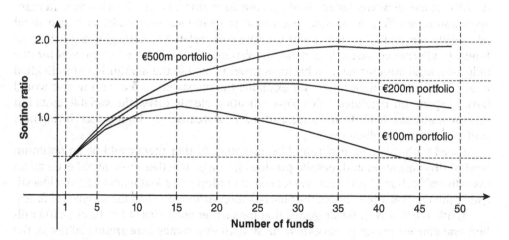

FIGURE 9.6 Sortino ratio versus number of funds per portfolio

Rather than over-diversification, inefficiency appears to be more important in practice. Using the CE concept, Sidenius and Ballek (2022) looked at the composition of peer groups in a private market benchmark and found diminishing benefits of diversification, simply because the number of truly different funds is limited. An additional point not even considered here, as it goes beyond diversification, is the bounded supply of 'top' funds.

How to set a 'satisficing' number of funds?

For the typical institutional investor's large allocations to private capital, the question of an optimum number of funds practically does not matter. This does not mean that the costs and diminishing fund quality associated with excessive diversification are irrelevant, and therefore, LPs should commit to the lowest number of funds possible. This number is the overall amount to be committed to funds divided by the maximum amount the LP can commit to any one fund on average – which will vary depending on whether the allocation is to VC funds or to mega-buyouts with a size of $5 billion or more. Taking this number as given, the LP should select fund with different styles to maximise CE to assure the best achievable diversification under these circumstances.

PORTFOLIO IMPACT

We can measure the impact of new commitments on the portfolio's diversification to engineer a portfolio that is resilient to adverse developments in the market. We also need to take the dependencies between funds into consideration when aggregating individual fund forecasts to a forecast for the portfolio of funds.

Commitment efficiency timeline

The CE timeline (see example in **Figure 9.7**) measures the impact of new commitments on the portfolio. Whenever a new fund is added or a fund matures and thus drops out of the portfolio, the CE changes.

In the example, the existing funds approach the end of their lifetime, and as they mature, the portfolio increasingly concentrates and therefore its CE goes down. Regularly committing to new funds improves CE. It is not the mere fact that new funds are added that leads to this improvement; it is also explained by spreading the commitments over vintages that assures a higher distance from the other funds in the portfolio.

Portfolio-level forecasts

Dependencies have a major impact when we aggregate the cash-flow forecasts for the individual funds to a portfolio-level forecast. As market stress goes up, we need to assume that funds with similar characteristics will increasingly behave in sync, i.e. all having a better or worse outcome together. The Monte Carlo simulation (MCS) captures this behaviour through treating funds that are in the same cluster consistently.

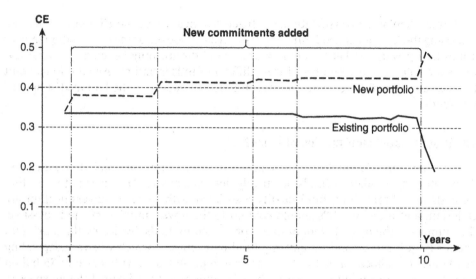

FIGURE 9.7 CE timeline

Figure 9.8 outlines the approach. During the first cluster step, funds A and B are assumed to be in two different clusters and thus treated as independent. For each individual cluster, the MCS samples one pair of random numbers, each between 0 and 1,

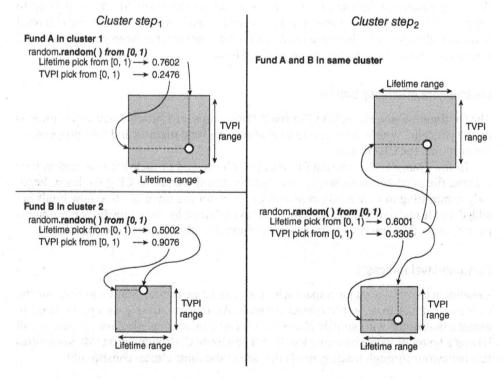

FIGURE 9.8 Randomly pick samples, reflecting membership to cluster

and applies to all members in the cluster. Here, for the first cluster, a pessimistic random number of 0.7602 for lifetime, and an also pessimistic random number of 0.2476, consistent with a low TVPI, is picked.[26] Fund B is in a different cluster, and the simulation picks an about average lifetime and a high TVPI.

In the second cluster step, funds A and B belong to the same cluster, and only one pair of random figures for lifetime and TVPI is sampled and applied to each fund's forecast ranges, with the degree of 'pessimism' expressed by the random numbers for lifetime of 0.6001 and for TVPI of 0.2205 being the same.

APPENDIX A – DETERMINING SIMILARITIES

A practical way of determining the similarity between classifications is a scoring approach. This can be done in several ways:

- Scoring based on the normalised distance (such as the transport way connection in the case of dimension 'geography').
- Scoring yes/no (e.g. does country X belong to a trade-bloc Y?).
- Scoring based on an expert's assessment of similarities.

Greenberg (2015) looked at using expert judgement to estimate correlations between distributions in situations where sufficient historical data are not available. He recommended not to use more than five scores as otherwise it becomes too difficult to differentiate between classes[27] (see **Table 9.A-1**).

How can the geographical distance between, for example, trade areas like the European Union and a single country like Japan be dealt with? One way would be to average over the pairwise distances between Japan and each EU member, i.e. Japan – Austria, Japan – Belgium, Japan – Bulgaria, etc.[28] Alternatively, one could take the country (or the countries) with the minimum distance to Japan;[29] assume that this country is the 'gateway', like the UK was pre-Brexit.[30]

For a scoring, we need to accept simplicity. Trying to capture minute details and dependencies only leads to an endless loop of questions.

For example, does 'geography' relate to the fund's style or to the private assets held by the fund? Probably, the fund's location is the 'best guess', but some are operating in several countries. How relevant is it anyway for VC, where technology is increasingly becoming global? Does the stage focus relate to the stage of the portfolio company at the

TABLE 9.A-1   Scoring similarities (based on Greenberg, 2015)

Similarity score	Similarity classes
1.0	Entirely similar
0.75	Strong similarity
0.50	Medium similarity
0.25	Weak similarity
0.0	Completely dissimilar

time of commitment or its current state? A seed investment five years later may already be in its pre-IPO stage. For all such questions, certainly rules can be drawn up, but it can become quite complex and we also have to ask ourselves the question of how we can manage this. For most of these dimensions, only a 'low resolution' will be practical.

Scores for different dimensions can be aggregated by averaging or taking their maximum score.

APPENDIX B – GEOGRAPHICAL SIMILARITIES

Geographical diversification is the practice of spreading a portfolio across different countries and regions to reduce risks and enhance returns. This is based on the observation that foreign markets rarely move in perfect tandem with each other.

Many countries are not highly correlated with each other as they are developing at different paces, due to climate, threats from nature (earthquakes and tsunamis), culture, and stages in economic development. Developing countries may offer greater growth potential than developed economies but expose investors also to higher risk, for instance, caused by unstable political systems, riots, and revolutions.

Geographical diversification for private capital

The private capital industry has traditionally been fragmented along national lines. Funds have been raised, investments have been made, and exits have been achieved primarily domestically. Since the mid-1990s, private markets have increasingly internationalised.

This trend has been especially pronounced in the growth of cross-border capital commitments done by funds. Heikkilä (2004) found that there are 'surprisingly few papers' on how investors create their portfolios of private equity funds and that assessing benefits of geographical diversification of a portfolio was extremely hard. Consequently, many of the investors explained that their geographical diversification principles are based on rules of thumb rather than on systematic analysis.

According to Heikkilä (2004), investors usually do not consider diversification at country level, but rather between areas like Northern Europe versus the UK, or even Europe versus the US. The classification group 'geography' could, for illustration, be decomposed into about a dozen classifications associated with continents or larger regions, referred to here as geographical blocks. This is assuming that geographical proximity is indicative of comparable economic conditions.

Regional groups

A simple way of approaching geographical diversification would be just to treat two countries that fall into different regional groups as completely dissimilar. Such broad regional groups are, for example, defined by the United Nations (UN):[31]

- Sub-Saharan Africa
- Northern Africa and Western Asia
- Central and Southern Asia
- Eastern and South-Eastern Asia

(A) Geographical blocks

Countries X and Y in different geographical blocks are <u>completely dissimilar</u>. If countries X and Y belong to different geographical blocks but are sharing a border, their similarity is <u>remote</u> (unless one country makes up the major part of the geographical block, like China or Russia).

- North America
- Central & South America
- Western Europe
- Central and Eastern Europe
- Russia & Belarus
- China
- Japan, Korea, Taiwan
- Australia & New Zealand
- South Asia
- South-East Asia
- West Asia and North Africa
- Sub-Saharan Africa
- South Africa

(B) Geographical distance

Similarity	Definition
Strong	X and Y are neighboring countries (share a border)
Medium	One other country separating X and Y; or X and Y are neighboring countries but separated by sea gate
Remote	More than one other country or sea separating X and Y

(C) Economic distance

If countries X and Y belong to the same free-trade agreement zone (e.g. EU, USMCA) their similarity score is <u>medium</u>.

The similarity between countries X and Y is defined as the maximum of (A), (B), and (C)

FIGURE 9.A-1   Geographies

- Latin America and the Caribbean
- Oceania
- Europe and Northern America

This, however, is likely to be over-simplistic and ignores other important factors related to the barriers between geographies, like trade and political blocs, distance, and languages (see **Figure 9.A-1**).[32]

Arguably, some regions (for instance, Western Europe) are more relevant for institutional investors and, therefore, call for a refinement, introducing higher granularity and similarities between the countries in such a region (see **Table 9.A-2**).

Trade blocs

A trade bloc is an intergovernmental agreement where barriers to trade such as tariffs are reduced or eliminated among the participating states. The prime example is the European Union's promotion of international trade among its member countries.

TABLE 9.A-2   Scoring similarities within region

Score	Definition
1	Strong similarity, X and Y are neighbouring countries (share a border)
0.66	Medium similarity, one other country separating X and Y; or X and Y are neighbouring countries but separated by sea gate
0.33	Near similarity: more than one other country or sea separating X and Y

However, a wider economic integration is not the only achievement of the European Union. In 2012, it was awarded the Nobel Peace Prize for over six decades contributing to 'the advancement of peace and reconciliation, democracy and human rights in Europe'. Whitten et al. (2022) saw this as evidence for better political relations and a greater volume of international trade going hand-in-hand. Their paper provided an empirical test of the conjecture that a warming and cooling of political ties between two countries is accompanied by expansion and contraction of their trade activities with each other.

This can be enhanced by grouping countries into 'developed economies', 'economies in transition', and 'developing economies', as defined by the UN's World Economic Situation and Prospects.[33] This reflects that, for instance, developed industries operate in similar trade blocs and under comparable infrastructural, legal, regulatory, and policy conditions.

Transport way connection

The proximity of one country to another is one indication of their similarity. Naturally, the transport way connection is a major entry barrier between two geographies. Brakman and van Marrewijk (2007) found that trade between two countries decreases by 9% when the distance increases by 10%.

German management consultant and author Hermann Simon coined the term 'hidden champions' for small, highly specialised world-market leaders, that, often deliberately, catch a low level of public awareness. He pointed to the fact that many of these hidden champions are in German-speaking countries and explains this with a geostrategic unique location.[34] He argues that the physical and practical limits of globalisation are based on immutable facts. Earth is a sphere, where day and night and time zones still matter. The German-speaking area and the neighbouring countries are the only region (in the northern hemisphere) in which you can make calls to the whole of Eurasia (including Japan) and America (including the west coast) within slightly extended office hours (9 hours). This advantage applies in a similar way to travel and favours globally operating companies that are based in the German-Austria-Switzerland (DACH) region.

Language barriers

In most businesses, a certain level of personal, direct communication remains essential. Ribeiro and Ferro (2017) focused on the relationship between international trade and language barriers. They found that language does play an important role in the choice of foreign trading partners. Where trading partners do not share the same language, a trade barrier will be imposed implying an additional cost to commercial transactions.

Limits to geography as diversifier

In practice, Heikkilä (2004) points out that institutional investors appeared to be more careful in diversifying their portfolios across what he referred to as 'investment stages' (defined in this book as 'fund strategies') – specifically VC versus buyouts – than across geographical areas. Some claimed that rather than spending too much time calculating potential benefits of geographical diversification, the more relevant issue is to consider the management teams of the funds. In any case, geographical diversification is not a panacea; the global economy remains interconnected so that different regions are not as independent as it may appear.

APPENDIX C – MULTI-STRATEGIES AND OTHERS

Simplistically, funds are either specialists or generalists. Specialists focus on an industry (e.g. biotech) or a country (say, Japan). There are generalist funds that have no industry sector focus or funds that focus on multiple industries. There are also funds that focus on multiple countries or broad geographies like the European Union.

One cannot assume that 'multiple' is an own geography that is independent from the other geographies. It is certainly similar to several of the geographies. Let us take as example a fund that is running a multi-region strategy with geographies US and Europe. This can be dealt with in two ways:

- Create in the similarity matrix for geography a class 'transatlantic' that is 50% similar to EU and 50% similar to US and assign the fund to this geography.
- The 'lazy' way, where you just allocate the fund to class 'multiple'. Here, we need to assume that there is an overlap with all other geographies (which is the default to be set).

'Multiple' ('don't care') is similar to 'Others' ('don't know'). With 'others' we need to be careful as they can be multiple themselves or heavily similar to one specific; therefore, we assume another, higher, default for 'Others'.

APPENDIX D – INDUSTRY SECTOR SIMILARITIES

Spreading investments across managers with skills in different industry sectors protects against a sector or technology going out of favour or against cyclical industries. In practice, it may be better to just consider coarse categorisations such as, in the case of VC, Life Sciences (biotech/pharmaceuticals), Green Technologies (Industrial/Energy), and ICT.[35]

Figure 9.A-2 shows a prototype similarity matrix for classification group 'industry sector focus'.

APPENDIX E – STRATEGY SIMILARITIES

Many LPs consider fund strategy to be one of the most important sources of diversification. Here, strategies are modelled as four dimensions, 'Target', 'Value Creation', 'Funding', and 'Stage', to which individually scores 0: dissimilar; 0.5 medium; and 1: similar are assigned. The average of these scores is then mapped onto one of the five similarity classes.

| | | Default for 'multiple' | 0.2 |
| | | Default for 'others' | 0.3 |

	Financials	Technology	Health	Diversified	Others
Financials	1	0	0	0.2	0.3
Technology	0	1	0	0.2	0.3
Health	0	0	1	0.2	0.3
Diversified	0	0	0	0.2 (1*)	0.3
Others	0	0	0	0	0.3 (1*)

* If fund identity

FIGURE 9.A-2   Industry sector focus

- **Target** means the underlying assets. In the case of VC, growth, buyouts, and distressed, they are similar (all companies); the targets for real estate and buyouts are (at least most of the time) dissimilar.
- **Value creation**: Growth and VC follow a similar value creation approach (build companies), buyouts use a lot of debt (and therefore only have medium similarity) to create value, and turnarounds create value through drastic restructuring and as legal play. For natural resources, value is created in a completely different, i.e. dissimilar, manner.
- **Funding:** VC, growth equity, leveraged buyout, and distressed equity are equity-based strategies. Direct lending, mezzanine, and distressed debt are debt-based strategies. There are clearly some overlaps. For example, the line between VC and growth equity is occasionally difficult to draw (e.g. in the case of VC in later stages). Mezzanine financing is a hybrid of debt and equity financing, and distressed equity and distressed debt meet in similar spaces.
- **Stages**: Note that stages (the state of a target at time of investment) are integrated in strategy similarities instead of treating them as an own dimension. Early stage is very similar to VC and late stage to buyouts, so incorporating them here avoids a double counting.

APPENDIX F – FUND MANAGEMENT FIRM SIMILARITIES

The number of fund management firms, with their specific 'style', strategy, and their specialised expertise in a particular segment of the market, is one of the key dimensions to consider when building a portfolio.

Maintaining a relationship with the same firm extending over several funds reduces the need for screening and pre-investment due diligence work and thus saves the investors time and money. This diversification dimension captures predominantly operational risk. During the normally 10 plus 2 years lifetime of a fund, it is quite likely that a fund management team will go through a crisis situation, such as tensions among the team members, the departure of a key person, or the spin-out of part of the team. Having relationships with several firms mitigates the potential over-reliance upon few key investment professionals.

Generally, management firms will be independent from each other, and therefore, the similarity between management firms will be defined by the unitary matrix.[36] As operational and ESG-related risks mainly depend on the management firms and are thus uncorrelated between them, these risks can efficiently be diversified away.

APPENDIX G – INVESTMENT STAGE SIMILARITIES

As discussed before, there are significant overlaps between strategy and investment stage as diversification dimensions, and arguably dealing with investment stages in the context of strategies avoids this double counting. Some investors, however, prefer to look at investment stages as a diversification dimension in its own right.

Spreading investments across companies at various stages of maturity also leads to a staggered pace of realisations and thus less dependence upon market conditions at particular points in time. Furthermore, the risk profile of a private capital investment appears to be significantly different depending on its stage focus.[37] **Figure 9.A-3** shows a prototype similarity matrix for classification group 'investment stage focus':

	Pre-seed	Seed	Start-up	Early expansion	Growth	Late expansion	Pre-IPO
Pre-seed	1	0.66	0.33	0	0	0	0
Seed	O	1	0.66	0.33	0	0	0
Start-up	O	O	1	0.66	0.33	0	0
Early expansion	O	O	O	1	0.66	0.33	0
Growth	O	O	O	O	1	0.66	0.33
Late expansion	O	O	O	O	O	1	0.66
Pre-IPO	O	O	O	O	O	O	1

FIGURE 9.A-3 Stage focus

As portfolio companies often quite rapidly advance from one stage to another, the definitions are blurred and also depend on how the fund managers define the fund. This matrix, therefore, defines significant overlaps between the different stages.

APPENDIX H – FUND SIZE SIMILARITIES

Related to strategies and investment stages, investors classify funds by their sizes, usually as classes 'small', 'medium', 'large', and 'mega'.[38] Size matters and is indicative for risk because the more capital a fund has available, the more likely it is to be diversified. The definitions are blurred, and like in the case of the investment stages, the similarity matrix needs to define significant overlaps between the different stages.

In any case, the classifications are not straightforward as they vary depending on the broad investment strategy. Moreover, what is 'small' or 'mega' has been changing significantly over the past few years. In the early 2000s, VentureXpert defined *venture and buyout fund sizes* as shown in **Table 9.A-3** (see Mathonet and Meyer, 2007).

TABLE 9.A-3　Investment sizes by strategy

Size classification	Venture capital	Buyouts and other private equity
Small	Up to $25 million	Up to $250 million
Medium	$25–50 million	$250–500 million
Large	$50–100 million	$500 million to $1 billion
Mega	>$100 million	>1 billion

At the time of this writing in 2023, for private equity, vehicles of a size of $5 billion or more are viewed as' mega-fund', and the $20–25 billion range appears to be a soft cap. A VC fund of less than $100 million is not viewed as viable any longer. VC generally is said not to be scalable, although in 2019 Softbank managed to raise the $100 billion Vision Fund, aiming to invest in emerging technologies like artificial intelligence, robotics, and the Internet of Things.[39]

NOTES

1. The methods discussed here are applicable to co-investments as well, but this is out of scope for the chapter.
2. See Kasumov (2020).
3. See Barry (2022).
4. See https://en.wikipedia.org/wiki/Battle_of_Agincourt, accessed [2 February 2022]: 'This battle is notable for the use of the English longbow in very large numbers, with the English and Welsh archers comprising nearly 80 percent of Henry's army [. . .] Early on the 25th, Henry deployed his army (approximately 1,500 men-at-arms and 7,000 longbowmen) across a 750-yard (690 m) part of the defile. [. . .] It is likely that the English adopted their usual battle line of longbowmen on either flank, with men-at-arms and knights in the centre. They might also have deployed some archers in the centre of the line.'

5. See https://www.merriam-webster.com/dictionary/commit, accessed [2 February 2022]: 'to pledge or assign to some particular course or use commit all troops to the attack'.

6. In the context of private equity, Brown et al. (2020) define *capital commitments to newly raised funds* as exposure. Their rational is similar: 'This occurs, in part, because investors can only time their commitments to funds; they cannot time when commitments are called or when investments are exited'.

7. Comparable to a covariance matrix for portfolios of listed assets, signifying the interdependence of each stock on the other.

8. On portfolios of hedge funds but applicable in the context of private capital funds as well.

9. See Browne (2006).

10. An occasionally mentioned additional diversification dimension is the transaction type (primary, secondary, and co-investment). Transaction types relate more to the way how the portfolio is built and, therefore, conceptually fall out of the scope of this discussion.

11. Reinvesting, also called 'recycling', of capital is possible under certain conditions but does not materially change this picture.

12. See various definitions for 'vintage year' in **Glossary**.

13. The main dimensions of private equity portfolio diversification according to Erturk et al. (2001) are: strategy, the vintage year, the stage focus, the broad industry sector, the geographical region (e.g. the US, Asia, Western Europe, Eastern Europe, and emerging markets), the currency, and the agent or counterparty concentration, i.e. the exposure to a specific fund manager.

14. The so-called 'insufficient reason criterion'.

15. See Meyer (2014).

16. According to Kshetrapal (2016), while 'funds categorize healthcare as one unified sector, the risk-return profiles of sub-segments within healthcare vary immensely. To illustrate, Pharma companies mimic the performance of technology companies with large investments in R&D followed by bumper returns with an extremely low hit rate of success (drug discovery). Hospitals mimic the cash profiles of hotel chains, except with much higher margins.'

17. For instance, all high or all low performance, albeit adjusted for each fund's specific maturity and strategy.

18. Also, traditional risk measures for portfolio of funds like the Sortino suggest diminishing benefits to diversification.

19. See for example http://cs229.stanford.edu/proj2017/final-posters/csoo.pdf

20. $n+2$ is the maximum number of steps; the minimum is 1 step (n funds never forming any cluster).

21. However, this assumption does not critically impact the methodology described here.

22. See Artinger, Florian, Malte Petersen, Gigerenzer, Gerd and Jürgen Weibler. 2015. 'Heuristics as adaptive decision strategies in management.' *Journal of Organizational Behavior*. Vol. 36. 33–52.

23. See Mascarenhas and Aaker (1989).

24. Styles can also relate to vintages, for instance, by continuation funds or side funds.

25. See Loretan and English (2000).

26. Simplistically, it is assumed that TVPIs and lifetimes are uniformly distributed within the ranges forecasted for each fund, instead of using PDFs built from private market benchmarks.

27. That is, no (0), weak (0.3), medium (0.5), strong (0.9), and perfect (1) correlation. The approach presented in Greenberg (2015) only relates to positive correlations.

28. Essentially this is average linkage, measuring the similarity of two clusters by averaging of distances between all pairs, where each pair is made up of one object from each cluster.

29. This is single linkage, measuring the similarity of two clusters by taking the distance of the most similar pair.

30. See Ring and Du (2018).

31. See https://unstats.un.org/sdgs/indicators/regional-groups/, [accessed 22 March 2023]
32. Other criteria like the stage of a market's development could be factored in as well; see https://en.wikipedia.org/wiki/Developed_country, [accessed 23 January 2023]
33. See https://www.un.org/en/development/desa/policy/wesp/wesp_current/2014wesp_country_classification.pdf, [accessed 22 March 2023]
34. See Simon (2007).
35. This is based on past experience. For instance, in the wake of the dot-com crash after 2000, investments in Life Science companies were almost unaffected, contrary to ICT.
36. However, there can be (albeit rare) exceptions, for example, in cases where firms entered into partnerships which to some degree show similarities.
37. Stages also apply to other alternative assets such as infrastructure, e.g. greenfield and brownfield.
38. For buyout funds, Pevara differentiated between BOUT LARGE, BOUT MEDIUM, and BOUT SMALL.
39. Recently, Tiger Global Management was reported to raise a $10 billion fund for technology start-ups and Insight Partners as seeking $12 billion for a similar vehicle (see FT, 5 May 2021, 'Tiger Global aims to raise $10bn for technology venture fund').

CHAPTER 10

Model Input Data

The cash-flow forecasting model is built to produce quantitative outputs, notably the timing and size of a fund's cash flows. This suggests a reliance on quantitative inputs. Concerns regarding input data – 'garbage in, garbage out' – are particularly pronounced for private markets. Here, we are faced with gaps in or even the absence of quantitative data. We can use qualitative inputs to address this problem, but they are often associated with being subjective and thus of 'low quality'. Practically, all models rely in varying degrees both on quantitative and qualitative inputs, which call for comments.[1]

CATEGORICAL INPUT DATA

Relevant for our cash-flow forecasting is the subset of input data (see **Box 10.1**) that can be categorised in the form of rankings, scores, ratings, and grouping.[2] While these categories are non-numerical, they can be arranged and be mapped onto a numerical scale to approximate quantitative model inputs that can then be used for mathematical calculations.

Box 10.1   Examples for cash-flow forecast model input data

QUANTITATIVE DATA

- Fund lifetimes and total value to paid-in capital (TVPI) are absolute figures. As example, according to one data set, for the 2006 vintage year, EU buyout peer group TVPI (5% percentile): 0.67 and TVPI (95% percentile): 2.68;
- Based on expert opinion, the real lifetimes for funds are typically between 8 and 15 years;
- The contribution schedule gives the percentage of the remaining commitments to be contributed for the period in question, here expressed as figure between 0% and 100% (max);
- The frequency of cash flows is controlled by the probability of a cash flow for a given period, between 0 and 1. For frequency set to minimum, there will be just

---

one contribution to the fund and one distribution from the fund to its investors. The maximum frequency would be one contribution/distribution in each period;

- The control parameter for the volatility of cash flows is between 0 and 1. For 0, the average cash-flow amount given by the Takahashi–Alexander model is assumed. 1 defines the maximum volatility possible for the next period;
- The bow factor is between 0 and infinity and controls the distribution rate's change over time;
- The management fee schedule, defining frequency, and amount of management fees and on which basis they are to be calculated;
- The fund's yield, i.e. its fixed income component, for which another schedule defines frequency and amount of payments and on which basis they are to be calculated.

CATEGORICAL DATA (QUALITATIVE)

- The pairwise similarity score between two fund's diversification dimensions, defined as between 0 ('completely dissimilar') and 1 ('entirely similar'), with similarity score of 0.5 as 'medium similarity', and with the diversification impact being between –1 and 1;
- The fund's rating (e.g. 'top', 'bottom' expected performance) and the scoring needed to derive these ratings.

In the case of categorical data types, parameters are 'named', i.e. classified into several ordinal categories, such as 'high', 'medium', 'low', that have an inherent order to the relationship among the different categories. To these categories, a 'scaling' is applied to determine quantitative measures.[3] Practically, we map the categories' ordinal scale onto a scale representing historically observed outcomes, such as a probability distribution function of TVPIs.

PERCEPTIONS

There is the perception that quantitative data are of high quality, neutral, and cannot be argued, as they are based on measurement or verifiable facts. In private markets, this comes with complications as there are biases that jeopardise objectivity, such as survivorship bias well known to be inherent in the data made available by private market benchmark providers, or the selection bias where investors collect their own data but only have access to a limited subset of the market.[4]

Regulation

Particularly, financial regulation promotes the use of quantitative data. The implicit assumption is that quantitative data are more rigorous, objective, and relevant than their qualitative counterpart. This is expressed, for illustration, in the best execution requirements described in the Conduct of Business Sourcebook for meeting the regulatory demands of posed by MiFID II. They stipulate that information given to clients needs to be based on reasonable assumptions supported by 'objective data'[5] and that future projections must be 'based on appropriate assumptions, supported by objective data and not simulated past performance'.

Richards (2021) gives as an example the case where the cash-flow tool takes in a historical index of returns and creates a forecast by sampling returns from this index – this would not be allowed. Just simulated past performance in this view cannot be used for forecasting future performance. Instead, we should model or make assumptions how this might change in the future.

Risk managers

Risk managers are tasked with the implementation of regulation. In this context, François-Serge Lhabitant suggested that a strong opposition exists between academics, who emphasise objectivity, and practitioners: 'Predictably, neither side really understands or even tries to understand the purpose or motivation of the other.' The root of the conflict, he argues, lies in a fundamental difference, i.e. that practitioners look to the future and forecast.

> *Consequently, practitioners' models rely entirely on intuition, are not validated by any type of established theory and are frequently changed in line with the reality of the market. Academics, in contrast, seek to understand how and why things work, and the only way to explain how things work is often to look back. Consequently, academics' models may be very good at explaining but they are usually very poor at forecasting, with the result that little value is attached to them by practitioners.*
>
> Lhabitant (2004)

Practically, risk managers have to base their assessments on categorisations that reflect combinations of qualitative and quantitative criteria. This necessarily involves judgement and is, therefore, often criticised as overly subjective.

Can data be objective?

This apparent conflict may also be caused by unrealistic expectations. 'We all think that data are so objective [. . .] but they are actually as interpretable as Shakespeare.'[6] For modelling private capital funds, we are faced with two main problems regarding input data: first, return figures like TVPI can only after several years be seen as indicative for a fund's performance on realisation. The only reliable growth estimates for the Takahashi–Alexander model funds relate to vintages older than at least five years. We can boost the available sample size by also including data for younger funds, but the reliability of these figures is naturally decaying over time with the changes in the overall market environment.

Second, few of the funds that represent these vintages are truly comparable with the ones for which the future development needs to be forecasted. We have far more data samples for US funds than for, say, emerging markets, but do these two really show similar behaviour? Can we use general fund data, for example, to model venture capital funds? The trade-off is between working with a limited set of closely matching data or with a higher sample number, not all of which will fully match the situation to be modelled. The choice of what available data to leave in or out brings in significant subjectivity.

Forecasting arguably is too centred on the historical performance of the assets that need to be modelled. This will not capture the risk/return trade-off going forward. The limited historical data available may be too similar and miss outliers. On the other hand, ranges of historical performance are one meaningful hypothesis regarding the future development. It is a reasonable assumption that past performance of an asset class reflects its 'laws of gravity' – to quote Martin van Creveld: 'Often in the past history has proved itself a poor guide to the future. But it is all we have'. In fact, input data are as much error-prone as a model itself.

MOVING FROM WEAK TO STRONG DATA

The shorter the time horizon of the forecast is, the lower the degree of uncertainty. Therefore, the accuracy of predictions will decrease as the horizon increases – in other words, forecasts are more accurate for shorter than longer time horizons. For the cash-flow forecasting model, the input data need to be complete and accurate, so that we can rely on its forecasts. But here there comes an additional problem: there is a significant input data error that depends on time as well and it is caused by the gap between existing market data and forecast horizon.[7]

In forecasting, Saffo views traditional research habits that are based on collecting strong information critically and views lots of interlocking weak information as 'vastly more trustworthy'. Form a forecast as quickly as possible and then set out to discredit it with new data. The forecasting model should be implemented in such a way that input data are regularly corrected and updated, and a new forecast is produced accordingly. This assures that the gap between market data and forecast horizon is shrinking, the input data are becoming stronger, and the input data error is going down. Effectively, the quality of the forecasts depends most of all on how often they are produced and less on how complex the model and its inputs are.

NOTES

1. The line between the two is not clear cut anyway. For instance, there are statistics for venture capital funds and for buyout funds, but there are many other situations that can fall 'in between'. Even if the data are objective, in this categorisation, there is already significant subjectivity and 'fuzziness'.
2. See blog 'Qualitative Data – Definition, Types, Analysis and Examples'. Available at https://www.questionpro.com/blog/qualitative-data/, [accessed 27 October 2022]
3. Phillips (1971) defines *scaling* as a 'procedure for the assignment of numbers (or other symbols) to a property of objects in order to impart some of the characteristics of numbers to the properties in question'.

4. In case data are reported from multiple sources, they could be confirmed. However, private market data even if reported by different sources are deficient. They have overlaps, but they are not identical and anonymised, so a confirmation in many cases is not possible.
5. See COBS 4.5A.14UK01/01/2021 in https://www.handbook.fca.org.uk/handbook/COBS/4/5A. html, [accessed 27 September 2022]
6. Mike Potter, chief technology officer of Qlik, as quoted from The Economist, 22 February 2020. 'The new AI-ssembly line'
7. If we try to forecast for a fund with a 10-year lifetime and the only reliable market data relates to vintages that are at least five years old, then we are faced with a gap of 15 years!

CHAPTER 11

Fund Rating/Grading

How can we model a fund's idiosyncratic risk? Limited partners (LPs) are predominantly doing primary commitments into a so-called 'blind pool', i.e. the fund has not started its investment activity and there are no private assets yet that could form a basis for assessing where the fund is going. Essentially, for making this decision the LP can only take historical data and qualitative criteria into consideration, like the fund management's track record, the fund's peer group's performance, how the managers are incentivised, or how the fund is structured. Here, the question is, of course, how comparable the assumed peer group to the fund in question really is and how indicative its historical data are for the fund's future development.

The traditional approach to deal with comparable issues in the context of assessing credit risk is a rating system. The rating of borrowers is a widespread practice in capital markets. It is meant to summarise the quality of a debtor and, in particular, to inform the market about repayment prospects. All credit rating approaches are based on a combination of quantitative and qualitative components. The more limited the quantitative data, the more the rating will have to depend on the qualitative assessments.

In this discussion, we will be using the terms 'rating', 'grading', and 'ranking'. In publications on investment management, these terms are often used somewhat interchangeably, which could make this subject highly confusing. The term 'rating' is typically used in the context of credit risk models and is associated with default probabilities of loans or bonds. While the term 'rating' is occasionally mentioned in the context of funds, funds do not 'default' in a sense of a credit.

PRIVATE CAPITAL FUNDS AND RATINGS

Publications on this topic approach this mainly as so-called 'fiduciary ratings' or rankings.

Fiduciary ratings

A fiduciary rating is an approach to assess an asset manager's quality of management and client services, and its sustainability of operations.[1] It focuses on the assessment of the management firm and takes criteria like the quality of investment process, the financial strength, the quality of risk management, the avoidance or the mitigation of conflicts of interest, the quality of controlling, customer service, or management strategy into consideration. For illustration, PACRA (2005) defines the highest rating as 'AM1: Asset manager meets or exceeds the overall investment management industry best practices and highest benchmarks in all criteria under review'.

There is no direct link between fiduciary rating and future performance. A good fiduciary rating is not necessarily indicative for good investment performance. As the scales are often similar to those used for credit ratings, this could cause confusion, as the fiduciary ratings do not aim to quantify the risks of defaults.[2] Fiduciary ratings have been promoted in the private capital industry, too, but they have apparently found little interest, neither among firms nor investors.[3]

Fund rankings

The ranking of private equity firms proposed in Gottschalg (2021) aims to answer the question: 'Which firm(s) generated the best performance for their investors over the past years?' For this ranking, Gottschalg's method uses a data set on fund performance provided by Preqin and directly from the firms to calculate the aggregate historical performance of a firm based on different performance measures for all the funds managed by it. While this ranking is certainly interesting for LPs screening the market for investment opportunities, it is only of limited value for monitoring the risks of funds held within an LP's portfolio. Rankings, like fiduciary ratings, are based on the assumption that successful or well-managed firms will deliver high returns in the future as well, but they do not attempt to quantify future financial performance or risks of the fund in question.

Internal rating systems

Among LPs, private capital fund 'rating' systems in various forms are apparently quite common. However, these are all 'home brew' solutions;[4] there is very little published on practical experiences, and there is no consensus on rating practices or even definition of *rating scales*.

The classifications that had been used by CalPERS in a rating-like approach for assessing their active portfolio are one example. CalPERS differentiated between 'Exceeds expectations', 'As expected', 'Below expectations', 'Below expectations/with concern', and 'Too early to tell'.[5] This early approach was very judgemental and anchored in the specific environment of the dot-com bubble. CalPERS then expected for seed capital investments a 30% return on invested capital and set targets around 25% for early- and late-stage venture capital. For buyouts and later-stage investments, a 20% return was expected, and for mezzanine capital, a 15% return target was set. These were exceptional conditions that for most of these strategies did not hold post-2000.

Also, the approach presented by one fund-of-funds player is illustrative. The objective of this internally developed tool was to assess the quality of a general partner. The tool covered the dimensions team quality, track record, investment strategy, legal structure and fund terms, and fund operations.

Each dimension was ranked on a scale from lowest to highest, and the weighted average of these ranks resulted in an overall fund rating. Combined, the dimensions team quality and track record had more than half of the weight in this assessment.

For assessing the investment strategy, various criteria were evaluated and ranked as well:

- A fund's sourcing capabilities, viewing proprietary deals as preferable to club deals and auctions.
- A team's degree focus on key sectors and strategies performance, viewing a straying away from this focus as weakness.
- A fund's positioning and coverage of key markets, viewing the fund managers' deep networks in these markets as important.
- A fund's approach to value creation, ranking this from a real hands-on approach as strong point, over the employment of financial engineering techniques, to just being a passive shareholder.

In this case, the rating was not confined to the fund in question, but the investment decision also took the proposals style and its attractiveness relative to the LP's overall portfolio into consideration.[6]

Further literature

To the extent that work on rating systems in private capital and similar asset classes has been published, it has been authored by practitioners and commercial entities. Examples include Troche (2003) and Meyer and Mathoner (2005) on private equity, Giannotti and Mattarocci (2009) on real estate, and Ruso (2008), who discusses a rating system comprising a governance and risk rating for closed-end real estate, ship, and private equity funds. In many ways, the proposed techniques are similar in the sense that the risk rating consists of several criteria for which either negative or positive points are awarded, depending on whether they increase or decrease the risk level. However, none of these studies links rating classes to quantitative measures.

PRIVATE CAPITAL FUND GRADINGS

In Meyer and Mathonet (2005), we suggested for funds an assessment based on comparisons. For expressing this comparison in a standardised way, we proposed to use the term 'grading',[7] also to avoid confusion with ratings. Like credit decisions for small lending exposures, such a grading is also based on techniques such as 'scorings' and 'rankings' and notably aims to quantify a fund's risks and returns.

Scope and limitations

The grading is not conceived as a tool for due diligence and pricing, for instance in the case of secondaries, which are subject to negotiation and aim for superior investment decisions. Of course, comparable techniques as described here can and are used for such purposes, e.g. in the context of due diligences, but this is not the aspiration here.

Purpose of the grading system is to quantify a fund's risk and return profile. It is also a tool for monitoring and revisiting assumptions as the fund is developing. The grading should be consistent over time and as objective as possible, in the sense that different users would come to similar results.

Selection skill model

An approach comparable to the one proposed in Meyer and Mathonet (2005) was described in Jeet (2020), who presented a scale for measuring the value of LP fund-selection skills, according to different 'skill types'. For this purpose, Jeet divided funds of a given vintage into quartiles based on their subsequent since-inception total value to paid-in capital (TVPI) performance. An LP's fund-selection skill types were defined by their fund-selection probabilities, by quartile, at the time of commitment (see **Table 11.1** and **Figure 11.1**).

TABLE 11.1   LP selection skill model (according to Jeet, 2020)

| | Probability distributions over fund quartiles | | | |
Skill type	Q4	Q3	Q2	Q1
Poor	0.35	0.25	0.25	0.15
Hit or miss	0.5	0	0	0.5
No skill	0.25	0.25	0.25	0.25
OK	0.15	0.35	0.35	0.15
Some	0.15	0.25	0.25	0.35

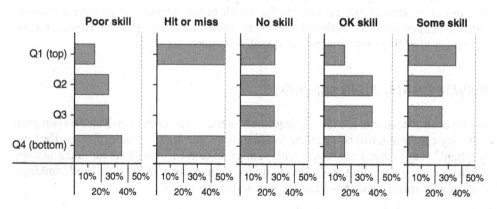

FIGURE 11.1   LP selection skill model (according to Jeet, 2020)

Jeet presented five skill types as representative. An LP with 'poor' skills, according to this scale, is more likely to select funds from the bottom quartile and less likely from the top. In the case of 'Hit or Miss', the LP selects from either the top or bottom quartile, with equal probability. An LP with 'OK' skills tends to avoid both top and bottom quartile funds, whereas 'some skills' describe an LP that has an increased probability of selecting from the better quartiles while avoiding bottom quartile funds. Jeet assumed for an LP investor that had no fund-selection skill that she would simply pick funds at random and in this case set the ex-ante probabilities as equal for each quartile with 25%.

Assumptions for grading

This scale and its underlying assumptions call for comments. Ex ante, the quality of a fund and selection skills (i.e. an LP's ability to recognise its quality) are equivalent concepts. Importantly, a random pick does not mean 'simple'. 'Random' implicitly not only requires that the LP knows and has access to the entire population of funds searching for investors; it is also based on the assumption that all the funds out will be able to close and thus become a member of the vintage year's peer group, all of which in reality is not the case. Also, additional funds will close and join this peer group afterwards, but they will not have factored in the LP's assessment. For these reasons, the 'random pick' rather represents the usual LP's approach to sourcing and assessing fund investment opportunities, based on incomplete information on alternatives.

Also, for private capital funds, the concept of default does not apply. For a long-term-oriented investor, the risk is rather to be seen as generating a return below a set threshold, but through this an LP is not granted any rights and remedies. As for closed-ended funds structured as limited partnerships, there is no risk-adjusted pricing mechanism,[8] we can assume that the peer group statistics covers mainly funds where investors after a rigorous due diligence committed to because they were convinced that these funds would deliver a 'top' performance.[9]

The equal ex-ante weighting in **Table 11.2** is in line with the 'no fund-selection skill' scenario defined in Jeet (2020). However, this rather models the situation where a competent LP has followed a proper due diligence and selection process and these ex-ante weights are consistent with expecting the fund to perform well. It, therefore, would better be described as 'no fund-selection skills better than the average LP' scenario.

TABLE 11.2 Equal ex-ante weights for quartiles, neutral scenario

4th quartile	3rd quartile	2nd quartile	1st quartile
0.25	0.25	0.25	0.25

PROTOTYPE FUND GRADING SYSTEM

The grading system draws upon analogies from established rating techniques for credit risk. In Krahnen and Weber (2001), a rating of a company in the context of credit risk is defined as the mapping of the expected probability of default into a discrete number of quality classes or rating categories. Formally, a rating system is a function:

$$R: \{companies\} \rightarrow \{rating\ values\}.$$

In principle, a private capital fund grading system should fulfil the same requirements as a rating system. The main difference between a rating and a grading for funds is that the grading system is marking a fund to a group of comparable funds, i.e. its peer group, taking its specific lifecycle characteristics into account. The historical performance statistics of the peer group forms the basis for the valuation. Intuitively, LPs focus on comparing interim performance results between funds, an approach that makes sense to apply for a fund grading as well. The grading aims to determine the current position of a fund compared with its peers, as defined in a benchmark expressed by quantiles. The funds of the same vintage year represent, in benchmark statistics form, the peer group.

We define a *private capital fund grading system* as a function:

$$\left(G:\left\{funds;\ peer\ group\right\}\rightarrow\left\{\left(expectation\ grades;\ risk\ grades\right)\right\}\right).$$

To model a fund's expected returns, the grading values, or short 'expectation grades', are defined as categories $\{x_1,...,x_n\}$. An expectation grade x_i can be ranked against grade x_j, $\forall i \neq j$:

$$x_i \succ x_j.$$

An expectation grade x_i is identical to grade x_j:

$$x_i \sim x_j.$$

In the same way, to model a fund's risks, the grading values, or short 'risk grades', are defined as categories $\{r_1,...,r_n\}$. A risk grade r_i can be ranked against grade r_j, $\forall i \neq j$:

$$r_i \succ r_j.$$

A risk grade r_i is identical to grade r_j:

$$r_i \sim r_j.$$

To quantify the impact of expectation and risk grades, we take private market benchmarking data as a proxy. The grading system maps the fund on performance quantiles that are representative of its peer group. How this is done will be explained in detail in the following chapters, but the first question is how to set the ex-ante weights for these quantiles?

EX-ANTE WEIGHTS

Ex ante, for a commitment to a blind pool, a fund's ranking within its peer group will be based on qualitative criteria only and thus will reflect aspects that – based on practical historical experience – are considered either as weaknesses and thus problematic or are deviations from standard practices.

Expectation grades

At the fund's inception, the highest expectation grade x_1 is consistent with a fund that, compared to the typical peer group member, shows no weak points and is thus likely to

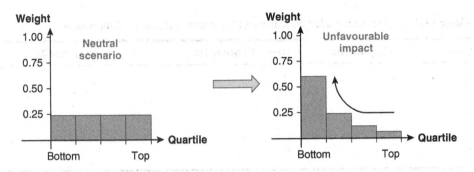

FIGURE 11.2 Asymmetric downward stress to capture diminished expectations

perform in line with the peer group, i.e. with equal outcome probability for each quantile, i.e. the cut-off points dividing the range of a probability distribution into continuous intervals with equal probabilities.

'Poor' in Jeet (2020) describes the unfavourable impact (**Figure 11.2**), whereas 'some skill' would describe a favourable impact scenario. The worst expectation grade x_n describes a fund that, either compared to its peer group or generally, shows an accumulation of weaknesses and problems and thus is either likely to fail entirely or is nearly certain to show bottom performance. Following this reasoning, **Table 11.3** shows the ex-ante weights for the $n = 2$ quantile benchmark.

TABLE 11.3 Expectation grades' ex-ante weights for a 2-quantile grading system

Grade	2nd half	1st half
x_1	0.5	0.5
x_2	1	0

In most cases, it makes sense to consider more quantiles for benchmarking and thus also a number n of grades that is equal to the number of quantiles (see **Table 11.4**). This is done by looking at the two extreme grades x_1 and x_n and interpolating the weights. Generalising, for $n > 2$ quantile benchmark, the kth grade x_k assigns a weight $w_{k;j}$ to each of the $j = 1, \ldots, n$ quantiles.

For the first, i.e. best, grade x_1, all weights are equal:

$$w_{1;j} = 1, \ j = 1, \ldots, n.$$

For the nth, i.e. worst, grade x_n:

$$w_{n;1} = n$$

and

$$w_{n;j} = 0, j = 2, \ldots, n.$$

TABLE 11.4 Expectation grades' ex-ante weights for an n-quantile grading system

Grade	nth quantile	$(n-1)$th quantile	$\ldots$	1st quantile
x_1	$1/n$	$1/n$	$\ldots$	$1/n$
$\ldots$	$\ldots$	$\ldots$	$\ldots$	$\ldots$
x_k	$\ldots$	$\ldots$	$\ldots$	$\ldots$
$\ldots$	$\ldots$	$\ldots$	$\ldots$	$\ldots$
x_n	n/n	0	$\ldots$	0

For grades x_k, $k = 2, \ldots, n-1$ and quantiles $j = 1, \ldots, n$:

$$w_{k;j} = \frac{w_{1;k}(n-k) + w_{n;k}(k-1)}{n-1}.$$

There is a trade-off: the higher the number of grades, the more nuances can be captured. On the other hand, the fewer grades are considered, the lower the scope for errors. Increasing the precision/granularity of grades increases the likelihood that they are assigned incorrectly.

However, in the private capital industry, the most common form of looking at outcomes is by quartiles, which will be assumed for the following discussion (**Table 11.5**).

Expectation grades reflect a fund's 'weaknesses', identified through qualitative and a quantitative scoring described in the following chapters, and defined here as, based

TABLE 11.5 Expectation grades

Grade	Label	Description
x_1	Neutral	Standard quality fund with no weaknesses or adverse signals so far.
x_2	Under-performance	Presence of weaknesses and/or adverse signals that – if no appropriate measures are put in place – would likely result in underperformance compared to a standard quality fund.
x_3	Low performance	Presence of weaknesses and/or adverse signals that – if no appropriate measures are put in place – would likely result in a fund's low performance.
x_4	Bottom performance	Presence of weaknesses and/or adverse signals that – if no appropriate measures are put in place – would likely result in a fund's bottom performance.

TABLE 11.6 Expectation grades' ex-ante weights for quartiles

Grade	4th quartile	3rd quartile	2nd quartile	1st quartile
x_1	$\frac{1}{4} = 0.25$	$\frac{1}{4} = 0.25$	$\frac{1}{4} = 0.25$	$\frac{1}{4} = 0.25$
x_2	$\frac{2}{4} = 0.50$	$\frac{0.667}{4} = 0.167$	$\frac{0.667}{4} = 0.167$	$\frac{0.667}{4} = 0.167$
x_3	$\frac{3}{4} = 0.75$	$\frac{0.333}{4} = 0.083$	$\frac{0.333}{4} = 0.083$	$\frac{0.333}{4} = 0.083$
x_4	$\frac{4}{4} = 1$	0	0	0

on empirical or anecdotal evidence, a recognised relationship between a fund's specific practice and its subsequent underperformance or other problems its investors are faced with (see **Table 11.6**).

The majority of LPs will not accept weaknesses ex ante, but in some cases LPs consciously make the decision to commit to funds that, based on historical experience, have a higher probability to fail; for instance, Development Financing Institutions often back inexperienced teams in order to develop an emerging market. However, here, the peer groups emerging/frontier markets can be seen a class on their own, provided that sufficient statistics is available.

Risk grades

In the absence of quantifiable risk and risk-adjusted pricing for funds, what risk-taking is rewarded? In the context, the cause of risk and the associated opportunity is doing something different or doing things differently.[10] 'Doing' can refer to action as well as 'inaction'; it may also relate to the fund's structure. Increased risk is taken when one deviates from the practices followed by a majority of market participants.

The ex-ante assessment is based on the assumption that peer group membership has significant performance implications. The risk grade measures the deviations from the peer group 'centroids'[11] as proxy for risk.

'OK skills' in Jeet (2020) describes lower variability, whereas 'hit or miss' describes the higher variability scenario (**Figure 11.3**). **Table 11.7** describes the definition of the *risk grades*, which are here assumed only to reflect increases in risks that are controlled by a risk shift towards higher variability for the weights, as will be further explained in **Chapter 13**.

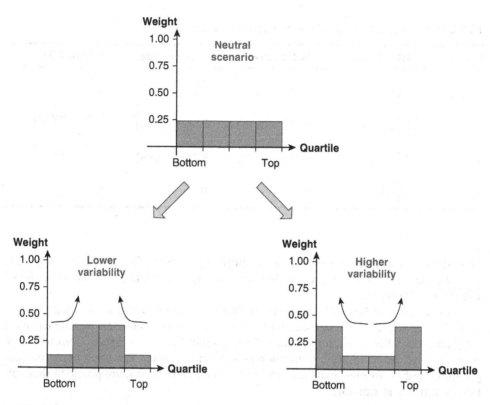

FIGURE 11.3 Symmetric stresses to capture risks

TABLE 11.7 Risk grades

Grade	Label	Risk shift	Description
r_1	Neutral	0	Standard fund with no significant deviations from peer group characteristics.
r_2	Increased risk	0.5	Niche funds are, for example, raised by GPs in emerging regions. They could be characterised by a strong specialisation or higher-than-average exposure to FX. Also, buyout funds with a higher-than-average degree of leverage could fall into the niche category. For such funds, it is assumed that they have potential for higher returns but also an increased probability of failure.
r_3	High risk	1	Funds that show an accumulation of deviations from its peer group practices, such as a very high level of leverage or hereto unknown markets. Outcomes are assumed as binary or 'barbell' with either high success or complete failure.

QUANTIFICATION

The main purpose of the grading system is the quantification of a fund's potential to reach a return and the associated risks. This is done in several steps. The next chapter describes how the LP's due diligence and monitoring is translated into a fund's qualitative score. Following on from this, the fund's interim return is benchmarked against that of its applicable peer group to determine a quantitative score. The quantitative and qualitative scores are combined into an expectation grade, essentially ranking the fund within its peer group. Then, the peer group's historical performance data is used for estimating the fund's returns and risks going forward. Finally, these estimates form the input into a cash-flow forecasting model, with an appropriate discount rate being applied to arrive at ranges for the fund's present value.

For credit ratings, the various rating classes like AAA, BB, etc. are associated with debt instruments and their respective probability of default. An AA-rated debt note from company X should have about the same probability of default as an AA-rated debt note from company Y. The grading for funds described here is defined per peer group but the 1st quartile performance for an US venture capital fund has a different quartile range than a 1st quartile for a European buyout fund. In other words, all matters like stage in the fund's life cycle being equal, an x_1 for the US venture capital fund implies a different performance range than x_1 for the European buyout fund.

The grading is an input into a model for quantifying fund's future performance, but it does not allow a comparison between funds from different peer groups. It is possible to define a unifying grading across various fund strategies, for example, through determining probabilities to exceed target rates. However, this goes beyond the scope of this discussion. Through the link to the private market benchmark, the grading model allows comparing the risk profile of buyouts against that of infrastructure, for example.

NOTES

1. See also Rating Capital Partners (2002) and Telos (2010).
2. See Meyer and Mathonet (2005).
3. As argued in Meyer and Mathonet (2005), an external rating service for private capital funds is unlikely to be a viable business model.
4. See Meyer and Mathonet (2005) for examples.
5. See Meyer and Mathonet (2005).
6. Looking at the fund's main strategy (e.g., buyout, venture capital) and its main geography (e.g. US, Europe), it assesses whether adding it improves or worsens the portfolio's diversification, and whether it would lead to an over-allocation.
7. *Collins Dictionary* defines grading as 'the act of classifying something on a scale by quality, rank, size, or progression, etc.' See https://www.collinsdictionary.com/dictionary/english/grading, [accessed 23 February 2023]
8. There are several mechanisms to reward the taking of risks with excess financial returns. For traditional asset classes, this is typically through risk-adjusted pricing, meaning that the higher the risk, the higher the premium required by the investor. The typical limited partnership structure, however, does not allow for risk-adjusted pricing. All primary positions are bought at par (i.e. without premium or discount), and there is no predefined coupon payment

but only an uncertain performance and a predefined cost structure. Reducing fees, particularly for smaller funds, has limits and cannot compensate for risks. Instead, the adjustment for risk comes in the form of reduced LP demand, leading to a lower size in combination with a lower probability of closing the fund. See discussion in Mathonet and Meyer (2007): this cannot be (at least not fully) replaced by a risk-adjusted pricing on the level of the private assets held by the fund.

9. See Mathonet and Meyer (2007).
10. See Meyer (2014).
11. The centroid can be thought of as the mean of all data points assigned to that cluster.

CHAPTER **12**

Qualitative Scoring

The grading supports a relative valuation[1] technique with its core assumption that a fund will perform in line with its group of peers, meaning funds that have been following a similar style.[2] It assesses the fund's risk and return profile relative to its peer group. To apply this relative valuation technique, we first need to identify the closest similar benchmark population as peer group. As this peer group is the reference point for quantification, we define it as it is identifiable within a private capital market database by its style.

To compare, we need to assess to what degree a fund shows similar features than its peer group and whether there are features where a fund is inferior to its peers. For alternative investments, there is, by definition, a tension with standardisation. Rich data support 'best practice' standardisation, implying consensus, and, in extremis, herding. It is a common fallacy to confuse absence of data with higher financial risk. In fact, the more is known about an opportunity and the longer it exists and a time series of data becomes available, the lower its potential going forward usually is. The scoring of qualitative criteria aims to address this tension.

What is here viewed as 'standard' is often referred to as 'institutional quality' funds.[3] There is no generally accepted definition of which funds are 'institutional quality' and which funds fall outside this category. At the end of the day, this can just be a grand way of referring to funds managed by established general partners (GPs) – nobody got fired for committing to Blackstone, Carlyle, and KKR. Rather than being guarantors of high investment performance, they should be seen as the benchmark population for quantifying risks. The approach is comparable to the Institutional Limited Partners Association (ILPA)'s Model limited partnership agreement (LPA) that is described as 'useful to LPs as a benchmarking tool to compare against existing LPAs they have signed, and funds they are evaluating, allowing them to have verified legal language they can compare against terms in the marketplace'.[4]

OBJECTIVES AND SCOPE

The qualitative scoring aims to assess a set of criteria that are relevant for the measurement and a meaningful categorisation in predefined classes. When designing a scoring template, important questions relate to the number of dimensions that should be reflected in the evaluation and the weighting of these dimensions.

This technique is designed to work with the information that is observable to a limited partner (LP) ex ante, i.e. when evaluating the private placement memorandum and the diligence material made available, and before committing to the fund. As the LP is committing to a so-called 'blind pool', a fund that has not invested yet and therefore no portfolio components do exist, only qualitative criteria can be taken into account.[5]

The scoring does not consider 'red flag' criteria like non-compliance with applicable laws and regulations related to fund structures, or industry reporting and valuation standards that would lead to LP rejecting the fund proposal right away. Also, the scoring does not lead to a recommendation whether to invest or not, which is the domain of the due diligence.

As mentioned above, several LPs developed scoring templates that aim to rank funds according to their quality and identify those that are likely to generate the best performance for their investors. However, one can only urge caution in making causal claims. Instead, the grading suggested here does not profess to result in superior investment decisions and lead to recommendations. Its objective is humbler.

There is no attempt to differentiate and rank, say, team experience – is 200 years accumulated team experience better than 50 years? It is rather whether the team's experience passes a minimum threshold. The presence of team's experience gives no advantage, whereas the absence of sufficient experience would be a clear weakness. There is certainly a subjective element in what is 'sufficient', and thus, the assessment requires a competent investment manager, but this approach is simpler to achieve and a more tractable objective.

Notably, the scoring does not take into consideration what the LP, based on her market research and specific insights, sees as desirable for picking the best funds but aims to reflect a market consensus view. What is here perceived as consensus relates to the perception of risks.

In fact, results in Mathonet and Meyer (2007) suggest that the probability that a 'weak' fund finds the critical mass of LPs and can close to start its investment activity is decreasing proportionately in line with the number and severity of its identifiable weaknesses. These findings also support the assumption that available industry statistics by and large represents a majority of funds that passed the rigorous selection process of experienced investors and where differences are more characterised by deviations than weaknesses.

Whether these risks will materialise or not is irrelevant, as the perceptions and the resulting best practices are based on the LP community's aggregate experiences. In many cases, these best practices are just based on anecdotal evidence, reflecting expert opinion. With increasing data as evidence and growing consensus, these specific insights cease to be a differentiator.

RELEVANT DIMENSIONS

In many situations, it will not be possible to assign a fund unambiguously to a peer group, in particular as peer groups comprise funds that are comparable but not identical regarding their characteristics. Examples for deviations are premium carry for perceived

TABLE 12.1 Scoring dimensions

Dimension	Explanation	Treatment
Investment style	Match of the fund's investment style with the peer group's style	Deviation
Management team	Is the management able to successfully execute this strategy?	Potential weakness
Fund terms	Are the fund's terms appropriate, based on prevailing market practices?	Potential weakness
Fund structure	Does the fund structure comply with the limited partnership fund structure?	Deviation
Incentive structure	Is the incentive structure in line with peer group's practices?	Deviation
Alignment of interest	If the fund is successful, are management team and LPs participating fairly in its success?	Potential weakness
Conflicts of interests	Are there outside opportunities that counteract incentives, and alignment of interest?	Potential weakness
Independence in decision-making	Are there outside influences that affect the team's decision-making?	Potential weakness
Viability	Does the fund have the right infrastructure and resources to execute the investment strategy?	Potential weakness
Confirmation	Do the management team's track record and the other LPs' give more certainty to the decision to commit to fund?	Deviation

'elite' funds, deal-by-deal versus fund-as-a-whole carried interest, and waiving management fees for higher carried interest.

Therefore, as a first step, we are using a fuzzy search approach (see **Appendix**) to find a peer group that is closest in its style to the fund to be assessed. Then, we assess the fund against the important dimensions that are generally viewed as indicative for its return potential and its risk and categorise them as either 'deviation' or as 'potential weakness'.

We have 10 dimensions, with four subject to deviations and six are prone to potential weaknesses (**Table 12.1**). Why are these dimensions considered and what do they tell us?

Investment style

When LPs look at a fund's investment style, they aim to understand how it will create value and differentiate itself within the private capital market. For a given fund with its specific investment style, we look for its closest peer group. Note that the quantification is based on the peer group's risk/return profile. We are not ranking, say, venture capital (VC) – represented by it specific peer group – against buyouts and make no assumption whether one style is more or less attractive compared to another one.

The qualitative scoring is based on how closely a fund is aligned with best practices within a given market environment at the time when it is launched. A fund that is well adjusted today is assumed to perform in line with earlier funds that were well adjusted at the time when they were raised, even if the criteria of what constitutes 'best practice' have changed since.

Management team

The next question is whether the fund's management is able to successfully execute this strategy. Researchers and practitioners alike highlight the importance of skills, industry experience, balance, and stability of a fund management team. Questions to be asked for assessing skills are, for illustration:

- Do a fund management team's core members have experience in the relevant aspects of a fund's value chain, i.e. deal sourcing and closing, value creation, and exit sourcing?
- Is the team size and breadth appropriate; for example, does each investment professional not oversee too many portfolio companies?
- Does the team have appropriate operational skills, such as investor relations, investment process, internal controls, risk management, and administration?

For assessing the management team's stability LPs could assess:

- Has the management team worked together sufficiently long or has it experienced significant staff turnover?
- Could skills critical to the investment process be covered by several team members (balanced team, succession issues covered), or is there a high degree of dependence on a key person (one-man show)?

The management team's quality is one of the few criteria where we can assume causality, at least related to a fund's failure. While it appears to be relatively straightforward to draw up a list of detailed criteria to evaluate a team, it is difficult to apply in practice. To quote Grabenwarter and Weidig (2005), a 'common objective such as raising a fund can convert individuals into great actors pretending perfect harmony in a team'.

Hüther et al. (2019) approached this by measuring the experience of all investment professionals in the fund at the time the diligence material was circulating and could be assessed by the LPs before committing to the fund. In their sample, these researchers found that the average investment team had 11.5 years of previous work experience in the industry. Hüther et al. (2019) pointed out that also first-time funds may comprise fund managers with a wealth of experience at previous firms, which is another reason why with a maturing private capital industry it is becoming increasingly difficult to differentiate in a meaningful way: the pool of experienced professionals has grown significantly, they move to other teams, and teams spin out and try to build their own firms.

Arguably assessing lack of experience is more prevalent in VC where LPs are regularly faced with new entrants coming from technology and entrepreneurship but with limited experience as investors.

It is easier to recognise issues related to the management team, like lack of experience in the industry or as a team. However, it will be difficult to rank qualified teams in the sense that team A is better than team B, or, even less, to determine how much better team A is than team B.

Fund terms

Are the fund's terms appropriate? Even if complying with local laws and regulations, a fund's terms and conditions may not be in line with what is perceived to be best practice internationally. There may also be laws and regulations considered to be less conducive to private capital investing than those followed in other jurisdictions.[6]

Rather than being considered as a driver of a fund's success, the terms and conditions need to assure that the LP's downside is limited. They are also aiming to avoid legal disputes with the associated costs, delays, and negative impact on reputation and relationships.

For the scoring, terms and conditions can be grouped into different categories:

- LP rights and protections.
- Corporate governance.
- Costs and non-performance driven fees.
- Liquidity and exits.

LP rights and protections

Downside protection is a common objective for investors and fund managers to avoid losses. Notably, for funds, there is no minimum return, or a return of principal guaranteed. Instead, LPAs foresee various termination rights, e.g., provisions to remove the GP in the 'no-fault' scenario or 'for cause'.

Investor protection clauses are evolving based on lessons learned. They are certainly 'important to have' and lack thereof, particularly if there are several cases of absence, will be a potential weakness.

Corporate governance

Is the right, i.e. best practice, corporate governance structure in place? While the establishment of a Limited Partner Advisory Committee (LPAC) is not mandated from a regulatory standpoint, it is usually its role to resolve potential conflicts of interest. The LPAC advises the GP on specific issues during the lifetime of a fund and approve material changes to the governing documents of the fund that require LP consent or approval.

Costs

Items to be considered here are:

- Are management fees not excessive?
- Is there a proper fee offset mechanism, so that the fund's management fees are reduced according to the fees collected by the investment professionals when managing the portfolio?

- Are the fund managers' salaries in line with market standards?
- Is the fund management company's budget realistic, aligned with market practices, and are there no unjustified surpluses?
- Do LPs that commit at later closings pay equalisation fees to compensate the LP that has committed earlier?

Variations in structures

Likewise, subscription lines were deviations in past, but have increasingly become mainstream, and may even become a standard feature, at least for some type of funds. These changes, however, do not change the dynamics for long; we see a Red Queen effect where successful improvements are quickly adopted by competing firms.[7]

Liquidity and exits

Funds are structured to be self-liquidating and thus often have lifetimes that are shorter than set in the LPA. Fund lifetimes can also be extended. Typically, this is permitted only in one-year increments, limited to a maximum of two extensions, and needs to be approved by the LPAC and the majority of LPs.

Another aspect of liquidity is the 'recycling' of capital, a mechanism that essentially increases the fund's commitment size. As a rule of thumb, only 85% of the committed capital will be called and invested in private assets to generate private-market-like returns.

When 'recycling' is allowed, usually only during the fund's investment period, returns from early exits can be used for new investments, which can have a positive impact on a fund's overall returns.

Some LPs prefer receiving distributions earlier and therefore either do not allow this or set a maximum amount that can be recycled, for example, only 20% or 25%. For illustration, recycling provisions in the fund's LPA may set a 20% limit for the total capital commitments. If the fund size is $100 million, not more than $120 million can be invested in private assets in total.

There can also be limit to the time after which early returns cannot be reinvested. For example, only capital can be recycled that was obtained from exiting a portfolio investment within two years from the investment date. All of this aims to ensure that capital is not locked up in a fund for too long.

Incentive structure

Even if the management team is of high quality and the fund is structured in line with best practices, the question remains whether the management team is really motivated to execute the investment strategy. Also, are fund managers and investors sharing success and failure in a proportional manner? There is a widespread preoccupation with fairness of the conditions with the perception is that contracts be 'LP friendly' or 'GP friendly'.

Management fees

Market practices suggest that management fees should not form the major part of the compensation. Instead, the fund's incentives are predominantly investment performance-based, structured around the distribution waterfall, setting out how distributions from a fund will be split and in which priority they will be paid out, i.e. what amount must be distributed to the LPs before the fund managers receive carried interest.

Carried interest

If the fund is successful, are GP and LP participating fairly in its success? The 'carried interest' share in the fund profits is the '20%' component of the traditional '2 & 20' compensation, with the '2%' relating to the management fee. As argued in Meyer (2014), the carried interest has ancient roots and reflects human's perception of fairness in the context of endeavours under extreme uncertainty, as typical for private market investing. A 20% carried interest is considered as a market practice, but there are variations. Carried interest is not a zero-sum game where the LP's gain or loss is exactly balanced by the losses or gains of the GP. A small number of mainly US 'elite' private equity firms manage to negotiate a 'premium carry' of 25–30%. Typically, these are VC firms, but also buyout firms have been reported to take a premium carry, albeit in combination with an increased hurdle of, for instance, 15%. Some funds give investors the choice of paying a traditional 20% carried interest after an 8% preferred return, or a 30% carried interest after a 20% preferred return. Occasionally, the carried interest split is contingent upon performance, e.g., 20% unless internal rate of return (IRR) to the LPs exceeds 25%, in which case it becomes 30%. Behind these variations is the assumption that with a higher fund manager motivation the cake will be getting larger.[8]

An IRR-based carry (particularly in combination with deal-by-deal carry provisions, see below) incentivises 'quick flips' where the company is bought and then sold at a relatively low multiple right afterwards, simply to get a high IRR.[9] Therefore, there are also TVPI-based hurdles (e.g., used by fund-of-funds and VC funds[10]) that use a multiple of contributed capital as the preferred return hurdle instead of an annualised percentage rate. Here, the fund managers would not take a carried interest before the LPs have received, for example, 2× of their contributed capital. According to Peterman et al. (2020) in the case of VC funds, this multiple is higher, e.g., 3×.

The so-called 'whole-fund' – also known as 'European' – carry provisions require that invested capital and fee are returned to LPs before the GP is entitled to earn any carried interest. The alternative is the 'deal-by-deal', or 'American', practice that allows the GP to earn carried interest on each deal as it is exited. As this can lead to situations where the GP receives carried interest even if the fund as a whole has not fully repaid the LPs, the American carry requires additional provisions, especially clawbacks.

European carry is perceived as 'LP friendly', while American typically is regarded as 'GP friendly'. For instance, Axelson et al. (2009) argue for the optimality of whole-fund compensation structures for buyout funds. Drawing from practical experience of investing in European VC funds, Grabenwarter and Weidig (2005) state that most fund managers were unable to present historical instances of where a distribution of carried interest on a whole-fund basis would have made a difference to them and that those rare cases where it mattered relied on one or two lucky winners rather than a systematic pattern of success. Notably, the ILPA promotes the 'whole-fund' carry, arguing that 'a standard all-contributions-plus-preferred-return-back-first must be recognized as a best practice'.[11]

However, an empirical analysis of US VC partnerships put forward by Hüther et al. (2019) suggests that the relationship between the timing of GP compensation and private equity fund performance is more complex. These researchers found that, actually, LPs earned higher net returns from their commitments to deal-by-deal funds than from funds with whole-fund carry provisions and, on average, did not experience better performance with the allegedly 'LP-friendly' provisions.

Hurdle rates

The hurdle rate, also often referred to as 'preferred return', is the return fund managers must generate for their investors before they can receive carried interest.

The use of hurdle rates demonstrates the different practices, depending on whether buyouts and VC, and in the US and Europe. While virtually all buyout funds and many growth equity funds offer their investors an 8% hurdle before they take a share of the profits for themselves, this is usually not the case for US venture capitalists. Morrissette (2014) referred a conversation with one of the 'top venture law firms' in the US that confirmed that 'nearly 100%' of VC funds do not have a hurdle rate.[12]

Fleischer (2005) explained this by the hurdle being more important as an incentive to properly screen the deal flow. Without it, buyout fund managers could pursue a low-risk, low-return strategy, for example by being inactive or by choosing companies that have little potential for generating large returns. A hurdle forces managers to make riskier investments to generate a return in line with the investor's targets. In the case of VC funds, however, investments are always risky, and the high risk, high-reward strategy makes it meaningless to bother about a hurdle.

In Europe, on the other hand, hurdle rates for VC funds are very common but are also criticised for creating the wrong incentives: rather than high returns, implicitly already returns above the hurdle rate are viewed to be a 'success'. The hurdle also delays the carry payment to the fund managers. Therefore, when the LPA foresees a recycling of capital, this becomes less of a priority and thus depresses the net return to LPs. US LPs investing in VC are said to view the presence of a hurdle as uncommon and maybe even as a signal for high risk.

To summarise, incentives are not a zero-sum game. LPs accept a certain degree of 'unfriendly' terms. Frequently, the conviction is stated that 'it is better to invest with a strong team and have mediocre terms, than to invest with a mediocre team and have strong terms' (quoted from Toll, 2001).

Alignment and conflicts of interest

In private capital, the alignment of interest is the major way to overcome the principal-agent problem, in situations where the fund manager as agent has a conflict in priorities with the LP as principal.

If the fund manager is successfully executing the strategy, will the LP receive her fair share of this success? One aspect is the percentage invested by the GP into the fund. In other words, is their 'skin in the game' significant enough to assure that their interests are aligned with those of the LPs?

The various mechanisms for incentivising and assuring the alignment of inter-ests between the GP and the fund's LPs will fail in situations where fund managers are seeking better opportunities elsewhere. For example, co-investments, side funds, and follow-on funds have the potential to create conflicts of interest where fund managers pursue interests outside the confines of the fund. Such conflicts of interest are likely to have a negative impact on a fund's performance and need to be considered as poten-tial weakness.

Independence of decision-making

Investors normally favour independently managed funds where investment decisions are either taken by the management team or a board where members are independent from investors and where the main source of fundraising is from third parties.

As mentioned, LPs consider the management team's quality and stability to be par-amount, with incentives aiming to make the team perform in line with its potential. However, this is only meaningful if the team can make its investment decisions fully independently.

This is typically not the case for the so-called 'captive bank funds' or 'in-house corpo-rate funds' with only few third-party investors.[13] In such cases, structures and incentives are quite different, for example, the carried interest – if any – is often less than 20% and a parent organisation as sponsor tends to be allocated a major part of it. This sponsor is the fund's main shareholder and contributes most of the capital from its internal sources.

The presence of a large, sponsoring investor does not necessarily mean a lack of management independence. The key issues are the decision-making process and the power to change the 'rules of the game'. Also, the allocation of carried interest is a key test. Independent teams usually receive most, if not all, of the carry and limit the scope for conflicts of interest with the sponsor.

Viability

Does the fund have the right infrastructure and resources to execute the investment strategy? This question brings the various dimensions discussed before together, but it is also not straightforward to answer.

One important aspect here is whether the fund size fits its strategy or, in other words, is there a minimum amount that will constitute a viable operation and maximum amount of capital that a fund can prudently manage? In fact, Kaplan and Schoar (2005) found a concave relationship between fund size and performance that suggest a decreas-ing return to scale of fund size.[14]

There is minimum feasible fund size, below which funds on average will underper-form. This is caused by a fund's fixed costs, insufficient diversification attainable, restricted deal flow as deals of a certain size simply cannot be done by the fund, or, in the case of early-stage-focused VC funds, dilutions in subsequent capital rounds. Fund sizes may also become too large. After achieving a peak at a certain size, average performance tends to fall with further increases. Where these thresholds are will depend on the fund's style.

VC is characterised as more labour-intensive and buyouts as more capital intensive. The crucial difference between the buyout and the venture business derives from the fact that a buyout manager's skill can be applied to extremely large companies, whereas a VC manager can add value to small companies only. For buyout funds, this implies increased scalability, allowing such firms to sharply increase the size of their funds, which will not work for VC firms. Particularly in the case of VC funds, a too rapid scaling up compared to the predecessor fund will likely lead to a decline in performance.

In this situation, GPs limit their fund sizes and become choosy about their LPs – a behaviour documented for the 'elite' Silicon Valley firms. This phenomenon is not restricted to VC. Also, some buyout firms have occasionally resisted the temptation to raise and invest ever-greater sums of money. This does not necessarily hold under all market conditions. With increasing institutional demand for VC investing, some of these 'elite' firms have abandoned these limits and gathered up more capital than initially expected.[15] Whether this is a temporary phenomenon or a general strategy shift remains to be seen.

A simple link between size and performance is controversial. For instance, in the portfolio analysed by Phalippou and Gottschalg (2009), no evidence for funds being too large was found. However, in broad terms, the result is widely accepted and plausible.

In fact, the answer regarding a fund's viability depends on a variety of factors, such as its investment focus, the anticipated size of deals, and the number of investment professionals. For instance, market best practices often refer to a maximum of five companies per investment professional.[16] Management fees depend on a fund's size and also have an impact on when the GP needs to raise a follow-on fund. Morgan-Lewis (2015) proposes the following formula as 'rough estimate' to arrive at the fund's viable fund size:[17]

$$\frac{A \times B \times C \times D}{1 - \left(E \times F \right)}$$

where:

 A = Number of senior investment professionals.

 B = Average number of new deals anticipated per year.

 C = Average anticipated deal size (including reserves for follow-ons).

 D = Expected investment period in years.

 E = Annual management fee rate.

 F = Term of the fund in years.

Confirmation

Under the extreme uncertainty associated with alternative assets, LPs use multiple indicators to confirm the soundness of the investment proposal. In this context, a GP's track record – such as, did they consistently perform within the first quartile of their peer group, and is the performance of previous funds fully relevant for the new fund? – is an important indicator. Lack of this kind of confirmation is particularly an issue with first-time teams, while no verifiable or poor track record usually leads to the proposal being rejected.

Since neither due diligence nor past performance is perfect predictor of fund performance, an LP would often base her investment decision additionally on confirmation from the market, i.e. the community of other experienced and reputable LPs. Rather than such confirmation giving a positive signal to invest, the absence of market confirmation in the form of high LP demand for a fund or LPs not reinvesting with a fund manager should be seen as warning and thus as potential weaknesses.

Dinneen (2004) emphasises the importance of the other LPs and saw several indicators for weak fund proposals, notably that they typically only attract inexperienced LPs, such as:

- Not being 'qualified' as third-party institutional investors with investment professionals that have experience in private markets;
- LPs being only 'friends and family' of the fund managers;
- Having no real third-party investors as fund is a 'captive' vehicle.

As guideline, Dinneen (2004) suggested that at least 50% of the fund's total capital be provided by qualified LPs. She saw as criteria for such 'qualified' third-party investors that they were experienced, with track record in managing LP portfolios and that their motivation was primarily generating high financial returns.[18]

Particularly when investing in new funds or market niches also, the help and pooling of resources from other experienced LPs can become important for dealing with problems during the funds' lifetimes.

SCORING METHOD

A good scoring method will result in classes where the intra-class similarity is high while the inter-class similarity is low. These classes should be somehow 'similar' to one another, so that the population of funds within the class can be treated collectively as one group.

It also does not make sense to look at too many classes and be overly detailed with the scoring. The lower the number of classes, the more robust the scoring method will be. The practical approach is a compromise between detail and robustness.

Tallying

A simple approach to guide decisions is 'tallying', adding up points, and, for instance, comparing them against a set threshold number. In this approach, analysts look for cues that might help to make a choice between two or several options, with the preferred option being determined by the greatest excess of positive over negative cues without bothering to try to rate them in order of importance.[19] Tallying looks over-simplistic as it takes no account of the relative importance of different factors, but this simple method was found to do consistently better in predicting outcomes than experts' intuition.[20] Statistical weighting of the different factors is a better fit for known data. However, risk managers are dealing with situations of high uncertainty where it is not known which weights to give to these factors. For extrapolating data into the future – what risk managers should primarily be concerned with – simple tallying works just as well and sometimes even better. Rather than operating with 'absolute truths', in essence, a risk manager – like a judge in a legal case – can only weight evidence pros and cons. Terry Smith followed a comparable approach in his 1992 analysis of accounting techniques.[21] He introduced 'blob' scores for companies (with a 'blob' representing the use of creative accounting techniques). For the companies he analysed, this 'blob' scoring had proved to be a remarkably robust methodology for predicting financial distress, in line with what Artinger et al. (2015) are arguing regarding heuristics.

Researching practices

A detailed discussion of features, their prevalence, and their development time falls outside the scope of this book. LPs need to continuously observe the market and research these practices, as they are doing in the course of their investment activity anyway.

The alternative investment industry continuously experiments with new structures that become widely adopted if successful. Therefore, a standard fund today may in terms of structure not have been a standard fund in 2000. The scoring, therefore, needs to be based on the market best practices that were prevailing at the time when the fund was starting its investment activity. Private market statistics reflect structures that were competitive and successful at the time, like dinosaurs that were well adapted to their environment during the Jurassic period.

Ex-post monitoring

LPs tend to tolerate deviations as these contribute to the diversification of their portfolio of funds, but it is a fair assumption that funds will only be raised successfully if there are no clear weaknesses. However, even if a fund is without weaknesses at the time of its close, there are many problems that occur or are discovered later, during the monitoring phase. Examples for this can be team issues, such as disagreements among team members, key persons leaving the team, major write-offs in the managed portfolio, and defaulting LPs. Such events are likely to have a strong adverse impact and, unless properly addressed and rectified quickly, are likely to depress the fund's performance going forward. Therefore, insights into the fund's operation observed by the LP can also lead to changes in the fund's qualitative score.

During the fund's lifetime, ex-ante assessments will change and thus need to be revised based on new information in the fund. One aspect is problems that potentially have an adverse impact on fund performance (**Table 12.A-1**).

Here, when events occur or issues are discovered, also checkmarks are assigned. This captures information that is conceptually close to event risk. These events – unless a mitigating action follows within the short to medium timeframe – are considered to be weaknesses and therefore expected to have a negative impact on a fund's performance.

Such signals can be the symptom of, as well as the reason for, underperformance. For example, tensions within a team are not necessarily the cause of a fund's underperformance. It could well be that the team understands the status of its portfolio far better than the LPs and does anticipate the fund's failure.

TABLE 12.A-1   Alerts, examples for signals indicative for fund problems

- Key person event
- Resignations, changes, and other problems within fund management team
- Too many private assets per fund manager
- Conflict of interest detected
- Contractual breaches
- Co-investing LPs discussing replacement of the management team
- Co-investing LPs want to sell their stakes in fund
- Defaulting LPs
- Litigation against the fund managers
- Significant deviation from the originally declared investment style
- Disagreements on valuations
- Auditors not signing off accounts
- Indications for fraud
- Financial information being faulty, inconsistent, 'creative', late, or missing

These events – unless a mitigating action follows within the short to medium time-frame – are expected to have a negative impact on a fund's performance. The LP's monitoring aims to identify these events and form a judgement on its severity. In essence, the grades have two functions: one is to alert in cases where 'red flag' events could have such an adverse impact that they need to be addressed right away, and the other is diagnosis, i.e. forming a judgement on the degree of the potential impact resulting in a priority setting for the monitoring corrective actions.

Certainly, an accumulation of problems is a sign that a fund is running off course and a sub-standard performance is to be expected. Assessing the severity of the event's impact is of course highly subjective. The Russian author Leo Tolstoy begins his novel *Anna Karenina* with the observation that all 'happy families resemble one another, but each unhappy family is unhappy in its own way'. In the same way, while it is meaningful to define a scoring for the 'happy' high-quality fund, it is futile to come up with an exhaustive list of issues that could lead to a fund's failure.

The other aspect is deviations from the standard funds that can only be discovered once the portfolio was built up. Important are the fund's leverage, its exposure to currency movements, and its level of diversification. The question, however, is not whether a fund is, for example, leveraged but whether the leverage is significantly higher or lower than that used by its peer group funds.

Regulatory reports like CSSF (2021) provide information on levels of leverage as reported by market participants that could be used for reference. But typically the assessment would be based on the LP's observations and experiences, for example, assessing whether a fund is over-diversified or highly concentrated.

ASSIGNING GRADES

To keep this robust, there is no attempt in the scoring to form a judgement on its severity and quantify the specific financial impact of these deviations and potential weaknesses.

Instead, we assign scores in case there is a potential weakness or a deviation or sum up them up. For the <u>Expectation Qualitative Pre-Grades,</u> the scores assigned for a 'potential weakness' result in:

- $\sum Scores \leq 1$: $x_1^{qualitative}$ (consistent with 'Neutral')
- $\sum Scores = 2$: $x_2^{qualitative}$ (consistent with 'Underperformance')
- $\sum Scores = 3$: $x_3^{qualitative}$ (consistent with 'Low performance')
- $\sum Scores \geq 4$: $x_4^{qualitative}$ (consistent with 'Bottom performance')

Together with the quantitative pre-grade described in the next chapter, this qualitative pre-grade will be the input to determine the funds' Expectation Grade.

For the <u>Risk Grades,</u> the scores assigned for a 'deviation' result in:

- $\sum Scores \leq 1$: r_1 'Neutral'
- $\sum Scores = 2$: r_2 'Increased risk'
- $\sum Scores \geq 3$: r_3 'High risk'

Even if we can assume that an LP will only commit to a fund that, based on a proper due diligence, is found to be clear of issues, in many cases, problems will manifest during the fund's typically about 10 years lifetime. LPs need to monitor potential deteriorations of quality and, where possible, intervene to fix problems.

APPENDIX – SEARCH ACROSS SEVERAL PRIVATE MARKET DATA PROVIDERS

How do we find private market data representative for the fund in question? Here, we are faced with a number of problems. From a practical perspective, the lack of any uniform classification scheme across the data providers (such as the International Securities Identification Number that uniquely identifies a security) creates a significant barrier to interoperability. Also, particularly for more innovative structures (e.g. subscription lines in recent years) or strategies, no or too few data exist.

INTEROPERABILITY

As the private capital industry becomes more global, internationally operating investors, such as sovereign wealth funds, require data from multiple countries and actually often use several data providers in parallel. However (and unsurprisingly), classification schemes are not standardised across different private market data providers. For the various private market databases, the classification schemes differ, often significantly. Examples are how regions and investment styles are labelled, and the labels' granularity, i.e. level of detail.

Not having any uniform classification scheme in place also creates problems for LPs who are faced with similar incompatibilities regarding how their fund holdings are classified within their own systems. In fact, many users of the data bemoan the high manual workload the translation between the various schemes regularly causes.

To facilitate the interoperability among different private market data sources, the critical step is to implement a method for mapping between various classification schemes. To integrate data from the different data sources that are organised along broadly comparable lines but have many idiosyncrasies, a single classification scheme is – as explained above – not enough. To overcome this obstacle, a mapping-dictionary-based approach is used to allow a fuzzy search for the data that match the required piece of information best.

Obviously, there is a trade-off between the match and the number of samples that can be found. Most of the time, there will be an insufficient number of samples that precisely meet the user's requirements. In this mapping dictionary, rules define the pairwise matches between classifications of various systems. The dictionary provides a ranking according to match, descending from closest to worst match. With this, the number of samples can be controlled as restrictions regarding the degree of match are gradually eased. This approach helps to access data across various providers and other sources.

MATCHING

There is a trade-off between sample size and representativeness. In the extreme, there are no data for the situation to be modelled. To overcome this problem, we can expand the samples by taking data from the 'next best' peer groups and measure the degree of match and categorise accordingly. As example, let us assume that we are looking for data on growth equity, a categorisation that we here, however, assume to not be adequately represented in the private market database.

Growth equity funds target companies that have the potential for scalable and renewed growth. They share similarities with buyout funds, but take minority stakes in mid-sized investments. Their focus is on growing a company's business. For this purpose, growth equity funds negotiate protective rights for investors, such as board representations or change of control provisions and get operationally involved, for example, by advising the company's management team. As investors growth equity funds come in later than venture capitalists but earlier than buyout funds.

There are similarities between growth equity and later-stage private equity. Later-stage private equity describes investment in companies that have considerable advanced in their expansion or turnaround and are close to an exit.

- 'Growth equity' has strong overlap (in terms of definition; see **Table 12.A-2**) with 'later-stage private equity'.
- 'Later-stage private equity' has a medium overlap with 'growth equity', in the sense that later-stage private equity comprises many other strategies as well.

This results in a match of 0.43 (see **Figure 12.A-1**).

Another example is looking at the dimension 'geography'. We could be looking for a 'German' fund, but database only goes down to the level of 'European' funds. Europe 'fully' overlaps Germany, but Germany is just a subset of Europe ('weak overlap'). The resulting match would be 0.25.

TABLE 12.A-2 Measuring the overlap between classification definitions

Overlap rating	Degree
Full overlap	1.00
Strong overlap	0.75
Medium overlap	0.50
Weak overlap	0.25
Possible overlap	0.10
No overlap	0.00

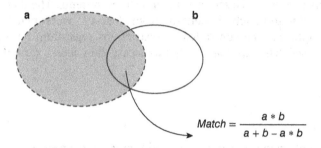

$$Match = \frac{a * b}{a + b - a * b}$$

FIGURE 12.A-1 Measuring overlap in definitions

Preqin (2017) outlines a comparable approach for dealing with situations where the peer group comprises too few members to be meaningful for benchmarking. In such instances, the peer groups will be expanded by including broader categories. This is either done according to set rules (see **Figure 12.A-2**) or by giving users the option to create tailor-made peer groups of funds and extract the benchmarking data accordingly.

When looking at similarities, another important criterion that needs to be taken into account is the vintage year. What is the difference in the economic environment a US VC fund starting its operation in November of 2010 is faced with and that of a US VC fund

Best case – most granular	**2014 / Europe / Growth**
Expand region focus	**2014 / All regions / Growth**
Revert to specific region and expand fund type grouping	**2014 / Europe / All-private equity**
Expand region focus	**2014 / All regions / All-private equity**
Revert to specific region and expand fund type grouping	**2014 / Europe / Private capital**
Expand region focus	**2014 / All Regions / Private capital**

*Preqin requires at least eight funds in
benchmark group (i.e., peer group)*

FIGURE 12.A-2 Benchmark expansion according to Preqin (2017)

TABLE 12.A-3   Measuring the overlap between vintage years

Distance to vintage year VY	Overlap rating	Degree
VY ± 0 years	Full overlap	1.00
VY ± 1 year	Strong overlap	0.75
VY ± 2 years	Medium overlap	0.50
VY ± 3 years	Weak overlap	0.25
VY ± 4 years	Possible overlap	0.10
VY ± >4 years	No overlap	0.00

that started in February 2021? It is a fair assumption that there is an overlap, and that the overlap depends on the distance between the vintage years (**Table 12.A-3**).

This idea was picked up and further developed in **Chapter 9**: we looked at vintage years as a major source of diversification, and where all diversification dimensions were modelled as time dependent.

When measuring similarities that take more than two dimensions into consideration (such as region, strategy, and vintage year), we cannot come up with an *overlap* definition that rebuilds any ranking – Arrows's impossibility theorem essentially says that with three or more candidates running, there can be no 100% perfect system of voting and selecting a winner, and therefore, such a ranking may not exist.

NOTES

1. Relative valuation, also referred to as comparable valuation, uses similar, comparable assets in valuing an asset.
2. Here, we are discussing the grading for funds; an approach for the assessment of, say, co-investments would follow similar lines.
3. CAIA defines an 'institutional-quality investment is the type of investment that financial institutions such as pension funds or endowments might include in their holdings because they are expected to deliver reasonable returns at an acceptable level of risk. [. . .] In commercial real estate, the term 'institutional quality' tends to conjure images of high-quality, Class A products located in core markets.' See https://caia.org/sites/default/files/caia_level_i_4th_edition_chapter_1_new.pdf, [accessed 10 April 2023].
4. See Peterman et al. (2020).
5. While private capital firms usually have a quantifiable track record, this only relates to their previous funds. Whether this track record or other quantitative data related to their history is 'good' or 'bad' requires the application of judgement.
6. An example is the discussions around the Alternative Investment Fund Managers Directive (AIFMD) being put in place in the European Union during the 2010s. 'For instance, ILPA reported that 52% of its members surveyed believe that the AIFMD requirements have in fact had a somewhat negative or very negative impact on the LPs in Europe.' See Black (2015).
7. See Meyer (2014).
8. See Toll (2001).
9. A real-life case is mid-market tech private equity firm Thoma Bravo having bought Digital Insight from Intuit for $1.025 billion, and then selling it four months later for $1.65 billion to NCR. This showed a high IRR of 316% but only resulted in a money multiple of about 1.6×

(assuming no debt/no debt repayment. See https://breakingintowallstreet.com/kb/leveraged-buyouts-and-lbo-models/cash-on-cash-return-vs-irr/, [accessed 31 May 2023]

10. See Peterman et al. (2020).
11. See ILPA (2011).
12. See also Peterman et al. (2020), who also saw a developing trend where about 30% of private equity funds have no hurdle.
13. See Dinneen (2004).
14. Fund size can be factored in various ways. For example, PEVARA, another private market data provider, differentiates buyout peer groups by large/medium/small buyouts. Statistics for these peer group can be used directly, i.e. without introducing stresses, as otherwise there would be 'double counting' for this criterion.
15. See Chernova (2022).
16. See Meyer and Mathonet (2005).
17. 'For example, for a firm of three principals doing three deals per year of $5 million each over three years and a management fee of 2.5% for 10 years, the formula yields a fund target of roughly $180 million.' See Morgan-Lewis (2015).
18. For explanation, Dinneen (2004) drew up these criteria in the context of emerging markets where many LPs investors are Development Finance Institutions or impact investors that aim to promote a development and/or political agenda, often at the expense of financial returns.
19. See Fisher (2009).
20. See Dawes (1979).
21. See Smith (1996).

CHAPTER 13

Quantification Based on Fund Grades

We assess a fund's risk and return potential by taking data for its peer group as a proxy. However, we need to address the high degree of uncertainty associated with a fund investment that lasts 'longer than the average marriage'.[1] There is very long time before reliable return figures can be calculated[2] and historical data are even less indicative for future performance than for traditional assets.

The A1*TAM and A2*TAM require a fund's expected growth rate to forecast a fund's cash flows and its net asset value (NAV) development. **Chapter 6** described how the growth rate is determined by sampling from the horizon total value to paid-in capital (TVPI) cumulative distribution function (CDF), but this technique does not take any qualitative assessment of the fund and the limited partner (LP)'s selection skills into consideration. The fund grading allows us to reflect these factors and improve on a fund's specific forecasts.

GRADING PROCESS

Chapter 12 described how a fund's qualitative pre-grade is determined. This chapter continues with the quantitative pre-grade. Both qualitative and quantitative pre-grades are combined to the fund's expectation grade. The fund's expectation grade together with its risk grade is controlling the model's convergence towards the fund's TVPI on maturity (see **Figure 13.1**).

This can be further refined by factoring in the LP's selection skills and the investor's degree of risk aversion.

QUARTILING

The quantitative pre-grade is simply the fund's current interim TVPI (here again referred to as $TVPI_{Interim}$) quartile position in its peer group benchmark. This can be calculated at any point in time during a fund's life based on the latest available data on its cash flows, NAV, measuring how it is performing, and ranking its performance against the peer group's benchmark.

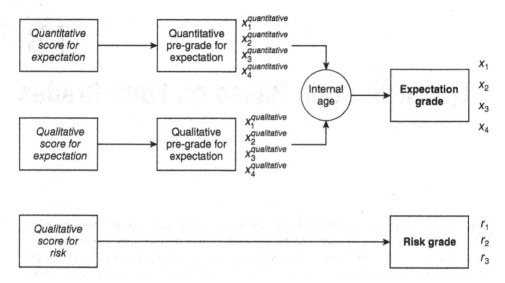

FIGURE 13.1   Grading process

Quantiles

Private market data providers report the peer group's performance in the form of quantile ranges. Quantiles are cut points dividing the range of a probability distribution into continuous intervals with equal number of population members. Quite common are terciles that divide a population into three equal parts (such as average performer, out performer, and underperformer) or deciles that create 10 classes. For quantiles, definitions can deviate. For instance, as discussed in **Chapter 5**, some benchmark providers exclude outliers, i.e. data points over the 95th percentile or below the 5th percentile. Nevertheless, the quantile ranges as reported by the benchmark provider are assumed as basis for determining the quantitative pre-grade.

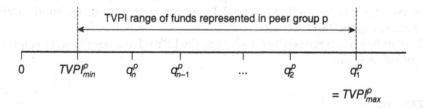

FIGURE 13.2   Benchmark TVPI ranges

Let $TVPI_{max}^p$ be the TVPI of the highest and $TVPI_{min}^p$ that of the lowest performing fund in the peer group. The quantile range for the kth quantile is $[q_{k-1}^p; q_k^p]$ (see **Figure 13.2**).

Quantile definitions become problematic for small amounts of data in a set. The grading is undefined if no quantile ranges are reported for the benchmark. The less data a set contains, the more of an issue this becomes. There is clearly a trade-off between detail and representativeness of the peer group.

Quartiling

Typical for private market benchmarks are quartiles that split a population of observations into four groups. Each quartile contains 25% of the total observations. A 'first-quartile' (or 'top-quartile') fund is typically defined as a fund that belongs to the 25% best performing funds in its peer group at the time of benchmarking. The model establishes a link between the strength of an ex-ante assessment of the fund's future quartile position and its quartile position ex-post, i.e. at time of realisation. For the peer group, it is assumed that TVPI quartiles are clearly defined.[3] For practical purposes, we can assume the first quartile's maximum TVPI to be the benchmark's 95% upper bound and for the fourth quartile as minimum TVPI = 0, even if not often observed in reality.

However, as the private capital market is opaque, the portfolio of funds to be graded is not always a full subset of the benchmark universe. In the extreme, the LP might even have invested in more funds within a vintage year than represented in the benchmark. This is not necessarily an obstacle in the methodology, as the benchmark only forms the yardstick for comparisons, provided that the funds to be graded have the same statistical characteristics as the benchmark.

As funds to be graded may not always form part of the peer group tracked by private market data providers, the following situation cannot be excluded:

$$\exists fund : TVPI_{fund} < TVPI_{min} \vee TVPI_{fund} > TVPI_{max}.$$

For this reason, the highest and the lowest quartile need to be extended to allow an unambiguous mapping of TVPI for fund i onto a quartile. A fund with $TVPI_{fund} > TVPI_{max}^{p}$ will be assigned to the top quartile and a fund with $TVPI_{fund} < TVPI_{min}^{p}$ to the bottom quartile.

Benchmark data can also be 'enriched' with in-house information and by combining various private market data providers (see **Figure 13.3**).

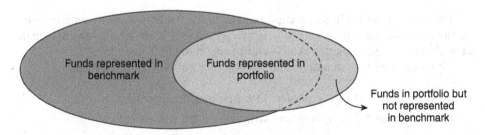

FIGURE 13.3 Funds captured by the benchmark

APPROACH

The approach for dealing with the forecasting problem is to reduce the complexity of forecasting a fund's TVPI to determining its expectation grade (see **Box 13.1**), i.e. the average of its quantitative and its qualitative pre-grades weighted by its internal age (IA).

This forecast aims to answer the question, 'if nothing else changes between now and the fund's maturity date, in which benchmark quartile does it end with which probability?'

Box 13.1 Expectation grade based on qualitative and quantitative scores

An alternative and more granular approach to setting the expectation grades is by using the fund's qualitative score for 'potential weakness' (see **Chapter 12**) and factoring in its so-called 'quantitative score'.[4] The scores are within defined ranges $0 \leq qual\_score \leq 4$ (there can be more than four 'potential weaknesses', but the cut-off is at 4) and $0 \leq quant\_score \leq 4$, with 0 being the best and 4 the worst score.

The quantitative score for $TVPI_{Interim}$ is the position in the peer group's quartile ranges. For example, let us assume the following quartile ranges $[0.77; 0.99; 1.16; 1.42; 1.91]$ with $[1.42; 1.91]$ being cut points that mark the first, i.e. top quartile. For a top-quartile fund with $TVPI_{Interim} = 1.6$, the quantitative score would be:

$$quant_{score} = 0 + \frac{1.91 - 1.6}{1.91 - 1.42} = 0.65.$$

A $TVPI_{Interim} = 1.05$ would be below average, therefore implying a quantitative score larger than 2:

$$quant_{score} = 2 + \frac{1.16 - 1.05}{1.16 - 0.99} = 2.64.$$

The fund's expectation grade is then determined by averaging quantitative and qualitative scores weighted by IA to a total score

$$total_{score} = qual_{score} * (1 - IA) + quant_{score} * IA.$$

For a young fund, a higher weight is given to the qualitative score, whereas for a mature fund, the quantitative score is overweighted – with increasing fund age qualitative findings cease to matter to have an impact on the final outcome.

The total score is then mapped on the scale for the expectation grades:

$0 \leq total\_score < 1 : x_1$ (consistent with first quartile most likely)

$1 \leq total\_score < 2 : x_2$ (consistent with second quartile most likely)

$2 \leq total\_score < 3 : x_3$ (consistent with third quartile most likely)

$3 \leq total\_score \leq 4 : x_4$ (consistent with fourth quartile most likely).

Example – how tall will she be?

For illustration, let us look at an everyday problem: 'Questioning your girl's height? Has a growth spurt come early, or late? What is the average height for girls?'[5] **Figure 13.4** shows a typical table that is showing the ranges for the height of girls from their second year until they turn 17. It is organised by quartiles that allow you to compare within the peer group, e.g. a five-year-old girl can be compared against those girls that are also five years old. Actually, this is technically the same way as looking at peer group benchmarks for funds.

Like in the case of private capital funds for which a J-curve can be observed, the table reflects a specific growth trajectory that also resembles a J-curve. For girls, first there is a kind of 'growth sprint', but the growth rate starts to flatten after 13 years and to plateau around 17 years. Because of this shape, we cannot take, say, the average growth rate between age five and six and assume that it would continue in the same way until she is 18 – this would imply an average height for girls in this age of about 195 cm.

More meaningful is to assume (there are some necessary refinements, but this is the principle) that a seven-year-old girl that is of above-average height as interim measurement (say, 128 cm) will be of above-average height when she is 17, too. According to this

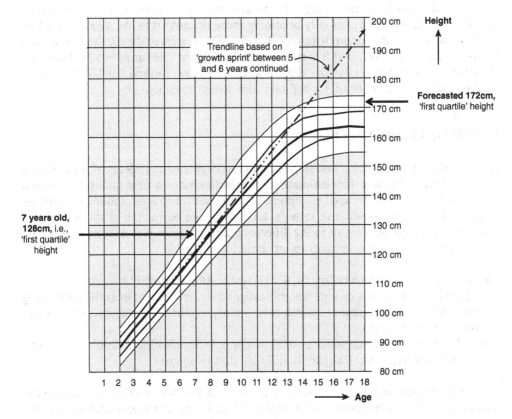

FIGURE 13.4   Height table quartiles according to girls' age

table, in this case, we would predict about 172 cm, as her 'horizon height'. As a forecasting method, this is of course simplistic, but the principle can be applied to forecasting fund performance, although we also need to take other criteria into account.

Probabilistic statement

The quality of the forecasting depends on realistic assessments and consistency of the process. The model's answers are probabilistic, giving weights to the quartile buckets in the applicable benchmark (ranked from top to bottom). One can of course argue that taking the quartile with the highest likelihood is the forecast, but this ignores the different ranges of the possible outcomes and be misleading.

When we are forecasting, we need an indication of the amount of uncertainty or error involved in this educated guess to give us probable upper and lower bounds on the unknown quantity – here the quartile forecasted at the fund's realisation. The certainty depends on the time horizon over which we need to forecast (the further in the future, the more uncertain), the facts available (the more, the higher the certainty), and the number of quantiles defining the possible outcomes (the more quantiles, the higher the scope for picking the wrong one; here only quartiles).

There is more variance in the model for a young fund than for a fund close to maturity. With the fund's increasing age, the general trend over time is towards declining uncertainty; the model is gradually becoming more precise.[6] It is like saying, based on available weather statistics, in three months from now at a given day D, the chance that it rains in London is 40%, that it is cloudy is 30%, and that it is sunny is 30%. However, these three months later at day D – 1, there will be more specific and reliable data, so the forecast for D will rather be that it will rain with 90% probability.

CONTROLLING CONVERGENCE

An estimate is more 'certain' and implies a higher degree of confidence if it provides a narrower range of values. This estimate takes quantitative as well as qualitative criteria into consideration. As LPs need to commit to a fund as 'blind pool', the initial estimate is primarily based on qualitative criteria. Over time, the narrowing of these ranges is controlled by assigning weights to the different quartile positions as outcomes, assuring that the forecast converges towards its outcome:

- Convergence from uncertainty (0, Knightian) to full certainty (1);
- The start point are the ex-ante weights assigned to the different quantiles, reflecting the grades for expectation and risk (uncertainty, qualitative assessment of a blind pool only, no history);
- End point: 1 for one quantile as final outcome, 0 for all other quantiles (certainty, quantitative assessment, portfolio, and cash flows known).

Let us assume that we are looking at a new fund and have no further insights into its quality relative to competing funds and opinions on its future development (i.e. the

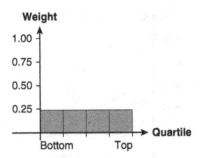

FIGURE 13.5 New fund / extreme uncertainty

'neutral' scenario). We are faced with extreme uncertainty and the best forecast we can make that all quartiles as outcomes (i.e. the fund's quartile position within its peer group of comparable funds at maturity) are equally likely and are, therefore, being given equal weight in the forecast (**Figure 13.5**).[7]

Once a fund and its peer group mature and come to the end of their lifetimes, we have complete certainty about its quartile position; in this example, the fund performed in the peer group's second quartile (**Figure 13.6**).

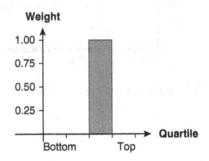

FIGURE 13.6 Mature fund / complete certainty

We measure certainty through the fund's IA. How is it in between, for instance if a fund is half-way through its lifecycle, i.e. has an IA of 0.5? Let us assume that fund is assigned as expectation grade 'Underperformance', suggesting that, based on an increasing amount of quantitative (the interim quartile position) as well as qualitative information, the fund will mature in the peer group's second quartile. Of course, over the fund's remaining lifetime, a lot can still happen.

In this case, the current weights will be the average between the fund's forecast ex ante (extreme uncertainty, with equal weights for all quartiles) and the final quartile position weighted by the IA. This results in a weight of 0.625 for the second quartile outcome and weights of 0.125 each for the other quartiles (**Figure 13.7**).

With IA equal to one, the fund is at the end of its lifetime and we have full certainty regarding its outcome.

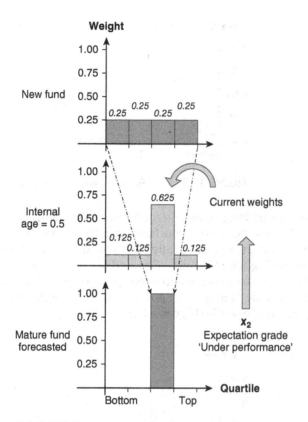

FIGURE 13.7 From uncertainty to certainty

LP SELECTION SKILLS

As argued in Jeet (2020), the LP's selection skills are an important factor. Probably, the most controversial aspect of qualitative model inputs is the investor's self-assessment. Most LPs believe in and boast their ability to pick 'top-quartile' funds. Investing in venture capital is said to be pointless unless you invest in the top-quartile or even the top-decile funds.[8]

Investing in alternative assets heavily relies on the opinions of experts. Individuals with specialist domain knowledge, or with superior understanding of due diligence, are called upon to determine the acceptability of an investment case. An investment manager's[9] market value depends on her judgement being believable and better than that of her peers, but this does not necessarily make the judgement more correct and will be a generally limited level of confidence in it.

Selection skills create a bias in the ex-ante weights of the forecast. Let us assume that the expectation grade suggests 'Underperformance', as for the fund a few weaknesses were discovered during the due diligence. However, the LP is convinced that the fund management team is very strong and will deliver a top-quartile return, nevertheless (see **Figure 13.8**).

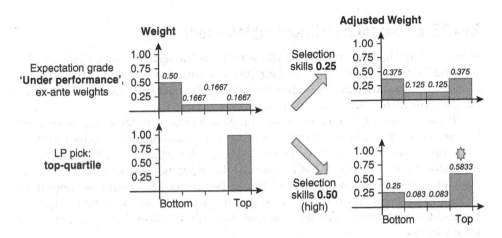

FIGURE 13.8   Modelling selection skills

The adjusted ex-ante weights for the forecast are the average between the fund's forecast for expectation grade 'Underperformance' (in this example) and the LP's 'Top performance' pick for the fund's outcomes on maturity. A selection skill parameter of zero suggests that the LP's forecast offers no additional information and leaves the one suggested by the expectation grade unchanged. A selection skill of 1 would be assuming that the LP has perfect foresight and then only the LP pick becomes valid as forecast. It is also possible that the LP gives a more nuanced forecast, for example, giving a weight of 75% to the top quartile and 25% to the second quartile.

Obviously perfect foresight is unrealistic but what selection skills are reasonable? One way of approaching this is assuming a normal distribution for selection skills. There may be good reasons to believe that an LP is systematically better in fund selection than her competitors, but measuring this on such a scale gives an indication how much better than the average the selection skill parameter would imply (and may give a pause to many bullish investment managers). These examples ignored the situation where LPs have worse selection skills than her competitors. Assuming this could, for instance, be meaningful for an LP to acknowledge being unfamiliar with the market represented by the peer group.

A warning when assuming selection skills: here, we need to factor in that there is only a limited population of high-performing funds, notably in a niche, and therefore, the selection skills are neutralised by high levels of diversification (see **Box 13.2**).

Finally, we need to factor in the risk grade. In the example depicted by **Figure 13.9**, the risk grade is assumed to be 'Neutral' so the risk assessment would lead to no further impact on the forecast. The expectation grade and IA imply the weights for sampling from the horizon TVPI CDF. In this case, still all outcomes have some likelihood, but the LP 'top-quartile' pick is already given less weight than the second quartile implied by the expectation grade.

Assuming that the fund would be eventually converging towards the second quartile performance, the LP's pick would become increasingly irrelevant as the fund is

Box 13.2 Sampling without replacement

Many LPs build highly diversified portfolio of funds, but usually Monte Carlo simulations (MCS) sample data for funds from given populations with replacement. Sampling with replacement makes sense if the samples can be considered as independent, i.e. if the covariance between them is zero.

If the population size of investable funds would be very large, the covariance between samples is close to zero and sampling with replacement does make no difference. For LP portfolios, the share of the funds invested compared to the universe of investable funds is often very high. Typically, the population size of investable funds per vintage year is around 100, and LPs can be assumed to commit to more than 10 new funds per annum. The extreme scenario would be an LP committing to all funds of the peer group – a situation where obviously selection skills would not matter any longer.

This suggests for the MCS that if sampling with replacement, a finite population correction factor needs to be applied. Alternatively, the MCS could sample without replacement. This, however, requires researching or estimating the number of funds that can be invested in and ranking them according to their TVPIs as sampled from the horizon TVPI CDF. Therefore, sampling without replacement is more complex to implement.

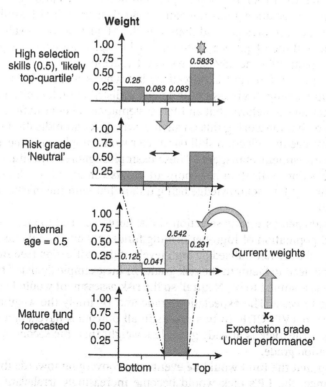

FIGURE 13.9 Selection skills and risk reflected in current weights for Expectation Grade and Internal Age (example 1)

maturing. This reflects that forecasts are never static. The future is always getting closer and the forecast itself is changing with new information, right until the moment when the future becomes the present.

IMPACT OF RISK GRADE

Increasing risks are reflected by overweighting the extremes of top and bottom performance compared to second and third quartile outcomes. The risk grade defines the risk shift, between 0 and 1. A risk grade 'Neutral' implies no change.

Increasing risks imply a higher risk shift (see **Figure 13.10**):

$$w_{Bottom\ quartile} = w_{Bottom\ quartile} + w_{Third\ Quartile} * Risk\ shift$$

$$w_{Third\ quartile} = w_{Third\ quartile} - w_{Third\ Quartile} * Risk\ shift$$

$$w_{Top\ quartile} = w_{Top\ quartile} + w_{Second\ Quartile} * Risk\ shift$$

$$w_{Second\ quartile} = w_{Second\ quartile} - w_{Second\ Quartile} * Risk\ shift.$$

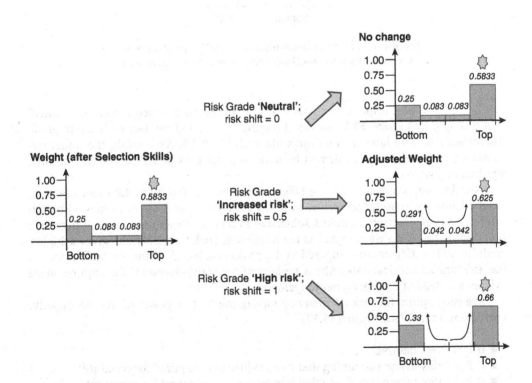

FIGURE 13.10 Risk impact

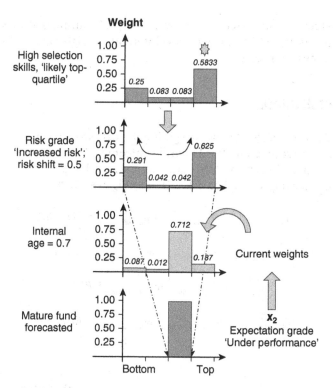

FIGURE 13.11   Selection skills and risk reflected in current weights for Expectation Grade and Internal Age (example 2)

A risk shift of 1 implies that only extreme 'hit or miss' outcomes are forecasted. The example in **Figure 13.11** shows the same case as before, but with a risk grade 'Increased risk' and later in the fund's life with IA = 0.7. As a result, the underperformance is increasingly confirmed by data, and the LP's pick's impact has become significantly weaker.

Another important factor to be taken into consideration is the LP's risk aversion, i.e. the tendency to prefer outcomes with low uncertainty to those outcomes with high uncertainty. As 'certainty' remains subjective to a large degree, we define it here as a function of IA. A decision-maker is overconfident (risk-taking) if she gives a higher credulity to her judgement compared to the projection based on the available evidence (i.e. the fund's historical data). She is underconfident (risk-averse) if she requires more evidence instead of relying on her judgement.

We can capture the risk adversity by raising the IA to a power of the risk appetite coefficient, i.e. IA^P (see **Figure 13.12**):

- If P = 1 risk-neutral.
- If P > 1 risk-averse (assuming that more evidence is required for certainty).
- If P < 1 risk-taking (assuming that less evidence is required for certainty).

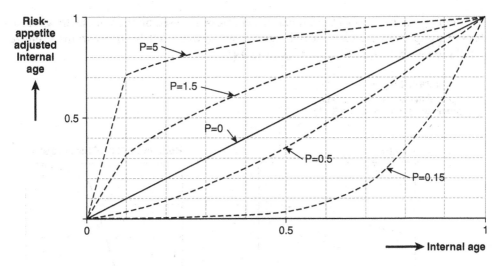

FIGURE 13.12   Internal Age reflecting risk appetite

TVPI SAMPLING

For the current weights given in **Figure 13.11**, the MCS samples TVPIs from the fund style's specific horizon TVPI CDF (see **Figure 13.13**).

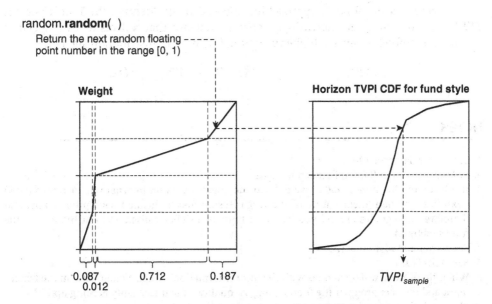

FIGURE 13.13   Sampling from Horizon TVPI CDF, reflecting current weights

$TVPI_{Sample}$ is the fund's TVPI on maturity forecasted based on the sample drawn from its peer group. Even as IA is approaching one, the sample is will be drawn from the entire population within a quartile (see **Figure 13.14**).

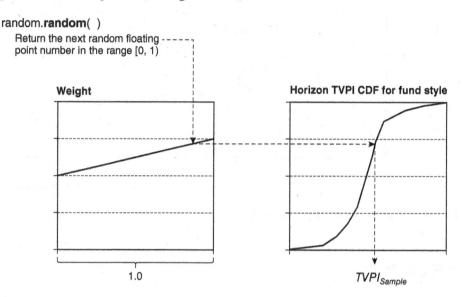

FIGURE 13.14   Mature fund sampling from Horizon TVPI CDF; assuming Expectation Grade 'Under Performance'

However, as the fund is approaching the end of its lifetime, the fund's current $TVPI_{Interim}$ is becoming an increasingly reliable predictor that reflects its own specifics and will, therefore, be given a higher weight in line with its distribution age DA:

$$TVPI_{Forecast} = TVPI_{Sample} * (1 - DA) + TVPI_{Interim} * DA.$$

NOTES

1. See Fraser-Sampson (2007).
2. Several years from the fund's inception date.
3. In Meyer and Mathonet (2005), we defined the grades based on internal rate of return (IRR) quantiles. The non-linear nature of the IRR measure makes this approach problematic, and therefore, here grades are defined based on horizon TVPIs (realised TVPI at the end of the fund's lifetime).
4. See Meyer and Mathonet (2005).
5. See Halls (2019).
6. When there are new data at odds with the prior information – in particular data on the benchmark and the peer group or the fund managers' quality – the uncertainty is going up.
7. More technically, maximum uncertainty implies maximum entropy, and the maximum entropy distribution is the uniform distribution.
8. Remember that we are talking here about the top quartile at the realisation after usually more than 10 years!
9. Person as well as organisation.

CHAPTER 14

Bottom-up Approach to Forecasting

The Takahashi–Alexander model and the stochastic models discussed in the previous chapters are top-down models, i.e. they look at a fund only from the 'outside' and do not take the specifics of the private assets held by the fund into consideration. For this reason, top-down models potentially ignore information that could significantly alter risk assessments and improve forecasts. Top-down is usually juxtaposed with a bottom-up approach to modelling. However, another term brought up in the context is 'look-through', which calls for clarification.

Simplistically, the look-through is a requirement to capture as much inside information on a fund as possible. Often such information is also provided by the limited partner (LP)'s investment managers as experts. Their insights, what is termed here as 'investment intelligence', can be assumed to be reliable and therefore will override the model's results. A bottom-up model is one way of using this inside information to generate forecasts. In the following, we are taking a closer look at the link between look-through, overrides, and bottom-up modelling.

LOOK-THROUGH

As discussed in Meyer (2023), various financial regulations for an internal-model-based risk measurement approach require that a look-through be applied to private capital funds. According to BIS (2020), the look-through is the most granular approach and thus assumed to give highest sensitivity to risk. It requires a bank to risk weight the fund's underlying assets as if they were held directly by the bank.

Regulation

Financial regulations like Basel III and Solvency II (applying to reinsurers and insurers that operate in the European Economic Area), have tightened capital requirements for investments in funds whose positions are not transparent and through punitive risk weights incentivise a look-through.[1] The Bank for International Settlements set out requirements that apply to banks' equity investments in all types of funds, including off-balance sheet exposures such as the unfunded commitments to subscribe to a fund's future capital calls.

Regulators expect that the look-through as mandatory requirement will benefit banks, insurers, and pension funds in their compliance, risk, and operational functions, and assume that decomposing positions held in this way represents the correct risks. This level of granularity allows LPs to identify fundamental risks such as alignment with the general partners (GPs), concentration, and leverage, and to manage contagion risk, i.e. risks originated by interactions between the individual private assets indirectly held by an LP.[2]

Fund ratings

Fund ratings as described in previous chapters appear to be a pragmatic way of address-ing the look-through requirement and make use of such detailed information. For exam-ple, a fund with a very concentrated or leveraged portfolio of private assets would be consistent with a 'high risk' grade (see **Chapter 10**).

In fact, in early 2000s, the Basel Committee on Banking Supervision saw it as sound practice to establish a system of internal risk ratings for equity investments, with different rating factors being appropriate for direct investments and funds,[3] but this recommendation never gained traction and, to the best of my knowledge, no internal-rating-based approach for private capital funds ever was presented and found supervisory approval.

Look-through in practice

Undoubtedly, the increased transparency associated with a look-through is an improve-ment of risk-management practices. However, the regulatory requirements related to internal models for private capital funds are conceptually and practically difficult to meet, and next to nothing has been published on this subject.[4] ISDA (2022) criticised the look-through to the individual components of funds mandated under the Basel III capital framework, arguing that fund exposures are generally managed at the level of the fund rather than the underlying assets, and that the look-through, in fact, does not necessarily provide the best view of a fund's underlying risk profile.

At the time of this writing, few, if any, regulated investors have implemented an internal model and thus a look-through for their portfolios of private capital funds. The workload and the associated costs for collecting, verifying, correcting, and maintaining data for thousands of the funds' underlying assets – a problem each LP needs to solve herself as these data are not public – is high, whereas many practitioners view the added value for portfolios that are already well diversified as limited.

The significant effort and the complexity of modelling and the difficult regulatory approval process are in contrast to a persistently benevolent environment for private equity investing. Many investors believe that the asset class's 'guaranteed' high outper-formance would sufficiently compensate for regulation's punitive risk weights. This has eroded incentives for financial institutions to invest in more sophisticated risk-management systems, a situation that has not changed in recent years.[5]

BOTTOM-UP

Confusingly, instead of 'look-through', also 'bottom-up' is used in a similar context. BCBS (2005) suggest view risk as 'bottom-up, namely from its components'. Munich-Re (2015) used the same term in the context of Solvency II. According to Vander Elst (2021), a bottom-up approach for private equity funds 'consists of forecasting the future proceeds for each underlying asset in a fund and then aggregate them at the fund-level'.

Viewing look-through as an approach that takes information of the fund's underlying private assets into account, and bottom-up as a technique that starts at the lowest level and aggregates results upwards, appears to be in line with these definitions. A bottom-up approach requires the look-through, but look-through is not equivalent to bottom-up.

Stochastic bottom-up models

Stochastic bottom-up models are forecasting the probability of various outcomes for every private asset held by the fund and arguably are the most challenging to operate as their performance depending on the quality of the statistical input data.

Bongaerts and Charlier (2008) presented an approach for measuring the risk of directly held assets. They modified the structural model based on the Merton approach – viewing the equity of a company as a call option on its assets – to capture stylised facts of private equity investments. Klüppelberg et al. (2010) proposed a stochastic model for assets held by a fund. These authors' model applied real-option theory, reflecting the assets' current valuations, their leverage, and their default probabilities. It also factors in critical assumptions on the investor's future projections and her self-assessment, which introduces subjectivity. The model described by Burkhard et al. (2013) decomposes the assets' returns into a set of factors to capture the different risk premia available in the financial markets. It infers the equity risk portion of unlisted private equity from a weighted average of the different option volatilities obtained from the Merton model as well, accounting for the different vintage years and debt levels in a portfolio of private assets.

Generally, stochastic models that start with the fund's underlying assets and add up these results to the fund's overall risk need to capture many details and interdependencies. For longer forecast periods, a bottom-up model needs a default/failure model for the private assets held by the fund. These cannot be assumed to fail independently, i.e. due to their own specific weaknesses, from the others. It is rather the fund manager who decides, taking the entire portfolio into consideration, which private assets to write off. Finally, a bottom-up approach needs a waterfall model to determine net cash flows to LPs. All of this renders a pure bottom-up approach fragile, cumbersome to operate routinely, and thus of little use for commitment pacing.

Machine-learning-based bottom-up models

Machine learning (ML) in theory can overcome such complexity and capture all relevant components and their interdependencies.[6] ML has also been applied to private equity fund cash-flow forecasting.[7] The major obstacle is the lack of statistically significant and high-quality time-series data that would allow training an ML model without making it prone to overfitting. Practical experience suggests limitations, finding that simple models often provide better results than the ML algorithm. Also, risk figures generated by an ML-based model are difficult to explain to decision-makers and supervisory authorities and to rely on.

OVERRIDES

Investment managers in the course of their work gather a significant amount of up-to-date information. Here, we discuss how these experts' insights can be used as overrides to adjust and improve the forecasts generated by a top-down model like the A2*TAM. These overrides relate to cash flows either on the fund or on the level of the private assets held by the fund.

Overrides will only explain part of the fund's forecast, so what we aim to achieve is a combination of a top-down and a bottom-up approach where the A2*TAM continues to forecast the share of the fund that is not covered by the override. To be compatible with A2*TAM's forecasts, the overrides need to be net cash flows to the LP.

Investment intelligence

Investment intelligence is the identification and evaluation of a particular organisation's investment insights. This term has connotations of military intelligence, i.e. information collection and analysis approaches to provide guidance and direction to assist decision-making.

Investment intelligence insights are gathered from alternative data sources, such as conversations with GPs and other LPs, due diligences on co-investments, monitoring visits, e-mails, memos, and presentations. These data sources are alternative in the sense that they fall outside the standardised reporting from GPs to their LPs. Occasionally information is confidential. It is, therefore, a fair assumption that in private markets, an LP's own investment managers are the best, often only, source of investment intelligence.

Advantages and restrictions

Decision-makers intuitively prefer an expert-based forecasting approach – it is less of a 'black box' – and particularly over the short term believed to be more reliable. In fact, most LPs started with collecting investment intelligence from their own investment managers by asking the GPs and incorporating this information into their own, mainly spreadsheet-based, bottom-up projection tools. The clear advantages are that there is no need for expensive and difficult to access historical data and no overly sophisticated modelling and implementation is required. Doing it this way assures high flexibility and allows inserting judgement into projections. In private markets, statistical models need to rely on usually outdated data, whereas human judgement has the potential to quickly adjust to new information, events, and observed changes in dynamics.

Practically and particularly for larger LPs, there are limitations. A cash-flow forecasting practitioner working for a large institutional investor commented that, interestingly, they were not asking the GPs for estimates. In his view, LPs should critically reflect on the additional strain this would be causing the GPs, on top of the continuously increasing demands for more detailed financial reporting and information requested for environmental, social, and governance (ESG) compliance. Also, fund managers will feel reluctant to disclose information on likely financing or exit events before the deals actually close, for example, to protect their negotiation position. Another interviewee commented that in the past, they also looked at individual portfolio companies, but it was difficult to go down to a company level and get meaningful information. The end result was not good as too many errors and imprecisions caused by vague assumptions added up.

Treatment as exceptions

Bottom-up modelling has the potential to be more precise over the short term, but the investment intelligence quickly becomes obsolete and the huge effort to keep data up-to-date stops an LP from updating them in a rhythm to keep forecasts sufficiently near time. The major limitation here is that meaningful judgement cannot be applied across all underlying assets for larger fund portfolios.

Non-standardised data gathering requires (typically manually) analysing large datasets, often unstructured and inconsistent across funds, with time lags, quality, and completeness being problematic. These unstructured data need to be converted into the structured data required for the cash-flow forecasting. The effort for the LP would be enormous. Actually, only for a minority of assets, superior insights exist, and usually for a major part of the private assets, there will be no new information.

Investment managers as highly paid professionals will reject repetitive work that they view as largely superfluous. Cash-flow forecasting is not necessarily the most important or value-adding information for them and generally investment managers appear to be reluctant to put much currency in a 'simple' model-based approach. Investment intelligence only works in exceptional situations, when concrete events are announced or planned. It tends to be incomplete as investment managers do not have the time to cover the entire portfolio consistently and routinely.

Integration of overrides in forecasts by a top-down model

According to Lawrence et al. (2006), the accuracy of judgemental forecasting improves if an expert has important domain knowledge or when more up-to-date information exists. Practically, experts tend to focus on the movers in the portfolio and where there is certainty, and for these cases want to have the option to override a top-down model.

Typically, such information will be only valid over the short term, not more than four months. It will be based on inside information or hunches what is going to happen next, gained from intimate knowledge of a fund's operation.

For these reasons, the expert's estimate for the future cash flow's amount CF_e and the time the cash flow is assumed to be 'true' – or at least more certain than the top-down model's forecast. If the estimated cash flow CF_e relates to a capital call for investments, the fund's contribution age CA(t) at time t where the forecast starts needs to be adjusted as:

$$CA'(t) = \frac{\sum_{i=0}^{t} C_{(i)} + CF_e}{CC}.$$

In case the cash flow relates to a realisation, we need to adjust the fund's distribution age $DA(t)$ (see **Chapter 6**). This means that we add the estimated cash flow CF_e to the enumerator that gives the sum of all cash flows so far and decrease $NAV_{(t)}$ in the denominator – by which amount? By the share of the private asset to which the realisation relates to. This, however, requires a look-through onto the fund's entire portfolio. In case this information is not available, we approximate the new distribution age reflecting the override with:

$$DA'(t) = \frac{\sum_{i=0}^{t} D_{(i)} + CF_e}{\sum_{i=1}^{t} D_{(i)} + \max\{0; NAV_{(t)} - CF_e\} + Undrawn_t}.$$

$\max\{0; NAV_{(t)} - CF_e\}$ addresses the situation where an exit generated more proceeds than the most recent $NAV_{(t)}$.

With these adjustments of contribution age and distribution age, and as a consequence, the changed internal age, we can reflect these overrides. The increased internal age leads to a narrower range of fund lifetimes and TVPIs from which the A2*TAM samples (see **Chapter 6**). The next step is to insert the estimated cash flow CF_e (see **Figure 14.1**).

We need to assure that after the insertion of CF_e for each cash-flow scenario, the respective $TVPI_{Target}$ is maintained. For this purpose, several strategies can be meaningful.

Let us assume that the A2*TAM has generated a scenario of J contributions and K distributions. The contributions are one array $(C_1, \ldots, C_J)$ and the distributions are another array $(D_1, \ldots, D_K)$. The A2*TAM has assured that

$$\frac{\sum_{i=1}^{K} D_i}{\sum_{i=1}^{J} C_i} = TVPI_{Target}.$$

One way of inserting the estimate D_e while keeping $TVPI_{Target}$ unchanged would be a proportional rescaling of the other distributions. So for $\left(D_1, \ldots, D_e, \ldots D_K\right)$ that means to apply a factor of

$$\frac{\sum_{\forall i \ne e} D_i - D_e}{\sum_{i=1}^{J} D_i}$$

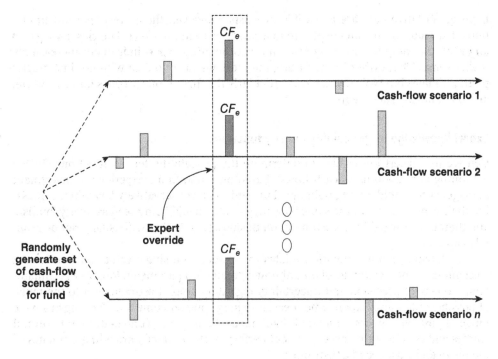

FIGURE 14.1   Inserting expert override into set of cash-flow scenarios

to the original distributions $(D_1, \ldots, D_K)$. While it is simple, this strategy may distort the volatility of the cash-flow scenario. An approach more consistent with the A2*TAM generated cash-flow scenario would be to randomly pick a distribution and reduce it by D_e or, in case the picked distribution was lower than D_e, remove it entirely, and randomly pick the next distribution, continuing the process until the full amount D_e is deducted from the scenario's other distributions. Implicitly that would reduce the frequency of the fund's cash-flows.

However, it is possible that

$$\frac{D_e}{\sum_{i=1}^{J} C_i} > TVPI_{Target}.$$

This would imply that the expert is certain that fund's TVPI on maturity will exceed the $TVPI_{Target}$. Analogously, the same procedure can be applied in case CF_e is a contribution. Of course, the expert can estimate an entire series of cash flows.

PROBABILISTIC BOTTOM-UP

When relying on investment intelligence, we are utilising subjective and intuitive information to make our forecasts. The great advantage is that this approach works even if no quantitative data are accessible or exists. However, there are important limita-tions. Estimates of distant events are inaccurate or even incorrect. The closer we get to an event, the more we learn about it and incorporating expert judgement increasingly makes sense. The further in the future, the more we need to deal with not just precise point estimates but typically ranges, particularly the further one projects into the future, and probabilistic statements.

Expert knowledge for probability density functions?

Can we use expert knowledge to determine the probability density functions (PDFs) for timing and amounts of cash flows? Based on the author's experiences, investment managers often hold 'strong opinions' but tend to be conservatively low when express-ing their expectations. In the same way, they tend to avoid being seen as overly 'bullish' and therefore 'low ball' their estimates on upsides, so volatility will usually not be prop-erly captured.

In statistics, point estimation relates to calculating a single value that serves as a 'best guess' or 'best estimate' of an unknown population parameter. Ranges in estimates relate to lack of precision and uncertainty regarding a point estimate, not to the range of possible outcomes. Experts find it easier to judge one outcome than looking at a wide range of possible outcomes and their likelihoods. Bansal et al. (undated) refer to several studies and conclude that experts do not perform well at directly providing estimates of the mean and variance of a distribution.[8]

Moreover, a bottom-up approach is vulnerable to idiosyncratic biases, with either fund managers or the LP's investment managers being overly conservative and notably reluctant to forecast extreme cash flows. As a consequence, the 'law of large numbers' will not work, and the bottom-up model will neither get expectations nor variances right. If a bottom-up approach is applied to the entire portfolio, biases get amplified and lead to a poor-quality forecast for the effort spent.

Estimating ranges

Experience suggests that estimates of cash-flow amounts, which are based on estab-lished valuation standards, will more likely to be accurate than those of the cash-flow dates. Cash-flow dates can be estimated only over a short time horizon. Typically, after more than six months, estimates cease to be of relevance and model-based forecasting techniques become more important.[9]

Distributions from funds to their investors are obviously sensitive to short-term information and changes. Estimates can be significantly improved through closer inter-action with fund managers and through incorporating judgement.

To measure the uncertainty of cash-flow amounts and dates, Delgado Moreira (2003) described a probabilistic methodology. Cash-flow amounts and dates are uncertain and continuous variables. For this bottom-up approach, investment managers are routinely asked to provide estimates for an early, foreseen (i.e. 'best guess'), and late cash-flow date, and a low, medium, and high cash-flow amount, which can be used as param-eters for a triangular distribution (see **Figure 14.2**). Assuming no correlation between

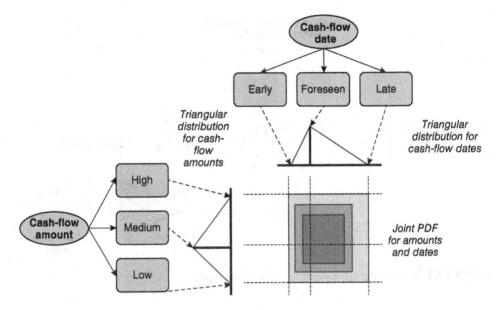

FIGURE 14.2   Investment manager's estimates for cash-flow amount and timing

amounts and dates of cash flows, the sampling leads to a joint PDF that characterises these continuous random variables.

Alternatively, each estimate can be assigned a probability, so that all estimated probabilities for amounts and times, respectively, add up to not more than one. That these probabilities for cash flow dates do not necessarily add up to one caters for the situation where the cash flow is not certain to take place at all. The expert's estimates define the inputs of a discrete distribution. The combination of three amounts and three dates gives nine possible outcomes per cash flow. A relatively simple Monte Carlo simulation (MCS) helps to determine the range for possible outcomes. If the sum of probabilities is one, it is assumed that there is no chance of a cash flow not taking place. The standard deviation of the cash flows and, therefore, the judgement on risk is implicit in the format of the estimates.

We can also take the expert's point estimates and apply a normal distribution, defined by its mean and standard deviation for both amount and date (see **Figure 14.3**).

As the normal distribution is unbounded, this model assumes small chances of a write-off and of a large positive cash flow.

For short-term estimates in a bottom-up approach, the funds and the private assets they hold are analysed in detail. When aggregating estimates for several private assets into a net amount to be paid to the LP, the fund's structure is also relevant. For example, the waterfall's hurdle rate can heavily distort the cash flow to the LP. With 100% catch-up, the LPs are effectively out of the money until the GP has made a full recovery. It is obvious that a thorough bottom-up analysis is a resource-intensive exercise, and therefore, especially for large portfolios, parameters for all assets cannot be continuously kept up to date.

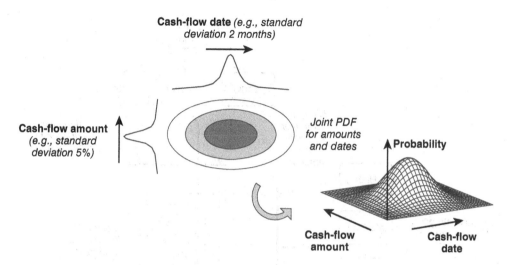

FIGURE 14.3   Translating estimates into probabilistic model

COMBINING TOP-DOWN WITH BOTTOM-UP

While a top-down model may leave important details out, a pure bottom-up approach is impractical to operate for large portfolios of funds, with often thousands of underlying private assets.

Forecasters give preference to up-to-date and detailed data (typically investment intelligence) forecast, where available; if such data are unavailable, a forecaster can use a model that does not depend on them. The main advantage of the top-down approach is that exactly it does not rely on many data and thus tends to be robust and works even under adverse circumstances.

The override technique described before allows us to combine the top-down with probabilistic bottom-up in an MCS. The starting point is N forecast scenarios generated by the A2*TAM. For those private assets for which experts have estimated a cash-flow date and amount, the MCS picks one sample date and amount, respectively, as overrides for the nth scenario. Then, as described before, we integrate these overrides into the A2*TAM result and aggregate all scenarios, each weighted by $1/N$.

NOTES

1. See EIOPA (2015). For the European Union's Alternative Investment Fund Manager Directive, the look-through requirement relates to a depositary's safekeeping duties in relation to keeping a client's assets in a secure area; see ESMA (2023).
2. See Hannover-Re (2021).
3. See BCBS (2001).
4. EVCA (2013) put forward a principle-based approach for developing private equity risk measurement models.
5. See Bongaerts and Charlier (2008).

6. See Vander Elst (2021).
7. See Karatas (2022).
8. They refer to research findings that experts have serious misconceptions about variances. In statistics, point estimation involves the use of sample data to calculate a single value (known as a 'point estimate' since it identifies a point in some parameter space) which is to serve as a 'best guess' or 'best estimate' of an unknown population parameter and acutely underestimates the variance. Even when estimating the mean – the first-order moment of a distribution – experts perform poorly. As Rae and Alexander (2017) point out, probability calculations are frequently counterintuitive and expert groups may adopt 'socially plausible but inappropriate' strategies.
9. See Meyer and Mathonet (2005).

CHAPTER 15

Commitment Pacing

imited partners (LPs) manage their exposure through commitment pacing, for which we in the previous chapters have developed the basic toolset. This aims to build a private capital investment programme that is much more nuanced and specific to the investor's objectives. The main assumption is that a well-constructed portfolio comprising primary commitments, and commitments to secondary and co-investment funds, and funds of funds (FOFs), can deliver superior and more sustainable risk-adjusted returns beyond what each of these individual components can achieve in isolation.

We approach commitment pacing in two steps: first, a pacing plan is defined, and in the second step, run a Monte Carlo simulation for the plan's progression and to assess its outcomes. Various dictionaries define *pacing* as moving or developing something at a particular rate or speed, however, typically without a particular destination. *The Cambridge Dictionary* provides another, quite fitting, definition: 'to walk with regular steps in one direction and then back again, usually because you are worried or nervous'.[1] This captures the iterative, probing aspects of commitment pacing and the thinking about probabilities with which scenarios could happen.

DEFINING A PACING PLAN

An LP can steer her exposure to private assets through timing and sizing of commitments to funds and the choice of the funds' respective styles. The pacing plan lists what amounts need to be committed at which time to which kind of fund (see **Figure 15.1**).

By its very nature – there is no detailed information available on funds that are still to be raised in future years – commitment pacing relies on a top-down modelling of funds. In the pacing plan, funds are defined by their style (e.g. US venture capital (VC), European buyout, and infrastructure) and their commitment type (primary commitment, secondary fund, co-investment fund, and fund-of-funds) with their specific contribution schedules, lifetimes, return ranges, and distribution patterns.

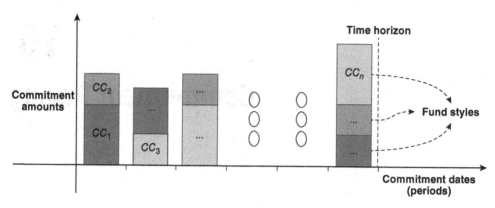

FIGURE 15.1   Pacing plan

Assuming that the plan covers a number of n funds with a committed capital of CC_i, the sum of all commitments to be entered in within the given time horizon cannot exceed the available resources R of uncommitted capital:

$$\sum_{i=1}^{n} CC_i \leq R.$$

Generally, the committed capital is an upper bound of the total capital finally called by a fund. However, a significant part of the initial capital is never invested. Therefore, it is not always meaningful to restrict R to the amount the investor has allocated to private capital, and instead, this amount can be leveraged through over-commitments (see **Box 15.1**).

Periods are set according to the pacing plan's granularity. If yearly, a flexing of the plan will not be necessary. If more granular, however, such as quarterly, we need to consider that funds will not necessarily close as foreseen. In this case, when simulating the plan, it makes sense to randomly allocate inception dates to quarters within a, say, one-year time window.

Commitment pacing is often perceived as a one-off exercise, done when launching an investment programme and for proposing and explaining an investment strategy to stakeholders for signing off. However, pacing plans can, or rather should be, rolling, i.e. continuously extended and updated based on new data and revised with new projections.

PACING PHASES

Commitment pacing is typically discussed in the context of starting an investment programme from scratch, i.e. assuming that there is no allocation to private assets yet. Practically, this is rarely the case; typically, there is already an existing allocation to private assets, so the starting point is rather an assessment of the current portfolio status versus the targeted allocation.

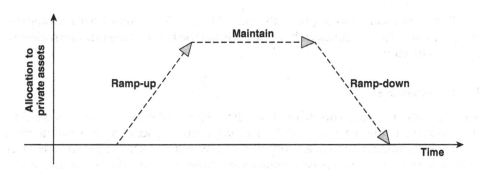

FIGURE 15.2   Pacing phases

The main assumption driving allocations to private capital is that illiquid private assets will yield a significant premium over liquid assets. Indirectly and with a time lag, the commitments result in an exposure to private assets. To harvest the premium from such investments, this true exposure needs to be maximised and kept stable. There are different phases for achieving a steady-state exposure to private assets: the 'ramp-up', the 'maintenance', and the 'ramp-down' phase (see **Figure 15.2**).

Ramp-up phase

An LP starting an investment programme would plan for an initial ramp-up period of more and/or larger commitments to build up this real exposure to private assets. Funds are often sourced opportunistically, without their specific styles being the major consideration. This aims to decrease the time to reach the targeted exposure while controlling for the risk of overshooting the target or breaking liquidity limits.

Maintenance phase

After a sizeable portfolio (and also relationships with fund management firms) has been built, adhering to a plan and diversification targets start to become important as concentrations can create unrewarded risks and also as a lack of exposure to wished segments of the market can increase the likelihood of not meeting the programme objectives. The ramp-up would be followed by the maintenance[2] (also called 'steady-state'[3]) phase.

LPs cannot passively maintain constant exposure. A consequence of the funds' limited lifetime and their self-liquidating nature is that LPs need to have a recommitment strategy to maintain their portfolio constantly invested at the targeted allocation and while balancing opportunity cost and risk of liquidity shortfalls. Two factors play together in creating high uncertainty regarding when and with which precision an allocation is met, and restrict the stability with which it can be maintained:

- The time lag between the commitment and the capital calls and their sizes that result in the investments;
- The uncertainty of the timing and size of the distribution of invested capital to the LP.

During this maintenance phase, the funds in the LP's portfolio distribute capital to be re-committed to new funds with the excess being used for funding other activities and investor's liabilities.

Ramp-down phase

There can also be a ramp-down, or 'unwinding', phase, where an LP decides to reduce her allocation to private assets, by either slowing down the pace of new commitments or by stopping commitments and exiting the asset class entirely. These phases can interact. Some LPs have over the years been oscillating between reducing allocations and rebooting their programme.

Box 15.1   Over-commitments

To minimise the opportunity costs associated with the undrawn commitments, LPs can follow an over-commitment strategy, where they commit more than the available resources and rely on expected cash distributions to fund future capital calls. Assuming that the LP has a targeted allocation to private assets of €10 million, with an over-commitment ratio (OCR) of 150% she would enter into commitments totalling €15 million.

This avoids the risk that resources are under-utilised and the exposure to private assets falls below 100% if committed capital is not called. The OCR of 150% is based on the assumption that the funds on average will call $100\%/150\% = 66.7\%$ of the LP's commitments. Some fund managers may reinvest proceeds from early investments to finance subsequent deals or use subscription lines, which could bring this percentage further down. On the other hand, fund strategies where on average 80% of the capital will be called would require a lower OCR:

$$OCR = {100\%}\big/{80\%} = 125\%.$$

Here, funding risk, in this context also often referred to as 'commitment risk', arises from market distortions that lead to a mismatch between contributions to younger funds in the portfolio and the distributions the mature funds generate. Funding risk notably materialises in situations where exit markets are depressed and, therefore, funds do not repay at the expected rate anymore, which hinders the LP's ability to use reflows to pay capital calls.

The risk of not being able to respond to a capital call naturally increases when the liquid assets of the portfolio decrease. To manage this risk, many LPs rely on tracking the OCR. The view on OCRs has evolved over time. In the early 2000s and with limited experience, investors targeted much higher OCRs, sometimes even 200%.[4] A survey conducted by Singelton and Henshilwood (2003) concluded that 150% of the strategic asset allocation be a suitable target to aim for in terms of commitments. Meanwhile, the perils of over-committing became clearer, and Kazemi et al. (2016) suggest lower OCRs between 125% and 135% as market practice.

Higher OCRs only make sense initially during the ramp-up phase, when LPs aim to put as much capital to work as possible and accelerate the time it takes to hit the targeted allocation.

During the maintenance phase, LPs cannot sign for more than what is expected as returns from their existing portfolio. Consequently, the long-term average return of a portfolio of funds sets a ceiling on over-commitments. In the case of buyout funds, average returns are historically higher, most of the time, than those of VC funds where returns also tend to be more volatile and where liquidity often dries up over protracted periods. For VC-focused investment programmes, OCRs tend to be significantly lower than those for other private capital strategies.

Controlling allocations

To increase an allocation, an LP could do more commitments or increase the amounts that are committed to each fund. Net asset value (NAV) exposure and liquidity required or generated are interrelated. Commitments can be accelerated, leading to an increased NAV exposure, but also require liquidity for the coming capital calls. The portfolio can be turned into liquidity by decelerating commitments, but that, in return, results in a reduced exposure to private assets.

Fund sizes, and with the fund sizes also the minimum and/or maximum commitment thresholds the funds impose on their LPs, vary between vintages, and therefore, an LP may not be able to consistently implement an equal-weight commitment strategy where the same amount is committed to each fund. An equal-weight commitment strategy implicitly overweights smaller funds in the portfolio. LPs can also take the same share in each fund. This would overweight larger funds in their portfolio.

In fact, through this, the LP is also controlling the level of diversification of the portfolio created. For instance, an allocation could be reduced by doing fewer funds, leading to a more concentrated portfolio. Alternatively, an LP could commit less to each fund, which would maintain the portfolio's level of diversification. More importantly, this would keep the established relationships with GPs alive, which would be needed in case the allocation to private capital needs to be increased again.

SIMULATING THE PACING PLAN

When drawing up a pacing plan, LPs assess the impact of potential new commitments on reaching the set objectives. However, the resulting exposure to private assets can only be forecasted imprecisely, and the LP cannot quickly adjust it. Prior to the mid-1990s, institutional investors had relatively low allocations to alternative assets. Also, at this time, stock markets showed exceptionally strong performance and the investors' primary concern was building up these allocations and gaining access to private markets.

Ratio-based commitment rules

Under these circumstances, for increasing as well as maintaining the allocation to private assets, simple rules of thumb were sufficient. Fixed commitment strategies assume that the LP makes commitments of a constant size within a period, typically per annum, for example:

- Cardie et al. (2000) suggested commit half of the capital allocated to private assets each year,[5] a strategy that, while simple and easily applicable for ramping-up, does not take the LP's specific portfolio and her expectations into account.
- To reach a targeted NAV, Shen et al. (2020) proposed to determine the commitment amount at the beginning of each quarter by multiplying the total amount of uncommitted capital at the end of the prior period by a factor.
- Jeet (2020) differentiated uncommitted capital (i.e. resources available and not committed yet) and undrawn capital related to existing commitments. Here, a fraction of the uncommitted capital is committed every vintage, with increasing aggressiveness: 50% (base case), 75%, and 100%. For ramping up the allocation, this factor needs to be set as greater than 100%; if less, the portfolio will be maintained and spread over the vintage years. Here, it is assumed that the pool of uncommitted capital is continuously replenished by distributions from prior commitments, aiming to make the allocation to private capital self-contained.
- Brown et al. (2021) recommended as rule of thumb that for a steady-state portfolio diversified across vintage years, LPs should be committing about 20% of their target allocation each year.

This approach also extends to the over-commitments, where OCRs of between 120% and 140% have been touted as 'best practices', but experiences are mixed and suggest that relying on fixed OCR ratios is insufficient for controlling risks.

In addition to the fixed commitment strategies, Brown et al. (2021) examined a dynamic one that conditions commitments based on the funds' current NAVs and their expected cash flows.

Dynamic commitments

Dynamic commitment strategies, on the other hand, take various criteria, notably a portfolio's current NAVs, expected fund cash flows, and information on economic conditions into consideration. For example, an LP could use an adaptive programme such as in Nevins et al. (2004) that determines commitments based on historic fund cash flows, taking the current status of portfolio and the rate of return on public and on private assets into consideration.

Instead of relying on ratios, we extend this dynamic approach to commitment pacing. With tools developed, we do not need to use rules of thumb but can simulate the portfolio's future development and adjust the commitment plan.

PACING PLAN OUTCOMES

LPs do not only aim to control their exposure to private assets, but also want to assure a suitable level of diversification in various dimensions. Diversification over time is

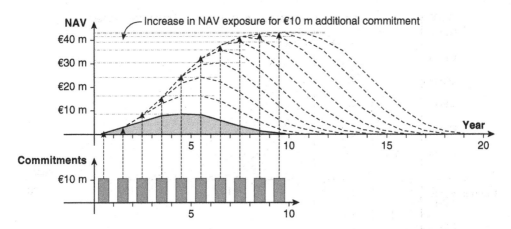

FIGURE 15.3 Equal commitments spread over 10 years (€100 m total commitment)

important in general, but in the context of commitment pacing, it is a major driver of cash-flow patterns and the resulting exposure. The critical spread over vintages is already assured by the very nature of commitment pacing.

In principle, LP can follow a 'slow and steady' approach to building up their allocation or attempt to reach their target as quickly as possible. Commitments should be consistent (see **Box 15.2**) and equally spread over vintage years, but this implies that the LP will take several years to reach a targeted allocation.

'Slow and steady'

According to Murphy (2007), with annual commitments of between 14% and 22% of a targeted allocation amount, LPs can reach this objective in about 10 years. In the example of **Figure 15.3**, 10 commitments of €10 million each spread over 10 years result in a peak allocation of less than €42 million (i.e. assuming that this would be the target allocation, requiring an annual commitment of 23% on average).

Accelerated pacing plan

Initially, most of the deviation from the target allocation comes from the need to get invested at all. The higher the steady-state NAV exposure sought, the longer it will take to build up the position. Larger positions require committing to more funds, which simply take time to find, and the committed capital is deployed over the funds' investment periods – there are opportunity costs associated with a slow build-up of a true allocation to private assets.

With a large initial commitment, this time can be shortened to six to seven years (see **Figure 15.4**), but this has the disadvantage that this creates concentrations in funds raised in the early years and puts the portfolio at risk should these funds underperform.[6]

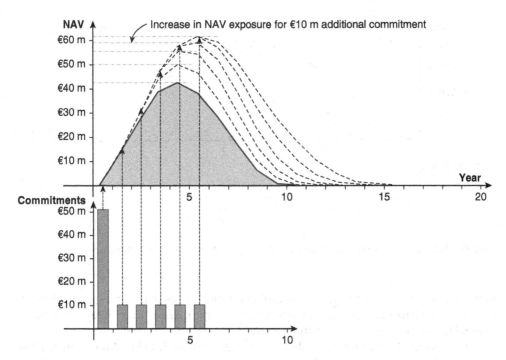

FIGURE 15.4 One large initial commitment to reach target exposure faster (€100 m total commitment)

In both cases, each additional commitment has a diminishing contribution to the portfolio's peak NAV exposure. The reason for this is that commitments are staggered over time, so that older funds are already liquidating their private assets and, as a consequence, their NAVs decline as well.

LIQUIDITY CONSTRAINTS

The main challenge of commitment pacing is finding the right balance between the time to reach a targeted exposure and the risk of overshooting the target or breaking liquidity limits.

Impact on cash-flow profile

The LP's liquidity requirements come from two directions: their assets, mainly comprising the portfolio of funds and the associated undrawn commitments on one side, and their schedule of liabilities on the other. Spreading commitments of €10 million per annum over 10 years is the base case we looked at before. It results in contributions as negative cash flows that on average do not exceed €10 million (see **Figure 15.5**).

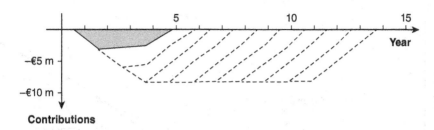

FIGURE 15.5 Aggregated contributions for equal commitments spread over 10 years

One large initial commitment is also, from the liquidity perspective, a more aggressive strategy and leads to an expected negative cash flow of nearly €15 million in year 4 before going down significantly. This strategy results in a less regular pace of commitments and resulting cash flows, and, consequently, a more volatile portfolio (see **Figure 15.6**).

Impact of commitment types

Though combining commitment types, LPs can manage their programme's cash-flow J-curve. **Figure 15.7** illustrates the different impacts of these building blocks on a pacing plan.

The reference point is the typical primary fund's cash-flow J-curve. Depending on the fund's style (specific to strategies, geographies, etc.), the contribution rates can look different. For VC funds, there tends to be a marked J-curve with the longest time horizons, while for other strategies, it typically is flatter and less pronounced. However, the strongest change in the J-curve comes from the main routes into private markets, i.e. funds focusing on co-investments and secondaries, and FOFs.

- For practical reasons, primary commitments will form the main components of a pacing plan. Secondaries and co-investments are assumed to be included at specific vehicles that essentially look like a primary commitment but show a different cash-flow pattern.

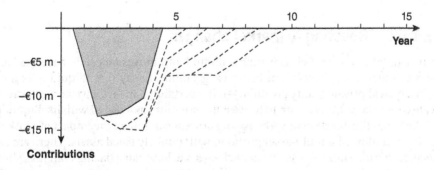

FIGURE 15.6 Aggregated contributions for one large initial commitment of €50 m; €10 m p.a. in year two to six

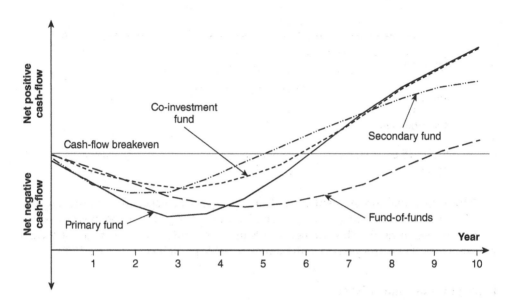

FIGURE 15.7   Cash-flow characteristics for different fund types (schematic)

- Co-investment funds tend to show a higher TVPI on realisation and an initially flatter J-curve. The cash-flow breakeven is comparable to that of the 'plain vanilla' funds.
- FOFs experience longer period for which net cash flows are negative, before eventually turning into a positive area. The typical FOFs tends to generate lower TVPIs compared to primary funds and has a significantly longer lifetime; on the other hand, it carries significantly less risk in terms of outcome ranges and randomness of cash flows.
- Secondary funds show the fastest cash-flow breakeven and thus also the highest IRR, which is their main attraction. However, they come with much lower multiples.

These patterns can be used to superposition J-curves for the different periods in the pacing plan.

Box 15.2.   Reacting to market changes

Private capital as an asset class is highly illiquid and moves at a slow pace. As ACG (2023) commented, it 'would not be an exaggeration to say that illiquidity is not a risk in a typical private equity portfolio—it is a certainty'. In fact, investors allocate to private capital because they aim to harvest the premium associated with its illiquidity.

The raises the question how the pacing process can reflect the impact of markets, also in the context of a multi-asset portfolio with publicly listed assets. There are two aspects to this question: across the asset classes, i.e. how can a pacing plan take short-term market swings into consideration, and within private assets – can LPs time the market and, for example, overweight better vintages?

MULTI-ASSET ALLOCATIONS

Maintaining pre-set allocation targets across multiple assets and keeping within set limits is an important part of an institutional investor's prudential apparatus. Either quarterly or annually, the market values of allocations, defined as the asset class's market value divided by the total portfolio's market value, are checked against these targets.

Practically, institutional investors find it difficult to keep a consistent exposure to private assets within a certain range, such as 15% to 20% bracket of the overall portfolio. Changing valuations on the traditional asset side, e.g. public equity or bonds, can lead to under-allocation or over-allocation to private capital within the total investment portfolio.

What stops institutional investors being consistent? Poor decision-making may occasionally be an issue, but there are also different dynamics in play. Many institutions invest in a collection of assets following a strategy defined as allocations like '40% equities, 30% bonds, 10% hedge funds, 10% private equity, and 10% infrastructure'. Following these rules implicitly let market quoted assets drive the portfolio dynamics.

A notorious example for the consequences is the so-called 'denominator effect', the typical impact that market downturns have on institutional portfolios. While the denominator (i.e. the total portfolio's value) shrinks, the numerator grows in relative terms: the NAVs reported by funds hardly change as write-downs in their valuations lag those of quoted asset classes. Even though nothing has really changed for the funds and capital continues to be deployed consistently, the percentage invested in private assets looks much higher than the targeted allocation. The problem with strict allocation targets is that the illiquidity of private capital is largely ignored, and reactions to this denominator effect are often improvised.

Occasionally investors, in line with their liquid assets losing value, aggressively write down their private assets, too, to be able to maintain their overall asset allocation. Often LPs freeze new commitments or even try to sell stakes in funds – over the short-to-medium term, this remains a very difficult task and usually only possible under highly unfavourable conditions, as secondary markets tend to dry up precisely when liquidity is needed. During downturns, secondaries regularly turn into a buyer's market.

Practitioners advice against selling down positions or reining in future commitments because public markets usually recover quicker than attempts to rebalance can take effect and outsized allocation tend to correct over the medium term.[7] Therefore, some LPs introduced 'grace periods' before a correction is supposed to take place.[8]

Also, LPs updated their asset allocation policies. In many cases, private equity, despite its fundamentally different dynamics, is lumped together with the public equity portfolio as one asset class 'equity' to avoid a premature sell-off.

Rebalancing to bring private assets in line with the denominator to a large degree is an act of self-harm. It is the result of overly rigorous application of allocation limits that are not appropriate for such crisis environments. Maybe investors are increasingly absorbing the lessons of past market crashes and have adjusted their internal rules. At least, a 2020 survey suggested that in reaction to the COVID-19 downturn, only 26% of investors were cutting their allocations to private equity.[9]

MARKET TIMING

Fund managers invest and divest the committed capital during the fund's lifetime at their own discretion. Jenkinson et al. (2022) found evidence that on average fund managers can create value by timing the financial markets. However, the LP's timing relates to their commitments and, therefore, cannot be precisely synchronised with the real investments in private assets. According to Brown et al. (2020), LPs can derive only 'modest gains, at best' from attempts to time the private equity market.

Timing the market is generally not seen as possible. LPs cannot predict which vintage year will be good, so it is important to consistently spread the portfolios over time. It is the fund managers who need flexibility regarding the private assets targeted and when to invest and divest. They are in a better position to time the market. If LPs try to time the market as well, the result is chaos.

CONSISTENT CAPITAL DEPLOYMENT

The illiquid nature of funds prevents tactical asset allocators from quickly increasing or decreasing allocations to private capital. When overshooting allocation targets, selling off fund stakes on the secondary market is difficult. When undershooting, due to the long lead times to source good opportunities, a quick scaling up to get back to the higher allocation target is impractical.

CalPERS head of private equity Greg Ruiz reflected on why its private capital investment programme has underperformed relative to peer benchmarks:[10] he identified the lack of consistent capital deployment and lack of strategic consistency as the main reasons. This behaviour contributed to the portfolio being concentrated in years when fund raising was booming and, in consequence, its lack of diversification.

The main lesson to be drawn from these observations is that LPs need to stay on course regardless of, largely short-term, swings in public and private markets. LPs should maintain a regular and consistent pacing of their commitments across the vintage years. Commitment pacing is not suitable for reacting to current market developments, but it is the most economical way for controlling allocations to private assets.[11]

MAINTENANCE PHASE

In a steady state, LPs in principle can aim for a constant target NAV (NAV focus) or for a liquidity focus, i.e. net zero cash-flow matching (CFM[12]), i.e. self-funding around a targeted allocation. In case of self-funding, distributions from older funds are used for paying the capital calls of younger funds.

This is managed through recommitments, where we need to take the uncertainty of future capital calls, distributions, and NAVs into account; exposure targets can only be reached and maintained within ranges and probability bands.

Recommitments

Distributions and maturing funds will reduce the exposure to private assets, requiring a recommitment strategy to new funds to maintain a targeted exposure going forward. When should new fund commitments be undertaken and for which size to achieve and to maintain a targeted allocation over an extended period, given that the cash inflows and outflows are (highly) uncertain?

A recommitment strategy requires assessing the current portfolio composition, maturity and return expectations to determine size and timing of future commitments approach. de Zwart et al. (2012) presented a first attempt relying on past portfolio development, aiming to maintain a stable exposure to private assets. Here, the level of new commitments in a given period depends on the current portfolio's characteristics, but do not take forecast for the funds' cash flows into account. Oberli (2015) extended this to multi-asset class portfolios including stocks and bonds.

Both approaches rely on handcrafted recommitment strategies. Future commitments are determined based on the ratio of NAV to NAV plus cash. If there is no cash, the ratio is one, and all what was distributed plus undrawn commitments for funds older than six years, i.e. after their investment period, is committed again. So far, only few works have been looking at such recommitment strategies needed for balancing several, often conflicting, investment objectives including performance, risk, and liquidity.

Target NAV

The target NAV aims to reach and maintain as exposure a targeted NAV, typically as percentage of an overall asset allocation. Various commitment and recommitment strategies have been looked at to achieve this objective. Shen et al. (2020) saw as drawback of the target NAV that it does not balance capital calls against realisations and thus affects the treasury part of the portfolio. **Figure 15.8** shows a simplistic pacing plan where

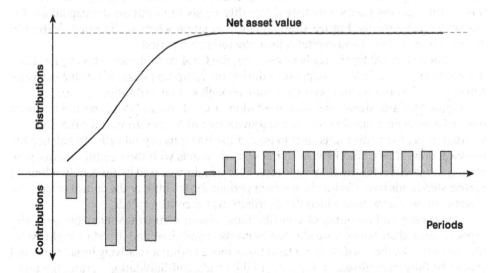

FIGURE 15.8 The Target NAV commitment strategy aims to reach and maintain a target NAV (example assumes positive growth rate)

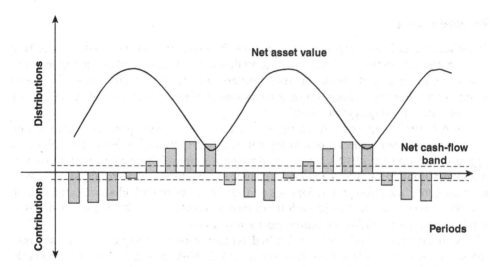

FIGURE 15.9   The Cash-Flow Matching commitment strategy aims keep the band for the port-folio's net cash flows close to zero (example assumes positive growth rate)

after 10 periods, a targeted absolute allocation is reached and kept at this level. As the funds are modelled with a constant growth rate of 5% per annum, from the 8th period onwards, this portfolio generates positive cash flows, which in later periods exceed what is needed for recommitments and thus can be used to fund other activities.

Cash-flow matching

As alternative to the target NAV approach, Shen et al. (2020) proposed a CFM commitment strategy. CFM is an investment approach that closely aligns a portfolio's cash flows with a pacing plan's anticipated liquidity needs to minimise the capital for the undrawn commitments. **Figure 15.9** shows the situation where realisations received in one period are used to fund capital calls in the following period.

At Shen et al. (2020) themselves observed, the CFM commitment strategy has limi-tations. In any case, CFM is not possible during the ramp-up phase, where the exposure still needs to be built up and become mature enough so that realisations set in.

Figure 15.9 also shows the main limitation of CFM. As an NAV exposure has been reached and again assuming a constant growth rate of 5% per annum for the funds, at a certain time, the realisations start to exceed the previous capital calls. To balance the two cash flows, LPs would have to sit out several periods with their commitments, gen-erating a jo-jo effect for the NAV exposure. This is mainly caused by the fact that limited partnership funds have distinct investment periods for the bulk of the contributions and divestment periods within which the distributions are concentrated.

The timing and amounts of contributions remain comparatively stable over vin-tages, whereas distributions are affected by market conditions and therefore highly vola-tile. Realistically, the portfolio's net cash flows move within a relatively broad band and cannot be fully neutralised. In fact, due to the funds' self-liquidating nature, the expo-sure to private assets would oscillate and a vintage diversification cannot be maintained.

This is clearly undesirable as now vintages and with this also some targeted funds would be skipped, and the portfolio becomes more concentrated in other vintages. For private capital allocations, a CFM strategy therefore is a more theoretical option.

ADDITIONAL OBJECTIVES AND CONSTRAINTS

Achieving the full potential of an allocation to private assets is very challenging. Reaching an allocation target is a process that stretches over years. The speed of change – or rather the lack thereof – is a problem.

This is complicated by the fact that other objectives, such as achieving diversification over different investment types, geographies, industry sectors, and strategies, are important as well (see **Box 15.3**). Specific concerns create constraints, such as upper limits on the total exposure to private assets. Also, passing on high-quality managers because they do not fit the allocation creates an opportunity loss. Such situations result in a return for the portfolio that is inferior to that which could be achieved without any constraints.

Commit to high-quality funds

The private assets' high expected returns can only be achieved by competent fund managers. The quality of the fund management teams is critical to investment success and therefore is the overriding criterion, arguably more important than other considerations.

Given the typical fundraising cycles, it is realistic to assume that LPs often know which fund management firms will be raising new funds and when. But practically, their knowledge will be incomplete, as, due to the nature of private capital, not all future funds are known or accessible. Also, funds typically do not close and start investing exactly as planned and often cannot accommodate the size of commitment the LP is aiming for. If the planned timing for commitments is observed too strictly, investors may miss good opportunities with some of their high-performing existing fund managers when they return to the market earlier or later than foreseen.

Moreover, even if a fund manager is identified and foreseen in the pacing plan, there may be new and potentially superior fund managers out in the market when the time arrives. A common criticism of pacing plans is that they may sacrifice quality for meeting an allocation target. When trying to rigidly stick to the plan, the investor would be tempted to accept lower quality managers and thus lower realised return in later years.

Building and maintaining relationships with management firms requires respecting their fundraising calendars. Skipping a fund that does not fit the pacing plan might limit the LP's future access to that fund manager. Finding a replacement and developing a relationship with a new fund manager can require a substantial effort. Instead, LPs could commit smaller amounts to maintain the option to continue investing with a known GP.

Achieve intra-asset diversification

Apart from the fund manager's quality, opportunities are typically evaluated based on size, sector, stage, geography, and, importantly, vintage year. How the portfolio of funds

Box 15.3   Balanced score cards

LPs are faced with additional and conflicting objectives, particularly when dealing with portfolios across assets and different short- and long-term dynamics. Combining several metrics into a single objective function does not work under these circumstances. Instead, balanced scorecards (BSCs) are used in management decision and control processes to assist with the balancing of multiple and competing objectives. Several key constraints prevent the institutional investor from achieving optimal performance. A BSC requires key performance indicators (KPIs) that reflect priorities and trade-offs and are measurable, relevant, and, most of all, actionable. Previous chapters have introduced such KPIs that are important for an LP, notably commitment efficiency (CE), exposure efficiency (XE), Sortino ratio, OCR, capital-call-at-risk (CCaR), and cash-flow-at-risk (CFaR).

However, managing a pacing plan against such a BSC is largely based on trial-and-error. An improvement to this unsatisfying state of affairs is an artificial-intelligence-based approach. Due to the commitment pacing's strong similarities to a control system, in Kieffer et al. (2023) we proposed a multi-objective reinforcement learning (RL) for 'learning how to recommit'.[13] We prototyped an RL algorithm to be applied to portfolios of private equity funds with the aim to solve the recommitment problem, using proximal policy optimisation (PPO) for a neural network.

This algorithm was inspired by biology and aimed to learn how to size and time recommitments through evolution. It generated a set of different equations for controlling the recommitments. These equations were expressed as a syntax tree and two operations applied to it many times: 'cross-over' for exploitation, procreating successful sub-trees as traits and 'mutation' to explore other traits. We then simulated portfolios of funds to train the RL model and used a PPO algorithm to discover reliable recommitment policies – an approach that is attractive as it avoids the burden to compute all state values to solve an optimisation problem.

The result was a policy expressed as human-comprehensible equation. A comparison to other policy approaches, such as the rules proposed by de Zwart et al. (2012), suggested that the trained policy was able to achieve high target allocation while bounding the risk of being overinvested and protecting LPs from the risk of defaulting on their commitments.

Secondary sell-offs actually suggest a failure of commitment pacing. In fact, the commitment pacing framework proposed by Shen et al. (2020) specified a penalty in the form of a subjective severity value to each type of liquidity event, the highest reserved for the illiquid NAVs that are traded on the secondary market. These penalties are ranked from 1 to 3 and, therefore, may not reflect the true relative 'damage'.

is diversified over these dimensions controls the risk/return profile of the allocation to private capital.

During the ramp-up period, the usual objective is to build up an allocation as quickly as possible. Clearly, the XE comes at the expense of CE.

The desire to reach a target asset allocation as quickly as possible is in conflict with the need to achieve diversification over time, so as not to risk becoming concentrated in a single sub-standard vintage. A minimum number of vintages is not only required to reduce this capital risk but also to smooth out cash-flow patterns for mitigating the funding risk associated with extreme capital calls. Like in the case of access to high-quality fund managers, for a desired portfolio composition, it may well be that no opportunities come up that would fit the allocation or that such opportunities are not accessible.

Minimise opportunity costs

For a young programme, the main objective is to meet exposure targets and minimise the capital not invested in private assets. The pacing model needs to inform us how much of the undrawn commitments need to be held in reserve in the form of low-yielding treasury assets to meet the future capital calls. The flip side of keeping these opportunity costs low is an increased funding risk in situations where liquid assets are insufficient when fund managers call capital for investing in private assets.

Instead of keeping undrawn commitments in cash only or investing everything in public equity, treasury assets should be tiered, so that the risk and investment horizon of each tier is aligned with the pacing of commitments it is intended to support.

Satisficing portfolios

How can we assess whether this is a 'good' or a 'bad' plan? A plan would certainly be unsuitable if it was based on unrealistic assumptions – for instance based on too high or too low expectations for the fund's growth, capital call rates, and realisations – and thus having no reliable reference for monitoring the investment programme's progress. Plans would also be considered as deficient if they:

- turn too little of the resources allocated to private assets into active commitments and subsequently into real investments in private markets, and thus incurring opportunity costs for the uncalled capital;
- run out of liquidity when capital is called and thus incur costs as other assets need to be sold off on short notice or alternative sources must be found. Unless the LP puts all resources dedicated to investing in private assets into cash, the probability of this happening will not be zero, but it needs to be weighted against the associated penalties;
- do not result the sought underlying private asset portfolio structure, e.g. not being well diversified (unevenly, over-diversified) or being too concentrated.

It is important to be flexible and allow for an opportunistic element outside of the model's constraints. Also taking the many, often non-quantifiable, trade-offs into consideration, with parameters that rely on quite heroic assumptions, an optimisation in a mathematical sense does not appear to be meaningful. Instead, we aim for satisficing, i.e. searching through the available alternatives until an acceptability threshold is met. In this respect, using a commitment pacing tool for engineering a portfolio of funds is more art than science, as the title of this book suggests, and has been viewed as such.[14]

CONCLUSION

The commitment pacing model needs to bring several tools together, fund forecasts, phases of the investment programme, the steady-state objectives, and the strategies with which they can be achieved. The result of this process is a plan and a proposed commitment budget to approach and maintain target allocations to the private assets.

However, no plan survives the first contact with the market. To deal with the unexpected developments, investment managers need to ask themselves 'what happens if' this scenario will materialise or not materialise? Stress scenarios are an indispensable part of a commitment pacing tool, to perform sensitivity analyses to test the effects of changing conditions on the portfolio's behaviour.

NOTES

1. See https://dictionary.cambridge.org/dictionary/english/pacing, [accessed 6 October 2022]
2. See Abrdn (2019).
3. See Brown et al. (2021).
4. See Mathonet and Meyer (2007).
5. See also Takahashi and Alexander (2002).
6. See Murphy (2007): 'It should also be noted that first-time investors in private equity often do not have the ability to access the top funds in the asset class, thus concentrating commitments in the developing years of a program may bias the portfolio composition away from top performers.'
7. See, for example, Samuels (2022).
8. See Murphy et al. (2022).
9. See McNulty (2020).
10. See Mendoza (2020).
11. See, for instance, Aalbers et al. (2019) and Samuels (2022).
12. See Shen et al. (2020).
13. Thomas Meyer co-authored this research paper.
14. See Samuels (2022).

CHAPTER 16

Stress Scenarios

A stress scenario is a collection of assumptions about potential future economic conditions over a time horizon relevant for a pacing plan. Also, incomplete data, poor data quality, and limitations of forecast models suggest applying stresses. 'Stress' is usually associated with adverse events, but generally it is a tool for sensitivity analysis, which allows evaluating the impact of varying assumptions and explaining the associated market risks and opportunities.

MAKE FORECASTS MORE ROBUST

Stresses are always applied to unbiased model projections. The analysis can give insights into how a portfolio will respond to future changes in market conditions over which limited partners (LPs) have no control and that could threaten the success of the investment strategy. Stress scenarios serve to make forecasts more robust as they reflect a much wider variation of possible futures and situations that have not necessarily occurred in the past. They simulate crises as well as boom periods with stress levels reflecting the degree of uncertainty.

Communication

The purpose of stress scenarios is not coming up with unrealistically conservative assumptions with catastrophic effects on the investment strategy that would render the exercise meaningless anyway, but rather to test the impact of changes in input parameters. Scenario analysis considers expert opinion and works even when there are no statistical observations for inferring valid likelihoods.

A stress scenario is not what is expected, but it should have a material probability to occur. The impact of possible events on investment objectives can be made transparent well in advance. Playing around with stress scenarios helps to critically questioning the validity of assumptions and to shaping the overall picture that is evolving. The important levers that determine the portfolio strategy can be revealed.

Another important aspect is a reverse stress test where several scenarios are applied simultaneously to assess how sensitive a portfolio is to changes in economic conditions.

Such a reverse stress is essentially a pre-mortem where an investment team imagines that the envisaged strategy has failed and then works backward to determine what potentially could have caused this. The objective here is to be more imaginative about the future and think about an array of probable events that in combination could lead to 'doomsday'. Hence, stress scenarios have an important role in encouraging conversations about the way forward and in building trust through more effective communications.[1]

Specific to portfolio

Historical events or other institutions' experiences may not be a suitable reference for comparison, as the LP's portfolio will have a different composition and the LP needs to consider the impact on the current and planned portfolio holdings and exposures and their sensitivity to fundamental drivers of risk and return. Unbalanced portfolios, for instance, with few funds and different commitment sizes, are prone to more extreme behaviour than portfolios that are evenly spread over vintages, strategies, geographies etc. Stress scenarios help us to determine where to focus. It is very likely that there will be scenarios that do not have a strong impact, and vice versa. Changing the portfolio's structure and concentrations can make it more or less sensitive to adverse scenarios or better positioned to exploit opportunities.

IMPACT OF 'BLACK SWANS'

When drafting a pacing plan, LPs will be concerned about the impact of a potential 'Black Swan' that could make all their efforts futile. Such events come as surprise, making them exceedingly rare from a probabilistic standpoint, and have a major effect, often in the form of a market crisis. Referring, among others, to the Asian Financial Crisis (1997–1998), and the Global Financial Crisis (GFC, 2007–2008) as examples, Reinhart and Rogoff (2009) describe the 'this-time-is-different syndrome', referring to the unrealistic optimism that afflicts investors and policymakers before such bubbles finally burst.

Usually, the unrealistic optimism turns quickly into a pessimism that, at least as far as private capital funds are concerned, seems to be equally misplaced. Regarding the financial returns, these crises and other 'Black Swans', like the dot-com crash, apparently had no discernible impact on outcome ranges (see **Figure 16.1**).

For funds that were raised during a crisis, average return in most cases did not go down; sometimes, they even went up. This should be expected, as because of LPs holding back fewer funds come to the market, they close later and subsequently face less competition and find better opportunities.

Vintages of funds being raised three to four years before a crisis should be exposed to it most, as their investments in private assets will be at their peak. However, also here no clear pattern emerges. Even if there is a downward pressure on the net asset values (NAVs), there is also sufficient time (more than five years) for the funds to mature, the market to recover, and the fund managers finding a better exit window.

NAVs of funds close to maturity with exits scheduled already should be strongly affected by a market downturn, but on the other hand, the bulk of their private assets

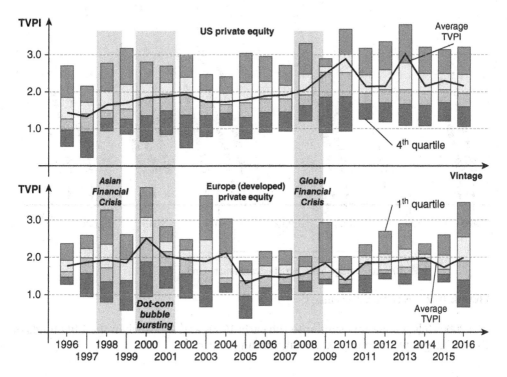

FIGURE 16.1 Quartile ranges for mature funds, by vintage year peer-group (source: Cambridge Associates)

will already have been realised and little of their portfolio remains that could materially change the fund's total value to paid-in capital (TVPI) on maturity.

From 1960 to 2020, the S&P 500 dropped more than 30% seven times,[2] i.e. on average every 8.6 years. Historically, next to every fund in its more than 10-year lifetime was exposed to at least two US presidential elections, recessions, wars, acts of terrorism, and epidemic outbreaks – in other words to at least one and sometimes more 'Black Swans' (often accompanied by '25-sigma market drops'[3]) (see **Figure 16.2**). The set-up of funds with their long lifetimes and the uncalled capital underwritten by deep-pocketed LPs has evolved to withstand such events.[4] As argued by Cornelius et al. (2011), funds are subject to structural illiquidity, thus offering investors a risk premium. The limited partnership effectively shields the private assets held from the financial market's vicissitudes and makes long-term investments value creating.

Interest rates and inflationary periods

Similar observations apply to other economic stress scenarios. Barrington et al. (2009) analysed fund performance data since 1986 and found no correlation between inflation and returns for leveraged buyout (LBO) funds. In line with the recommendations of the previously mentioned research reports, these authors' conclusion regarding the attractiveness of the environment at the time remained unchanged – in their assessment, the

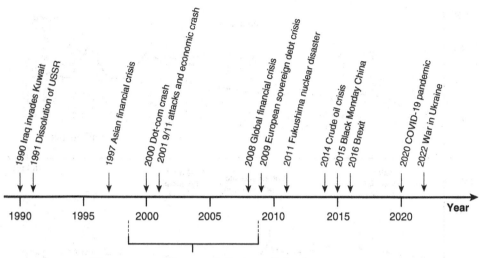

FIGURE 16.2   'Black swan' events

late 2000s felt remarkably similar to the early 1990s and 2000s when the LBO funds of those vintages went on to produce outstanding returns.

MODELLING CRISES

As far as we can rely on private market statistics, there is little impact of crises on the fund's performance outcomes over the long term, at least on the portfolio level. But how do crises show and how can stress scenarios model this? It is instructive to look at the recent market crises – dot-com bubble, the GFC, and COVID-19 – that were expected to fundamentally alter the private market landscape and what LPs observed.

Delay of new commitments

During the GFC, many LPs feared to become cash constrained as pensions and allow-ances needed to be paid, whereas there were the remaining commitments supposed to be called by the fund managers.[5] Under these circumstances and in response to the unanticipated liquidity shock, many LPs delayed new commitments. Unsurprisingly, there was not only a slowdown in commitments to new funds but fund holding periods became longer as well.

Changes in contribution rates

Capital calls as well as realisations tend to decline during market downturns as not only LPs but investors in general become stricter regarding their due diligence and potential sellers more reluctant to transact at close to bottom prices.

During the dot-com bubble, venture capitalists invested large amounts into Internet companies. When investors began questioning the viability of this sector, the bubble finally deflated and few new investments were undertaken, as evidenced by the sharp decline in

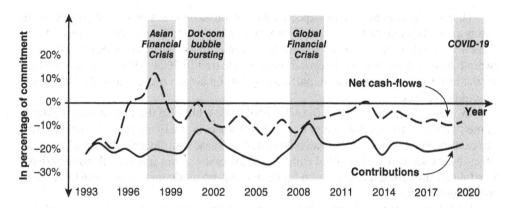

FIGURE 16.3 Contributions (averaged across 1–4 years old buyout funds in a given vintage year), netted against distributions (averaged across 7–13 year old buyout funds in a given vintage year). Source: Cambridge Associates, based on Murphy (2022).

contribution rates (see **Figure 16.3**). The GFC showed a similar pattern. In its beginning, LPs were suffering declines in value of their liquid assets and struggling to meet capital called from the private equity funds. In this situation, large institutional investors like CalPERS were even reported to have asked fund managers to delay capital calls.[6] Also, some firms themselves reduced the size of their funds or asked for fewer contributions.[7]

Schneider et al. (2022) analysed Preqin data (mainly North America) from 1992 to 2020, incorporating funds with at least five years of data, and found evidence for timing and sizing of capital calls being correlated with financial market movements. For private equity and private debt capital call rates, the authors found a slightly positive relationship to public market returns (a 0.33 correlation for debt and 0.46 for equity).

This pattern changes, however, as a crisis is prolonging. Contributions rise again, often significantly, for various reasons. Fund managers try to support their remaining promising investments. Because it is difficult to access external funding under depressed market conditions, the 'dry powder' of remaining commitments becomes the main source of financing. Thus, with a delay of two to three years, capital calls tend to accelerate and catch-up with the historical contribution rates.

Post-COVID-19, Murphy et al. (2022) reported that at a time when the crisis abated, a historically very high 40% of dry powder was in funds that were two to five years old, i.e. funds that were approaching the end of their investment period. The need to put capital at work quickly could have negative implications: pressured buyers focus at spending equity, thus paying higher multiples, reducing leverage, and syndicating less.[8] On the other hand, as the market is recovering, fund manager may be well placed to acquire private assets at more attractive valuations. Funds with adequate liquidity during down markets were found to harvest a significant return premium.[9] The pick-up in contributions later in these crises (as shown in **Figure 16.3**) is consistent with these observations.

Changes in distributions

During the GFC, an illustrative portfolio of private equity funds showed a contraction of distributions by 65%, while contributions decreased by 20% relative to the forecasts under normal market conditions.[10]

This is a development to be expected during a market crisis where valuations for all assets are collapsing, but in 2012 this impact was just over a relatively short term. Here, the same sample of private equity funds had caught up and its cash returns as well as its overall performance was well beyond what was feared in 2009.[11] Exits are also affected by the interest rate environment, particularly for the largest transactions that often rely on public listings.[12]

In crises, there is a shortfall in cash distributions, but also the contributions usually come to a standstill, so that the net cash-flow impact is relatively mild. However, there are caveats. For mature funds, realisations will decrease significantly. This decline is not offset by the slowdown in capital calls, so in this case the net impact will be negative.[13] Portfolios comprising mainly young funds in ramp-up mode may experience lower than usual net cash flows.

Cash-flow patterns also change over time, e.g. the downside scenarios observed during the GFC did not materialise during the COVID-19 crisis, where it looked quite different. Here, some portfolios even gained – with a kind of 'M&A boom' in various sectors like food delivery and online mail order – while notably travel and leisure were hit hard.

NAV impact and secondary transactions

When the market drops 30% or more, 'playing it safe' to avoid losses appears to be the only rational strategy, resulting in similar patterns as market participants follow the same instincts. The immediate impact of depressed markets is on valuations. This is often accompanied by a regulatory backlash, leading to punitive risk weights for alternative investments. Investment boards become concerned about risks. Under these circumstances, some LPs try to sell off stakes in funds on the secondary market, and secondaries become attractive for buyers. While this reaction is understandable, there could be no worse time than during a large market decline – 'exactly when one would want to put committed capital to work'.[14] Other LPs get concerned about the denominator effect and aggressively write down the private assets valuations to avoid the need of selling them off.

According to Gottschalg (2020), two observations during the GFC stand out: firstly, the shortfall in NAV amounted to only 4% relative to the forecasted NAV. Secondly, this impact was relatively short term in nature. In fact, the 2012 figures showed that the same sample of funds had caught up and that their investment returns were well beyond what was predicted for 2009. The funds experienced a longer J-curve but that on aggregate they eventually moved back into positive performance territory.

Lessons

A key lesson from the GFC period is the need for a consistent approach to committing.[15] As one representative from a pension fund observed in a roundtable discussion, in hindsight, institutional investors in private equity funds should have committed more in 2009/2010. There was little funding available at that moment, so if LPs were seeking access to funds and strategies, they would have found that very few funds were able to facilitate an orderly close, and these funds therefore faced less competition for investment opportunities afterwards. When the investment pace rebounded just after the crisis, the vintage year 2010 turned out very well. This anecdotal evidence suggests that LPs should not overreact to relatively short-term market developments.

Robinson and Sensoy (2016) looked at funds that called capital in down markets. They found that such funds perform about 36% better over their life in absolute terms and about 15% better in terms of public market equivalent (PME) performance. LPs who stayed the course and continued committing were able to benefit from above-average returns when the markets eventually recovered.

Making a portfolio safer by reducing exposure to illiquid assets seems to be the right response during a crisis, but choosing safety can be a mistake for long-term investors. Looking at stress scenarios that are appropriate for the prevailing market conditions can help LPs to get a more realistic look at the consequences of crises.

BUILDING STRESS SCENARIOS

Rating agencies test the robustness of their models for portfolios of private equity funds through various sensitivity analyses, notably increases in return volatility, longer/shorter fund lifetimes, earlier/longer contributions, later/lower distributions, longer drawdowns and lower distributions combined, and changes in interest and foreign exchange (FX) rates.[16] When looking at pacing plans, the following questions stand out for assessing factors that drive variations and where analysts want to flex their assumptions:

- What market environment will the portfolio be exposed to? Past is not future, so to what degree are past performance outcomes indicative for the scenarios that should be addressed?
- How will the outcome of the individual funds be affected, taking their historic development so far, their stage in the lifetime, their exposure to foreign currencies, and their chosen set-ups into account?
- What impact do dependencies have between the funds across their various diversification dimensions on the portfolio's outcomes and its extremes?
- How are cash-flow patterns affected by market changes and what impact does this have on the portfolio's liquidity?

Here, two approaches to flexing assumptions are considered. The first technique is running a range of sensitivity analyses on key input parameters[17] and/or applying transformations to the forecast models' results. These results are generated mainly through a Monte Carlo simulation (MCS). The second technique controls how the samples for the simulation are generated, i.e. by overweighting or underweighting specific favourable or unfavourable scenarios. This technique is applied to fund grades, their dependencies, and to replaying the market.

MARKET REPLAY

'The COVID-19 pandemic sent shock waves through the world economy and triggered the largest global economic crisis in more than a century'.[18] At the beginning of this

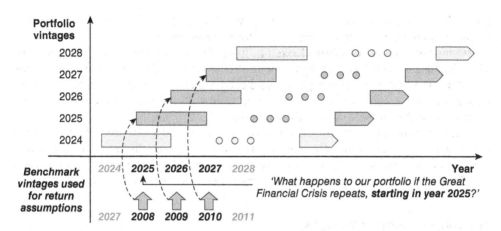

FIGURE 16.4 Replay of Great Financial Crisis

crisis and absent of a crystal ball, a reasonable way of looking at how this could unfold would have been to look at a comparable situation: for instance, what would happen to an LP's portfolio if the GFC repeats – an economic downturn of comparable severity, judged at the time to be the 'worst [. . .] in the U.S. since the Great Depression'.[19]

Any crisis features close similarities to earlier ones, which suggests that replaying them on the LP's current portfolio structure, with its different exposures to strategies, geographies, sectors, and fund ages, be a powerful way of understanding its vulnerabilities. Such a replay connects with decision-makers as such scenarios will not appear to be farfetched and unrealistic.

What happened in the past, while not being a perfect indicator for the future, provides insights into how a portfolio may react to similar events should they repeat in the future (see **Figure 16.4**).

There are many market factors that came into play during a historic period that are not all known and understood. Using private market data that were influenced by these periods can recreate these market conditions (see **Table 16.1**).

Not every crisis is a repeat of a previous one that can be explained by a replay story. Is the situation really comparable? Any analogy will be controversial and may even result in complacency ('this clearly never happened'). One way of stressing this additionally is simulating longer periods where conditions of historical crises continue to hold. Also, it makes sense to define hypothetical scenarios and assess the impact of multiple variables in combination to show the range of outcomes that could occur.

VARYING OUTCOMES

During market downturns, investors get worried that the reported valuations – for instance, due to delays – do not reflect the true situation. The LP would like to put stresses on current valuations and, implicitly and probably more relevant, performance

TABLE 16.1 Definition of vintage-year-specific market periods

Vintage year	Strategy	Geography	Industry	Market period
. . .	. . .	. . .	. . .	. . .
2000	Venture Capital	US	Internet	Dot-com bust
2001	Venture Capital	US	Internet	Dot-com bust
2002	Venture Capital	US	Internet	Dot-com bust
2003	Venture Capital	US	Internet	Dot-com bust
. . .	. . .	. . .	. . .	. . .
2008		Worldwide		Global Financial Crisis
2009		Worldwide		Global Financial Crisis
2010		Worldwide		Global Financial Crisis
. . .	. . .	. . .	. . .	. . .
2008		Eurozone		Medium inflation
2021		Eurozone		High inflation
2022		Eurozone		High inflation
2023		Eurozone		High inflation
. . .	. . .	. . .	. . .	. . .

outcomes. An obvious sensitivity analysis to apply is changing the fund's forecasted TVPIs on maturity upwards or downwards. For doing this, the portfolio needs to be split into an invariable past and future exposures and cash flows that are to be scaled and can be subjected to stresses.

Older funds with realisations and closer to maturity can be assumed as less exposed to changes in market dynamics than younger funds. Fitch considers stresses on the funds' performance, e.g. assuming returns to have deteriorated to third or fourth quartile levels, which negatively affects their projected distributions and other performance measures.[20] While easy to implement, it is difficult to apply this stress consistently across the portfolio. Assuming a fourth quartile level will not make sense anymore if a fund has already generated a realisation multiple that puts it in into, say, the second TVPI quartile.

Instead, using the fund grading methodology allows not only doing this consistently but would also work with realistic return figures. The fund expectation and risk grades are a function of quantitative and qualitative scores. Quantitative scores reflect a fund's historical cash flows that cannot be stressed any longer, and its NAV that can be subjected to reductions in, say, 10%, 20%, and 30% steps, as suggested by Fitch Ratings.[21] This in combination with notching qualitative scores downwards or upwards for the expectation grade models a decreasing or, respectively, increasing probability of a fund reaching a set return target.

Depending on the dimensions assessed, qualitative scores can also have an impact on the funds' risk grades, with downward notches corresponding to an increase in volatility of outcomes. The qualitative scoring also relates to the GPs' quality, evidenced by their track records in the fund types that are represented in the LP's portfolio. Moreover, it can capture the LP's own due diligence standards and manager selection skills and subject these assumptions to stresses.[22]

Foreign exchange rates

Also, increased volatility in currency markets is likely to have an impact on the valuations. To assess the outcome's sensitivity to different currencies, a cash-flow-based approach is the best-suited methodology, as shifts in currency pairs lead to upward and downward shifts in contributions and distributions.[23] This is not about trying to predict future FX rates. Rather, a suitable way of looking at this would be to replay market periods with their specific exchange rate fluctuation patterns. For funds, cash flows follow a specific pattern, e.g. investment periods with predominantly inflows and divestment periods with more and higher outflows. Here, exchange rate fluctuations do not necessarily offset each other, and their long-term trend can have a significant negative as well as a positive impact.

The impact on outcomes of taking on exchange rate risk is not necessarily negative. Essentially, a foreign currency can be seen as one of several assets comprising the LP's portfolio. Depending on to what degree the timing of cash flows to and from the funds are correlated with FX movements, the impact of committing to funds in various currencies can be beneficial for the portfolio's risk and return as well as its liquidity profile. Attempts to time the market increase the dependency between FX rates and cash flows and can have a negative impact on the portfolio's risk and return profile.

A sensitivity analysis would consider to what degree fund managers succeed in timing cash flows with an advantageous exchange rate. Such an analysis would assess the impact of allocating a specific FX rate to given cash flow. The base case is assuming no timing skills, i.e. randomly picking the FX rate within the given time interval and applying it to the cash flow.

Timing skills assume that the fund manager is able to pick the best FX rate and day with a set level of skills. This could be modelled by moving cash flows within a time window and then applying the prevailing FX rate. Zero skill would describe the situation where a fund manager consistently picks the worst FX rate, whereas a perfect skill of one implies that the cash flow is timed with the best FX rate within the time window.

VARYING PORTFOLIO DEPENDENCIES

A widely used sensitivity analysis is examining the effects of committing to fewer or more funds per vintage year.[24] However, this is not the only impact diversification, or lack thereof, can have. During a severe market crisis, it can no longer be assumed that within a portfolio the dependencies between fund cash flows and their performance outcomes remain unaffected. What happens if a large part of the portfolio starts to move in sync? Assessing this impact requires increasing or decreasing the dependencies between funds and the dependency of the cash flows across the portfolio.

Increasing and decreasing outcome dependencies

The approach to modelling diversification assumes that under increasing market stress, the funds in the portfolio form clusters and that these clusters grow in steps. The example in **Figure 16.5** shows a portfolio that concentrates from 10 independent funds to one cluster in steps at these cluster points: $c_0 = 0$, $c_1 = 0.25$, $c_2 = 0.5$, $c_3 = 0.75$, and $c_4 = 1$.

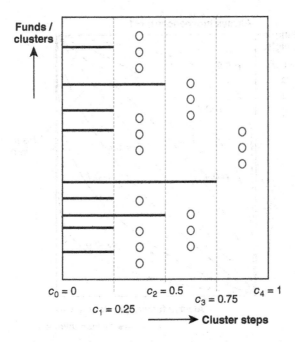

FIGURE 16.5   Decreasing / increasing dependencies between funds

In the MCS, an increasing dependency is modelled through generating more samples for steps where the portfolio is concentrated in few clusters. For the example, the extreme case is all samples being assigned to the last step where one cluster – where all funds change in sync into the same direction – only remains.

Weights are set for a given stress level $0 \leq s \leq 1$ for the market and a stress factor $-1 \leq r \leq 1$, with $r = 1$ describing a portfolio of funds that are independent under any stress level and $r = -1$ a portfolio of funds that are always fully dependent.

$$
w(s,r) =
\begin{cases}
s^{(1-r)} & \text{if } r > 0 \\
1 & \text{if } r = 0 \\
1-(1-s)^{(1+r)} & \text{if } r < 0.
\end{cases}
$$

$r = 0$ and $w(s,0) = s$ reflects the neutral scenario, where higher stresses are becoming increasingly unlikely, as described by a straight-line schedule. This schedule can be 'bent' by applying the stress factor r (see **Figure 16.6** and **Table 16.2**).[25]

$$
W_{i,r} =
\begin{cases}
\dfrac{\left(1-w(c_i,r)\right)+\left(1-w(c_{i-1},r)\right)}{2} * \left(c_i - c_{i-1}\right) & \text{if } r \geq 0 \\[4mm]
\dfrac{w(c_i)+w(c_{i-1})}{2} * \left(c_i - c_{i-1}\right) & \text{if } r < 0.
\end{cases}
$$

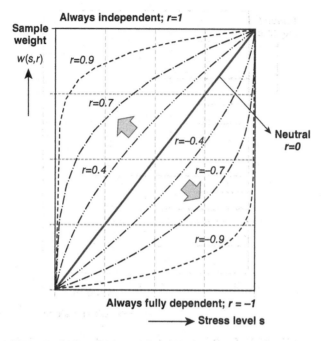

FIGURE 16.6 Controlling sampling in line with stress factors

TABLE 16.2 Sample weight schedule $w(s, r)$

Cluster step	0.25	0.50	0.75
$r = 1$	1	1	1
$r = 0.7$	0.66	0.81	0.92
$r = 0$	0.25	0.50	0.70
$r = -0.7$	0.08	0.19	0.34
$r = -1$	0	0	0

Assuming a sample size *Sample* = 1000 gives the following schedule with which samples are allocated to the respective clusters, for *n* cluster steps (see **Table 16.3**).

TABLE 16.3 Sample per cluster step $\dfrac{W_{k,r}}{\sum_{i=1}^{n} W_{i,r}} * Sample$

Cluster step	0–0.2	0.2–0.5	0.5–0.8	0.8–1
$r = 1$	1000	0	0	0
$r = 0.7$	603	238	122	37
$r = 0$	438	313	188	63
$r = -0.7$	37	122	238	603
$r = -1$	0	0	0	1000

Increasing and decreasing cash-flow dependencies

We cannot assume that the timing of cash flows from and to different funds that are active at the same time is independent. However, there tend to be many realisations in some periods and few in others. IPOs are avoided under depressed market conditions, while buoyant markets encourage companies to seek a public listing and investors to back the IPO.

A dependency between cash flows across funds can be modelled by simplifying an algorithm for the so-called 'gravitational clustering', an idea first proposed by Wright (1977). This is treating cash flows as 'planets' with masses and make them interact through 'gravitational forces'. The planets symbolise data points and are merged in several iterative steps until one large planet remains as the only cluster.

The stress scenario considers pairwise distances between the funds' individual cash flows and the total cash flows aggregated over the entire portfolios of funds that represent the clusters. Under increasing stress, it is assumed that the cash flows attract each other. The 'gravitational pull' between a cluster and the cash-flow 'planet' depends on the sum of their sizes (i.e. the 'mass') and the time interval that separates them as 'distance'. Dividing the 'mass' by the 'distance' determines the 'attraction', i.e. how far the smaller cash flow needs to be moved closer to the larger.

To apply this idea requires some tweaks. The stress is applied in iterations. In each iteration, first the 'attraction' is calculated. In the second step, it is determined which direction the 'attraction' takes, and the smaller cash flow is moved accordingly. Depending on whether inflows or outflows, the cash flows are either moved forward (more contributions being called earlier) or backwards (more distributions being delayed). Note that it is not possible that one fund's cash flows move before its inception date or that the fund's cash flows are moved to a period after its lifetime has already ended.

Here, the stress factor is defined as a number $r = 0, 1, 2\ldots$ that relates to the number of iterations applied. A stress increase is modelled through an additional iteration (see **Figure 16.7**). Each iteration reflects an increased dependency between cash flows. The algorithm stops eventually either when only one cash flow is left as 'black hole' or when for all funds cash flows cannot be further moved, due to the inception date and lifetime constraints. The gravitational clustering models longer stretches without liquidity and short periods with a higher-than-average liquidity.

Blanking out periods of distributions

Blanking out all distributions for some time interval is a simple way to assess the impact of closed exit markets and combine a stress on liquidity with lower TVPIs across the portfolio.[26] The impact on the individual funds will be different, depending on the respective stage in their lifecycle and how they are diversified over vintage years. Young funds still in their investment period will be less affected than mature funds where LPs had planned with their expected distributions. This stress is comparable to gravitational clustering, but gravitational clustering only changes the timing but not the amounts that are distributed. The impact of blanking out distributions will depend on the length of

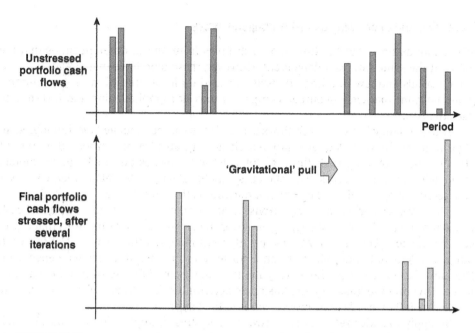

FIGURE 16.7   Applying gravitational clustering to cash-flows across funds (example for distributions)

the period, and for portfolios of mature funds, can have a significant negative impact on cash flows and return outcomes.

VARYING PATTERNS

A slower growth for a fund during challenging economic times is a reasonable scenario, but the more immediate impact is that cash flows are being accelerated or delayed, depending on the circumstances. For instance, from a practical perspective, the rating agencies recognise the peculiarities of illiquid alternative assets. Their methodologies for rating private equity securitisations are based on cash flow historically observed for comparable funds and put less emphasis on a fund's NAV.[27]

'Hot' markets tend to result in faster and higher capital calls, resulting on stresses on the fund's capital call schedule. In the same way, 'bearish' markets are likely to result in later repayments of lower amounts; in this case, the fund's distribution schedule needs to be subjected to appropriate stresses. Particularly, stresses of timing continue to be important elements in the models applied by the various rating agencies.[28] Stresses on patterns relate to increases and prolongations of commitments and to changing fund lifetimes, front-loading, and back-loading of cash flows, and changes in frequency, and volatility of cash flows. Currency movements are another important stress to be applied.

This assumes that, over many runs, projected capital calls to and distributions from a fund will still take the same amount of time, on average, to materialise as they have in the past, regardless of specificities of individual cash-flow scenarios. For each fund, stresses are proportional to its remaining lifetime and diminish with increasing internal age (i.e. the closer the fund is towards its maturity and the more historical data is becoming available for it).

Applying stresses to cash flows can lead to inconsistencies with the TAM, as the forecasts are not always reconcilable with the TAM forecasts. On the other hand, this also addresses the situation where the TAM does not describe the patterns of fund cash flows sufficiently well anymore, as the market dynamics have changed too strongly. Management fees and fixed returns are time invariant to changes in lifetime, front-loading, and back-loading of capital calls and realisations. Operational risk-related stresses are likely to have an impact on the fund's management fees, resulting in calling up a higher share of the management fee reserves.

Stressing commitments

Markets also have an impact on the pacing of commitments and their sizes. During boom periods many funds close faster than originally foreseen, so one stress is moving the anticipated inception dates forward and thus increasing the LP's risk of experiencing a liquidity shortfall.

During market downturns the new funds' closing dates will be delayed, therefore reducing the LP's exposure to private assets and creating opportunity costs. Under severe conditions LPs try to negotiate a reduction in commitment to the funds in their portfolio.[29]

There can also be attempts by fund managers to increase commitments through side funds.[30] Following the burst of the dot-com bubble, side funds – or similar structures – became quite popular as one solution to provide additional funding to VC funds faced with a difficult exit environment, which had forced them to support their still cash-burning investee companies over a longer than expected period. Moreover, the slow-down of the general economic growth had a negative impact on the revenue growth of most of them, further increasing their cash burn rates and postponing their cash break-even point.

A side fund is said to be in most cases linked to higher than planned cash needs of the investee companies, a wrong assessment of the market conditions, a failed investment strategy or its flawed implementation. Typical objectives are:

- To secure and further support the development of some investee companies with a real opportunity to become commercially successful.
- To enable the restructuring of companies that would otherwise have to be completely written off, with a view to selling the participation at cost or at slightly better conditions.
- To complement the investment capacity of a fund which, facing a stronger deal flow or an increase in the size of the targeted companies, has not sufficient resources to establish a sufficiently diversified portfolio.

In addition to that, when a general partner is not able to raise a follow-on fund, a side fund can be used to prolong the investment period of the current fund.

Extending and shortening of fund lifetimes

While fund's have contractual lifetimes, the reality is often quite different, a reason why assessing the impact of changes in lifetimes is an important part of a sensitivity analysis.[31] A typical stress would be increasing a fund's projected lifetime while maintaining its projected TVPI. This results in a lower internal rate of return (IRR), as distributions will be spread over longer time periods.

Doimi de Frankopan (2009) suggested as a possible response of private equity longer holding periods during deflation, as exits become more difficult. During inflation, there would be a flight to investments that have a much quicker turnaround. Also, the opportunity costs and risks related to the undrawn commitments are likely to be higher during inflationary periods.

The fund's cash-flow scenario is a series of cash flows $c_i \geq 0$ over n periods. A cash-flow scenario comprises either contributions or distributions. **Figure 16.8** shows two strategies for allocating cash flows to different lifetimes. If several cash flows are allocated to the same period, they are added and therefore the size of the cash flow in the new period can increase. When shifting, one cash flow from one previous period is mapped to one new period. When stretching, one cash flow related to one previous period can be split into different cash flows (according to the number of periods it is mapped to). The size of the cash flows changes in proportion to the relationship between old and new (remaining) lifetime.

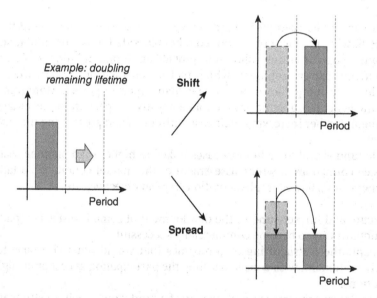

FIGURE 16.8 Strategies for extending the fund's lifetime

Stretching comes in most cases with a decline in volatility. Shifting, therefore, is more consistent with a stress as the cash-flow volatility is preserved. The extension or shortening of a fund's lifetime would come with a proportional stretching and compression of the fund's cash-flow pattern. **Figure 16.9** depicts the situation where a fund's lifetime is extended with its distributions shifted backward.

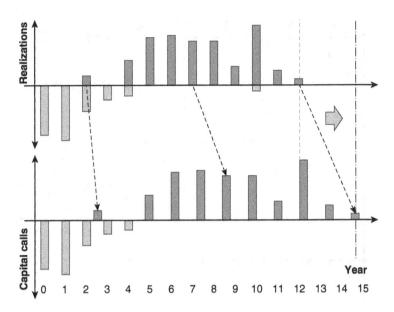

FIGURE 16.9 Extension of the fund's lifetime

Front-loading and back-loading of cash flows

A variation on this play is a sensitivity analysis where the fund's lifetime as well as its TVPI is kept unchanged, but where within the assumed lifetime, cash flows are accelerated or decelerated.

Typical stress scenarios are front-loading with positive stress factor (see **Figure 16.10**) of contributions compared to a normal schedule, back-loading with negative stress factor (see **Figure 16.11**) of the fund's distributions, or combinations of both, as both these stresses imply less liquidity for the LP.[32]

When the investment environment is unfavourable, investment opportunities are likely more difficult to come by, and therefore, contribution rates will be lower than under normal conditions.

With front-loading and back-loading, cash flows are 'squeezed' into shorter time intervals. Combining the front-loading of contributions with back-loading of distributions results in a lower IRR for the fund. The back-loading of contributions together with front-loading distributions has the opposite effect.

Foreign exchange rates and funding risk

More relevant than its impact of outcomes is the FX impact on funding risk. Exchange rate fluctuations outside the LP's control can well result in an unexpected over-commitment compared to the resources dedicated to the investments in private assets. Also, stresses that reflect the fund managers' attempts to time the market, as described before, are likely to lead to the acceleration or deceleration (moving investments/divestments

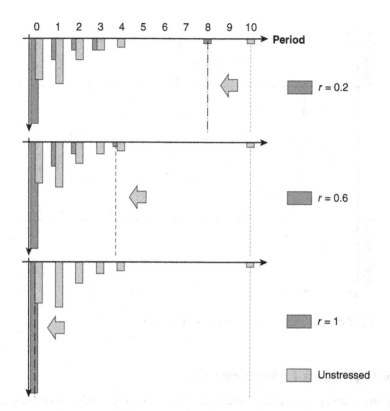

FIGURE 16.10   Front-loading of contributions (acceleration)

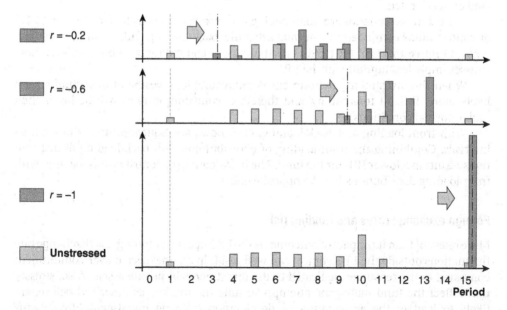

FIGURE 16.11   Back-loading of distributions (deceleration)

forward to coincide with an advantageous FX rate) and a clustering of cash flows (as several investments/divestments will be affected by this) compared to the base scenario.

To the extent that exposure to foreign funds introduces currency risk, additional cash-flow stresses are introduced if this risk appears to be significant.[33] The MCS to determine the portfolio's cash-flow-at-risk (CFaR) and capital-call-at- risk (CCaR) would consider a large number of potential future FX rate paths, aggregating them to fore-casted probability density functions (PDFs) for cash flows. It is also necessary to factor in the impact of parameters like frequency and volatility of cash flows.[34]

Increasing and decreasing frequency of cash flows

Variations caused by changes in frequency and volatility of cash flows are critical for liquidity risk management. Let m be the number of non-zero cash flows during the scenario's n periods. For the purpose of the sensitivity analysis, the frequency $0 \le f \le 1$ of this cash-flow scenario is defined as:

$$f = \begin{cases} 0 \; if \, n = 1 \\ \dfrac{m-1}{n-1} \; if \, n > 1. \end{cases}$$

For this frequency, there are two extremes: one non-zero cash flow for each period, giving the maximum frequency $f = 1$ and just one cash flow of maximum size $c_{max} = \sum_{i=1}^{n} c_i$ for $f = 0$ (see **Figure 16.12**).

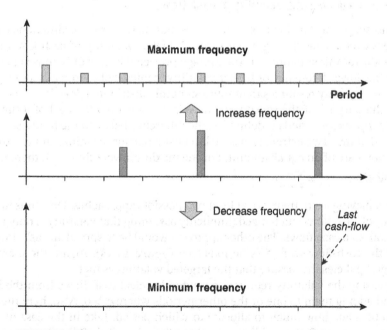

FIGURE 16.12 Decreasing / increasing frequency of cash-flows (example for distributions)

Assuming that changes in frequency have to maintain the fund's targeted lifetime and TVPI, for $f = 0$ and for distributions, the only remaining cash flow is allocated to the last period. In case of contributions, this cash flow is allocated to the first period; both treatments are consistent with a, from a liquidity management perspective, pessimistic scenario.

Unlike in the previous cash-flow-related stresses, there is no unique solution to changes of f. The base scenario described in **Figure 16.12** is three cash flows over eight periods, implying $f = 0.28$. Increasing $f = 0.50$ requires m of between four and five periods. Assuming five periods, we then need to randomly split the existing three cash flows and assign part of these splits to two randomly chosen periods without a cash flow.

Decreasing the frequency requires to randomly select cash flows from the base scenario and individually adding them to one of the other cash-flows in an again randomly chosen period. If we reduce the frequency to zero, m would be 1, meaning that we need to remove the other two of the three cash flows and assign them to the last remaining one.

The randomness inherent in picking cash flows, splitting them, and assigning them to remaining cash flows (when frequency is decreased) or empty periods (when it is increased) requires various choices. For decreasing as well as increasing the frequencies of cash flows, different policies are meaningful. For example, basing the decisions how much to allocate to which period on a skewed PDF would allow making the allocation of cash flows to periods closer to the fund's end of lifetime more likely. This illustrates that changing the frequency of a fund's cash flows requires several assumptions and is more complex to implement than the other stresses discussed so far. Similar complexities apply to changing the volatility of a fund's cash flows.

Increasing and decreasing volatility of cash flows

Past crises suggest a slowdown of capital calls, but there were also situations where LPs with more capital calls during down turns. A higher volatility of cash flows may be a better model for this situation.[35] If the average projected timing of both is kept constant, lumpier (i.e. lower frequency or higher volatility) capital calls and realisations put more pressure on liquidity resources than more smoothly distributed ones.[36]

For the purpose of the sensitivity analysis, the volatility $0 \leq v \leq 1$ of a fund's cash-flow scenario over n periods is defined as the difference between the fund's smallest and largest cash flow.[37] Two extremes need to be considered: for the minimum volatility $v = 0$, all cash flows are of an equal amount. For the maximum volatility $v = 1$, there is just one cash flow of size $c_{max} = \sum_{i=1}^{n} c_i$.

For achieving $v = 0$, there are at least two possible approaches. One aims to keep the frequency of cash flows unchanged, implicitly assuming that volatility is only measured for the non-zero cash flows. The other approach would be to spread all cash flows evenly over all the cash-flow scenario's periods (see **Figure 16.13**). Again, there are various meaningful policies that assure that the targeted volatility is met.

Increasing the volatility requires to randomly select cash flows from the base scenario and adding them to one of the other periods where $c_i > 0$. Also, here the decision needs to be made how much to allocate to which period. Like in the case of reducing frequency, a skewed PDF would allow making the allocation of distributions to periods

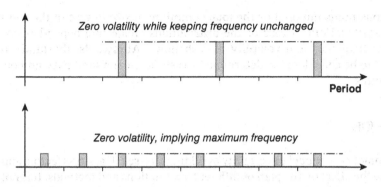

FIGURE 16.13 Strategies for decreasing volatility

closer to the fund's end of lifetime more likely. In case of contributions, the last cash flow would be allocated to the first period; again, both treatments are consistent with a, from a liquidity management perspective, pessimistic scenario (see **Figure 16.14**).

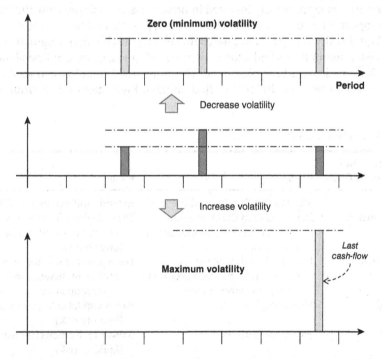

FIGURE 16.14 Decreasing / increasing volatility of cash-flows (example for distributions)

Decreasing a cash-flow scenario's volatility requires shifting amounts from the largest to the smallest cash flows so that they level out. We need to determine which cash flows need to be reduced by which amounts and to which other period's cash flows these amounts should be added.

The constraints imposed by the total commitment size in case of the contributions and the targeted TVPI in case of the distributions create interdependencies between changes in frequency and volatility of cash flows. Afterwards, the fund's new cash flows need to be considered to determine its cash-flow-consistent NAV and other exposure measures.

CONCLUSION

It is good practice to model uncertainty by adding stresses. The stress factors applied help to examine the effect on the plan of different assumptions and methods. It is not possible to say that a certain variation will have a positive effect only; there can be adverse effects, too (see **Table 16.4**). Stress testing taking combinations of the stresses into consideration helps investors to understand the range of potential future outcomes. These scenarios can have reinforcing as well as opposing effects and often cannot be clearly labelled as favourable/optimistic or unfavourable/pessimistic.

For example, early contributions place pressure on liquid resources but overall result in higher returns as more is truly invested in private assets. Delayed contributions exacerbate the opportunity costs associated with treasury assets and tend to create problems related to liquidity drying up or outcomes being less favourable than originally expected.

Also, faster distributions and shorter lifetimes of funds, despite at first glance being viewed as favourable, can be problematic. The unplanned liquidity can strain an LP's resources as it can be very difficult to find suitable investment opportunities during

TABLE 16.4 Summary stresses

Stresses on fund's projected cash flows	$r > 0$	$r < 0$
Lifetime	Shorten fund's estimated lifetime	Extend fund's estimated lifetime
Outcome return	Increased confidence in higher return, decreased confidence in lower return	Decreased confidence in higher return, increased confidence in lower return
Outcome risk	Increased confidence in less extreme returns, decreased confidence in extreme return	Decreased confidence in extreme returns, increased confidence in less extreme return
Front-load	Slower capital calls	Faster capital calls (increasing liquidity risk)
Back-load	Faster realisations	Slower realisations (increasing liquidity risk)
Foreign exchange	Lower volatility	Higher volatility
Volatility	Decreased volatility of cash flows	Increased volatility of cash flows
Frequency	Increased frequency of cash flows	Decreased frequency of cash flows
Commitment	Move back to originally planned commitments	Increased commitments (side funds)
Fee	Move back to budgeted management fees	Increased management fees

periods where asset prices are probably inflated. Moreover, this reduces the exposure to private assets and put pressure on recommitments to new funds. Late distributions, on the other hand, produce more cash for a given positive IRR.

NOTES

1. See Aven (2015).
2. See 'The Price of Panic'. 3 March 2022. Available at https://www.hartfordfunds.com/insights/investor-insight/client-seminars/media-replay/the-price-of-panic.html, [accessed 5 September 2013]
3. A 25-sigma loss event denotes a drop in daily asset returns of more than 25 standard deviations from the mean. According to Cotter et al. (2008) the probability of a 25-sigma loss event under the normal distribution can be compared to the probability of winning the UK National Lottery 21 or 22 times in a row or to 'being on a par with Hell freezing'.
4. See Meyer (2014).
5. See Aalberts et al. (2020).
6. See Aragon (2008) and, additionally, Lowe (2009): 'Clear signs began to emerge from the end of 2008 that pension funds and other institutional investors, particularly in the United States, were struggling with a lack of liquidity [. . .] Reports in the press suggested many institutions were struggling to meet capital commitments from private equity funds, with some putting pressure on general partners to delay such calls or to negotiate a reduction in commitment.'
7. See Vardi (2009).
8. See Murphy et al. (2022).
9. See Robinson and Sensoy (2016).
10. Gottschalg (2020), based of analysing a sample of 429 private equity funds from vintage years 1999 through 2008, derived from a larger cash-flow dataset maintained by Preqin.
11. See Gottschalg (2020).
12. See Hammond et al. (2023): 'Venture capitalists are advising start-ups to postpone plans to go public in the US until interest rates have plateaued, after choppy debuts for Arm and Instacart damped investors' hopes for a rush of tech listings.'
13. See Murphy et al. (2022).
14. See Schneider et al. (2022).
15. See Aalberts et al. (2020).
16. Regarding stresses applied, see Erturk et al. (2001) and Arozamena et al. (2006) on the methodology followed by Standard & Poor's, Kalra et al. (2006) on that by Fitch, Perrin et al. (2006) on that by Moody's, and Chen et al. (2018) on that by DBRS.
17. See Kalra et al. (2006).
18. See https://www.worldbank.org/en/publication/wdr2022/brief/chapter-1-introduction-the-economic-impacts-of-the-covid-19-crisis, [accessed 1 October 2023]
19. See Duggan (2023).
20. See Fayvilevich et al. (2018)
21. See Kalra et al. (2006).
22. See Erturk et al. (2001), Chen et al. (2018), and Jeet (2020).
23. See McGuinness (2020).
24. See Brown et al. (2021)
25. Note that stressing the dependency has no effect on the CE measure.
26. Kalra et al. (2006) consider portfolio-level fund distributions reduced by 5%, 10%, and 15% in each period.

27. Standard & Poor's takes the NAV into consideration in modelling CFOs when any of the structural features of the transaction are dependent on it. In such situations, the NAV is assumed to be equal to the cash invested less any distributions made (see Cheung et al., 2003a). Moody's performs modelling stresses in its assessment of cash flows and capital calls including severe adverse scenarios, which impact the overall level of returns. Furthermore, impacts on the alteration of the drawdown and distributions schedules have also been considered (see Perrin et al., 2006).
28. See, for instance, Fayvilevich et al. (2018).
29. See Lowe (2009).
30. Kalra et al. (2006) consider portfolio-level fund capital calls increased by 10%, 20%, and 30%, consistent with higher commitments.
31. Appelbaum and Batt (2014) discuss various research findings on the average lifetime of private equity funds. They find that a 'life span of ten years for a PE buyout fund seems to be a more reasonable estimate than five to six years. Other researchers consider ten years (or more) to be the typical life span of a PE fund.' See also Lykken (2018): 'Private equity moves at a glacial pace. While the average shelf life of a PE fund is often assumed to be eight to 10 years, many funds require considerably more time to wind down.'
32. See Perrin et al. (2006). Moody's assesses the impact of cash-flow-related stresses by front-loading the drawdowns (by up to two years) and delaying the distributions (by up to two years) to assess the impact.
33. See Chen et al. (2018).
34. See McGuinness (2020).
35. For instance, DBRS performs additional analysis assuming large distributions as a stress. See Chen et al. (2018).
36. See Kalra et al. (2006).
37. In statistics, *volatility* is defined for a given time interval. Here, to keep it simple, this interval is assumed to be the fund's remaining lifetime.

CHAPTER 17

The Art of Commitment Pacing

The previous chapters described the building blocks for commitment pacing and the important engineering principles for managing allocations to private capital: the need to diversify, notably over time, select funds run by experienced fund managers, and having sufficient liquidity to respond to capital calls. Most of all, limited partners (LPs) should avoid the temptation of trying to time the market and frequently change tack and instead invest steadily with a long-term horizon.

The models presented are built to work with the patchy and poor-quality data that is the signature pattern of illiquid alternative assets. They use the LP's internally available data on the assets under management, supplemented by data obtained from data vendors, triangulating with qualitative inputs to fill the remaining gaps. Where do we go from here? This is certainly not the end of the story and significant challenges remain. On the other hand, there are also new exciting opportunities.

IMPROVED INFORMATION TECHNOLOGY

For commitment pacing to this day, the Takahashi–Alexander model (TAM) is the industry's workhorse, usually implemented via spreadsheets. The TAM is often criticised as overly simplistic, but one practitioner commented, 'our own experience in using a simple model but running it frequently has proven to be much more useful than anything complex' – an observation that ties into the recommendation made by Saffo (2007): 'If you must forecast, then forecast often'.

The models we introduced can automatically update and self-calibrate the forecasting parameters and assure that the forecasts become increasingly precise and converge towards the final fund life and total value to paid-in capital (TVPI) outcomes. This overcomes a major hurdle, i.e. the usual manual burden of analysts needing to come up with rather heroic assumptions how the many funds in the portfolio will grow over the next 10 years. It helps us in changing assumptions and in simulating new commitments much more rapidly than previously possible.

Now, a strong toolset is available that builds on proven approaches but provides much richer details on the individual funds and on the entire portfolio. To determine how the irreversible commitments will be developing requires a simulation that is so complex and has so many scenarios that it cannot be done through spreadsheets any longer. We are now in a region where 'serious' IT can be employed and give an edge.

DIRECT INVESTMENTS

Direct investments, where investors are bypassing the traditional intermediation through funds, are increasingly part of institutional allocations to private assets. One motivation behind this is to avoid paying high management fees and carried interest. Other factors, such as better market timing, may play an important role. This also reflects the institutional investors' growing experience and confidence in their ability to successfully play in the private markets themselves. We touched upon these directs in the context of a bottom-up approach to cash-flow forecasting, but that was an exception, to improve fund forecasts in case superior inside information becomes available.

Direct investments sit uneasily in the context of commitment pacing as cash-flow forecasting story. Like funds, they are highly illiquid and could arguably be modelled like we did with co-investments through tweaking the TAM. As opposed to an LP who has no control over the investments and divestments in companies and thus delegates this to the fund manager, in the case of directs, usually everything is under the investor's control. In this situation, cash-flow forecasting by using statistics for capturing unknown intentions of a third party, i.e. the fund manager, does not make sense anymore.

Typically, direct investments are of a more strategic nature with models tailor-made for the transaction. Often they are also monitored within special administration systems, for instance in the case of real estate. Usually, here the modelling focus is rather the value development and the associated milestones, not the cash flows. In such cases, trying to come up with a general purpose cash-flow forecasting model like the TAM maybe futile; instead, importing the cash flow produced by these specific models into a portfolio forecast appears to be a pragmatic solution.

USE OF ARTIFICIAL INTELLIGENCE

So far, portfolio construction is based just on forecasts for expected cash flows and few scenarios. Optimisation is still out of reach, pacing plans are constructed more by trial-and-error, trying to satisfy and respect many trade-offs and constraints.

The promise of machine learning is to automate the trial-and-error and search for resilient portfolios. With the A2*TAM, we can obviously generate as many artificial cash-flow scenarios as needed. We successfully used this technique in Kieffer et al. (2023) and applied it to reinforcement learning for finding policies that maximise the exposure to private assets while respecting constraints, such as imposed by commitments.

Artificial intelligence can also help investors to better understand the risks inherent in their allocations to private assets. Simulations can produce a regular 'weather forecast' for a portfolio's development and to which market factors it would be susceptible going forward.

RISK OF PRIVATE EQUITY

To come back to the discussion on risk in the book's **Introduction** chapter and a number of misconceptions surrounding this question: various studies concluded that the performance of private equity would be lower than that of public markets.[1] For illustration, the CalPERS came under strong criticism because of the high amount of performance fees it paid to private equity firms. Observers like Appelbaum and Batt (2015) refuted the argument that those high fees were worth it because of CalPERS 'stellar' private equity returns and pointed out that these investments, in fact, had underperformed its risk-adjusted benchmark – assumed as the stock market – over the previous 10 years and in various sub-periods.

Such findings contradict the wisdom of crowds of LPs successfully investing in this asset class. The main assumption behind the perceived underperformance is that private markets are more risky than public markets, and for a multi-asset portfolio, it is generally believed that less risk implies a lower allocation to private assets, but this perception may not necessarily be correct.

While the criticism led them to rein in the private equity investment activities, CalPERS eventually had to revise this policy. In 2022, it was estimated that CalPERS missed out on $11 billion in gains during a 'lost decade' for private equity, during which the retirement scheme's private equity returns were trailing 1.3 percentage points behind those of other large pensions. There were various factors that have played a role here, but according to CalPERS's Chief Investment Officer, the 'biggest impact by far was the 10 years we took a break from participating in private equity'.[2]

A better explanation for this conundrum is that well-diversified portfolios of properly selected funds that are professionally monitored may be less risky than public markets, the risk/return relationship thus making private capital a value-adding component in an asset mix.

SECURITISATIONS

What is risk in private capital and how to measure it remains controversial: is it market risk (there is no real market for private assets) or is it closer to credit risk (a limited partnership fund somehow resembles a debt instrument)? The proof of the pudding is in the eating. The techniques described in this book – notably cash-flow forecasting and stress scenarios – were pioneered in the context of securitisations, i.e. collateralised fund obligations (CFOs), for portfolios of private equity funds.

Securitisations layer a pool of illiquid assets into tranches of notes with standardised risk characteristics that can then be traded on exchanges. This transforms the risk of an investment in illiquid limited partnership funds into two different sub-categories: default risk of a debt instrument and the levered long-term risk of equity. CFOs so far could only be done by few specialist asset managers with the larger rating agencies being able to analyse these structures.

While market liquidity so far was illusory, we can now quickly and consistently produce cash-flow forecast for private capital portfolios and in this way democratise the access to liquidity and transferring risks. Going forward, this could be applied to 'synthetic' (also known as 'balance sheet') securitisations where the ownership of the securitised exposures remains on the originator's balance sheet and the rights to the portfolio's cash-flows are sold off. This route to liquidity would be much more in line with the dynamics of private markets, as the LP remains committed and the assets themselves do not need to get traded in secondary markets.

JUDGEMENT, ENGINEERING, AND ART

The book's title suggests that commitment pacing be an art, often also described as 'judgemental work',[3] a thought also expressed in Samuels (2022). Investors in private assets operate in a market that consists of fleeting opportunities with limited lifetimes, fuzzy boundaries and overlaps with other asset classes, poor quality and lack of data, reliance on qualitative judgement, and, as a consequence, great scope for a cult of personalities, with highly paid professionals being not much different from artists.

The toolset presented here allows us to engineer better, i.e. more resilient portfolios of funds that are reliably meeting the LP's objectives while respecting the many side conditions. Engineering sounds dry, mechanical, and nerdy, but it is a tool for implementing ideas and turning creativity into reality.

We do not see the inner workings of, say, a mechanical clock, a Formula One car, an extreme ultraviolet lithography machine, or a graphical processing unit, but we are fascinated and see beauty in what they are doing or creating. The outcome of commitment pacing is a vision that can be amazing and qualitatively appealing, as it is a stake in the real economy and in building the future. We all love when this plan comes together!

NOTES

1. See Brinker and Polman (2023).
2. See Gillers (2022).
3. See Hall and Johnson (2009).

Abbreviations

AI	Artificial intelligence
AIFMD	Alternative Investment Fund Managers Directive
A1*TAM	First augmentation of TAM: ranges for TVPIs and lifetimes, annual expected contributions, distributions, and NAV
A2*TAM	Second augmentation; volatility and frequency of cash flows, monthly, quarterly, semi-annually randomly distributed cash flows (capital calls, management fees, realisations, and fixed returns), cash-flow-consistent NAV
B	Bow factor *(TAM parameter)*
BOSTON	Bow-Speed Time Option Normalised *(forecasting model)*
C	Contribution *(TAM parameter)*
CalPERS	California Public Employees' Retirement System
CA	Contribution age
C_i	Cluster step *(diversification management parameter)*
$Cl_{G_i;A}$	Classification of Fund A in Classification Group i *(diversification management parameter)*
CC	Committed capital *(TAM parameter)*
CCaR	Capital-call-at-risk
CE	Commitment efficiency
CDF	Cumulative distribution function
CFaR	Cash-flow-at-risk
CFO	Collateralised fund obligation
cr	Ratio of total contributions during the fund's life over the committed capital *CC (TAM parameter extension by Corvino, 2020)*
D	Distribution *(TAM parameter)*
$D_{A;B}$	Similarity between funds A and B *(diversification management parameter)*
DA	Distribution age
DACH	Germany (Deutschland) -Austria-Switzerland (Confoederatio Helvetica)
DCC	Distributed to committed capital
DCF	Discounted cash flow
DPI	Distributed to paid-in capital
ESG	Environmental, social, and governance
ETF	Exchange-traded fund
freq_ctrl	Frequency control *(A2*TAM parameter)*
FOFs	Funds of funds
FOIA	Freedom of Information Act

FX	Foreign exchange
G	Growth rate *(TAM parameter)*
G_i	Classification Group *i (diversification management parameter)*
GFC	Global Financial Crisis 2007–2008
GP	General partner
ip	Fund's Investment Period *(TAM parameter extension by Corvino, 2020)*
IA	Internal age
IBM	International Business Machines
ILPA	Institutional Limited Partners Association
IPEV	International Private Equity and Venture Capital Valuation
IPO	Initial public offering
IRR	Internal rate of return
KPI	Key performance indicator
L	Fund lifetime *(TAM parameter)*
LBO	Leveraged buyout
LP	Limited partner
LPA	Limited partnership agreement
LVaR	Liquidity-adjusted value at risk
M&A	Mergers and acquisitions
MCS	Monte Carlo simulation
ML	Machine learning
MPT	Modern portfolio theory
NAV	Net asset value
OCR	Over-commitment ratio
PERE	Private equity real estate
PDF	Probability density function
PG/LGD	Probability of default / loss given default
PIC	Paid-in capital
PICC	Paid-in to capital committed
PME	Public market equivalent
PV	Present value
qual _ score	The fund's qualitative score (between 0 and 4)
quant _ score	The fund's quantitative score (between 0 and 4)
r	Stress Factor (between –1 and 1, with 0 as 'neutral')
R	Total available resources for committing to funds
RC	Rate of contribution *(TAM parameter)*
RD	Rate of distribution *(TAM parameter)*
RVPI	Remaining value to paid-in capital (also residual value to paid-in capital)
s	Stress level for the market (between 0 and 1)
$s_{A;B}$	Similarity between funds A and B *(diversification management parameter)*
$\overline{s}_{A;B}$	Vintage-year-adjusted similarity between funds A and B *(diversification management parameter)*
TAM	Takahashi–Alexander model

TVPI	Total value to paid-in capital
$TVPI_{Interim}$	Fund's current TVPI
$TVPI_{Targeted}$	The targeted TVPI to be generated by the A1*TAM and A2*TAM
VaR	Value at risk
VC	Venture capital
vol_ctrl	Volatility control *(A2*TAM parameter)*
vy_A	Vintage year of fund A *(diversification management parameter)*
$w(s,r)$	Sample weight schedule
XE	Exposure efficiency
y	Year impact parameter *(diversification management parameter)*
Y	Yield *(TAM parameter)*

Glossary

Alternative Assets   Investments that fall outside of the traditional asset classes commonly accessed by most investors and mainly comprise hedge funds, private capital, natural resources, real estate, and infrastructure

Alternative Investment Fund Managers Directive   Regulatory framework applying to hedge funds, private equity funds, and real estate investment funds registered in the European Union

Blind Pool   Primary commitments are to blind pools, i.e. a fund that has not invested in private assets yet and where LPs have no visibility into where their capital will be invested

Bottom-Up   An approach for modelling funds that forecasts the cash flows for each underlying private asset and then aggregates them at the fund level. A Bottom-Up approach requires the Look-Through, but Look-Through is not equivalent to Bottom-Up

Bow Factor   A Yield and the Bow Factor together describe changes in the rate of distribution RC over time

Burgiss   Private market benchmarking data provider

Buyout Funds   Funds whose strategy is to acquire other businesses; this may also include Mezzanine Finance

Capital Calls   When investors commit to back a private capital fund, the Committed Capital is not needed at once but will be called once an investment is identified. The capital that has been called is defined as Contributed Capital. For this book, Capital Calls do not include the Management Fees

Capital-Call-at-Risk   The CCaR is the most capital a portfolio of funds will call within a given time period for a given confidence level

Capital Distributions   Short for Distributions

Cambridge Associates   Private market benchmarking data provider

Carried Interest   A bonus entitlement accruing to a Fund Management Firm or individual members of the Fund Management Team. Carried Interest (typically up to 20% of the profits of the fund) becomes payable once the LPs have achieved repayment of their original investment in the fund plus a defined hurdle rate

Carry   Short for Carried Interest

Cash Drag   Cash Drag refers to the portion of a fund's Commitments being held in cash rather than being invested in private assets

Cash-Flow-at-Risk   The CFaR is the maximum cash flow for a portfolio of funds within a given time period for a given confidence level

Cash-Flow-Consistent NAV   The Cash-Flow-Consistent NAV is applying a discounted cash-flow model to valuing the private assets held by the fund

Cash Management   See 'Treasury Management'

Closing Time where fund can start investing. A Closing is reached when a certain amount has been committed to the fund. Several intermediary Closings can occur before the final Closing of a fund is reached

Co-Investment Syndication of a financing round for a private asset between a fund and one or more of its LPs

Collateralised Fund Obligation Securitisation of a pool of private capital funds that transforms the risk of an investment in illiquid limited partnership funds into two different subcategories: default risk of bond and levered long-term risk of equity

Committed Capital Committed Capital is the total amount that the LPs promise to invest in a fund over its lifetime. It excludes the GP contribution to the fund. This committed amount is called over time by the fund managers as attractive opportunities to invest in private assets arise. The LP has an obligation to provide this capital when the GP asks for it

    Commitment Types Primary commitments, secondary transactions, co-investments, and funds of funds

Commitment Short for Committed Capital

Commitment Efficiency The CE measures how efficiently the funds' diversification dimensions are spread over the private capital market. CE as KPI is based on the assumption that an evenly and widely committed portfolio offers the best diversification and, consequently, the best protection against unforeseen future developments in the market and portfolio

Contributed Capital See 'Contributions'

Contribution Age A fund's CA is the relationship between the sum of contributions until time t and the expected sum of contributions over its full lifetime

Contributions Capital calls + Management fees. For this book, Contributions mean the fund's inflows in general. Contributions is the capital the LP is providing the fund with

Distributed Capital See 'Distributions'

Distributed to Committed Capital DCC is Cumulative Distributions divided by Committed Capital

Distribution Age A fund's DA is the relationship between the sum of distributions until time t and the expected sum of distributions over its full lifetime

Distributions Realisations + Fixed Returns. For this book, Distributions mean the fund's outflows in general. Distributions are the capital returned to the LP

Distribution Waterfall The Distribution Waterfall sets out how Distributions from a limited partnership fund will be split and in which priority they will be paid out, i.e. what amount must be distributed to the LP before the GP receives carried interest

Distributed to Paid-In Capital DPI (also referred to as the Realisation Multiple) measures the total capital that a fund has returned thus far to its LPs. DPI increases as exits are achieved and capital is distributed to investors. Once all distributions are made, the DPI becomes equal to the TVPI of a fund. DPI and RVPI comprise the fund's TVPI. DPI is net of fees and carried interest

Distribution-in-Kind Payment made in the form of securities or other property rather than in cash

Divestment Period The period during which the fund will hold, manage and then liquidate its investments

Drawdowns See 'Contributions'

Dry Powder Assets managed by fund but not yet invested; essentially the fund's Undrawn Commitments

Due Diligence The process of verifying the data presented in a business plan/sales memorandum, and completing the investigation and analytical process that precedes the decision to invest

Exit Liquidation of holdings by a fund. Among the various methods of exiting an investment are: trade sale, sale by public offering (including IPO), write-offs, repayment of preference shares/loans, sale to another private capital fund, sale to a financial institution

Expectation Grade A Fund's performance forecast categorised by 'Neutral', 'Underperformance', 'Low performance', and 'Bottom performance'

Exposure The capital remaining at a given point in time from the originally invested amount that an investor stands to lose should the investment fail

Exposure Efficiency XE measures how much of the LP's committed capital is really turned into invested capital. The portfolio's XE gives indications how the diversification implied by the commitments is reflected in the funds' underlying assets and their diversification

Firm See 'Fund Management Firm'

Fixed Returns Interest/principal or dividends (defined for debt)

Foreign Exchange Rate Conversion of one currency into another at a specific FX rate

Fund Closed-ended limited partnership fund as vehicle for enabling pooled investment by a number of investors in private assets. hedge funds and, except where otherwise noted, publicly traded or open-end funds are excluded

Fund Age The age of a fund (in years) from its first drawdown to the time when all the private assets have been exited

Fund Focus The strategy of specialisation by stage of investment, sector of investment, geographical concentration. Generalist funds do not have such a focus

Fund Grading System Expectation Grades and Risk Grades

Funding Risk For an LP Funding Risk is the risk of loss from higher funding costs or from lack of funds to finance contributions

Fund Manager Team of Investment Professionals involved in the fund's day-to-day management

Fund Management Firm Fund Management Firms take charge of all activities relating to the day-to-day operation of funds, e.g. overseeing the investment management, marketing and central administration of the fund, as well as establishing a risk management and due diligence that satisfies regulatory requirements and protects investor interests

Fund Management Team See 'Fund Manager'

Fund-of-funds A fund that takes equity positions in other funds (plural: funds of funds)

Fund Rating Other name for 'Fund Grading'

Fund Size The total amount of capital committed by the LPs and the GP of a fund

Fund Strategy For example, venture capital, buyouts, infrastructure, real estate

Fund Style Fund Strategy plus other diversification dimensions

General Partner A Fund Management Firm's GP has unlimited personal liability for the debts and obligations of the limited partnership and the right to participate in its management. Also see 'Limited Partner'

Horizon TVPI CDF Cumulative Distribution Function for the TVPIs of funds with an age larger than a defined time horizon

Investment Period The main part of the capital is drawn down during this period, typically four or five years, where new opportunities are identified

Grading System   The Grading System is marking a fund to a group of comparable funds, i.e. its peer group, taking its specific lifecycle characteristics into account and assigning Expectation Grades and Risk Grades

Gross Figures   The fund's TVPIs, IRRs, cash flows etc. before tax, management fees, carried interest and other expenses are deducted

Hurdle Rate   Usually Carried Interest is subject to a Hurdle Rate, so that it is only paid once investors have received their capital back and a minimum pre-agreed rate of return

Inception Date   A fund's Inception Date is the start date for its operations

Internal Age   A fund's IA is a figure between 0 and 1 and models the uncertainty regarding its outcomes. The IA reflects the fund's Contribution Age CA and its Distribution Age DA

Internal Rate of Return   A time-weighted return expressed as a percentage. For funds, the IRR is calculated as an annualised effective compounded rate of return, using cash flows to and from LPs, together with the residual value as a terminal cash flow to the LPs

Investor   Short for Institutional Investor

Institutional Investor   Investors, such as asset managers, insurers, pension funds, banks, endowments, sovereign wealth funds, and family offices, who generally have substantial assets and experience in investing. LPs describe the specific case of investing in private capital through funds as intermediaries

Invested Capital   Total amount of Called Capital which has actually been invested in Private Assets

Investment Manager   Member of the LP's team

Investment Period   The period during which opportunities are identified and investments are made

Investment Programme   For the purpose of this book, the general term for in-house programmes, captive or independent funds of funds focusing on investments in private capital funds

Investment Professional   Member of fund management team

J-curve   The curve generated by plotting the NAVs, returns, or net cash flows generated by a private capital fund against time from inception to termination

Leveraged Buyout   A buyout financed by a particularly high level of debt, much of which is secured against a company's assets

Limited Partner   The institutional investor that provides the capital for commitments to private capital funds. Also see 'General Partner'

Limited Partnership   A limited partnership is a business (here an investment vehicle) owned by two or more parties, with at least one serving as the GP who oversees the business

Liquidation Period   See 'Divestment Period'

Liquidity-Adjusted Value at Risk   The LVaR is the worst transaction price that could be obtained for a fund on the secondary markets for a given level of confidence

Look-Through   Requirement to capture as much information on the private assets held by a fund as possible. The Look-Through is the most granular approach to risk measurement and thus assumed to give highest sensitivity to risk. Look-Through is not equivalent to Bottom-Up

Management Fees   LP payment to Fund Manager for their asset management services

Mezzanine Finance   Provides (generally subordinated) debt to facilitate financing Buyouts, frequently alongside a right to some of the equity upside

Monte Carlo Simulation The MCS uses randomly generated numbers to recreate the inherent uncertainty of the input parameters for producing possible outcomes of an uncertain event

Multiple The Multiple reveals how many times investors have, or are likely to get their money back and make a profit from their investments. For funds it is the sum of the residual value of the portfolio plus Distributed Capital. The Multiple is net of fees and Carried Interest

Net Asset Value The fund's NAV reflects its managers' best estimate of the current market value of the portfolio companies held and other assets of the fund, less any fund liabilities

Net Figures The fund's TVPIs, IRRs, cash flows etc. after tax, management fees, carried interest and other expenses were deducted

Over-Commitments To minimise the opportunity costs associated with the undrawn commitments, LPs can follow an Over-Commitment strategy, where they commit more than the available resources and rely on expected Distributions to fund future Contributions

Pacing Plan A Pacing Plan lists what amounts need to be committed at which time to which fund. In the pacing plan funds are defined by their Fund Style and their Fund Type

Paid-in to Capital Committed PICC is the cumulative Contributions divided by the Commitments. PICC is net of fees and carried interest

Pari Passu Ranking equally and without preference

PitchBook Private market benchmarking data provider

Pledge Fund Type of investment vehicle where participants agree, or 'pledge', to contribute capital to investments. Unlike a blind pool, contributors to a pledge fund reserve the right to review each opportunity prior to contributing or refrain from investing

Portfolio Short for Portfolio of funds

Preqin Private market benchmarking data provider

Primary Commitments LPs come in before the final closing, under pari passu conditions

Primary Fund See 'Primary Commitments'

Private Asset Private assets are held in investments that are not publicly traded. The most common private asset investment types are start-up companies, real estate objects, infrastructure projects, like airports. Private Assets are either invested in through a fund or directly

Private Capital Set of investment strategies, mainly Private Equity, Private Credit, Real Estate, Infrastructure, and Natural Resources

Private Capital Investment Programme See 'Investment Programme'

Private Credit See 'Private Debt'

Private Debt Private Debt is the provision of debt finance to companies from funds, rather than banks, bank-led syndicates, or public markets

Private Equity Private Equity includes Venture Capital and Buyouts, and provides equity capital to enterprises not quoted on a stock market

Private Markets Private Markets are investments made in equity and debt of Private Assets not traded on a public exchange or stock market. Usually invested in through closed-ended funds, as well as related Secondaries and Funds of Funds

Private Placement Memorandum Brochure presented by a GP in the process of raising funds. This document is dedicated to potential investors (limited partners), and usually contains (among other information) a presentation of the Fund Manager's Track Record, terms and conditions, and investment strategies

Realisations   Proceeds of (partial) exits, usually equity, returned to LPs

Realisation Multiple   See 'Distributed to Paid-in Capital (DPI)'

Residual Value to Paid-in Capital   NAV divided by cumulative Capital Calls. The sum of RVPI and DPI equals TVPI. RVPI is net of fees and carried interest

Resources   Uncommitted Capital + Uncalled Capital

Returns   IRR, TVPI, multiple

Risk Grade   A fund's forecasted risk categorised by 'Neutral', 'Increased risk', and 'High risk'

Risk Shift   Increasing risks are reflected by overweighting the extremes of top and bottom performance compared to second and third quartile outcomes. The Risk Grade defines the Risk Shift, between 0 and 1. A Risk Grade 'Neutral' implies a Risk Shift of 0

Commitment Types   Primary commitments, secondary transactions, co-investments, and funds of funds

Secondary Market   Market for buying and selling interests in existing funds from their original LPs. A secondary transaction may comprise a single manager's entire fund or, more commonly, a portfolio of interests in a number of different funds

Securitisations   Through securitisation of portfolios of funds (also known as 'Collateralised Fund Obligations'), incorporated fund vehicles can offer interests to investors in the form of notes or bonds with credit ratings, including convertible securities

Selection Skills   A Selection Skill parameter of zero suggests that the LP's forecast offers no additional information compared to the model's forecast. A Selection Skill of one would be assuming that the LP has perfect foresight and thus fully replaces the model's forecast

Self-Liquidating   Private assets are turned into cash without the LP's initiative. Self-Liquidating funds address the problem of proper incentives as fund managers only get rewarded once cash has been returned and true performance has been revealed

Sharpe Ratio   The ratio of expected performance minus the risk-free rate to the standard deviation

Shortfall Risk   Probability that a portfolio will not exceed the minimum return set by the investor

Sortino Ratio   The excess return over risk-free rate (or a certain threshold) over the downside semi-variance

Track Record   A firm's experience, history and past performance of previous funds managed

Treasury Management   Treasury supports financial resource management and asset–liability management to facilitate the provision of contributions at the lowest cost possible

Uncalled Capital   See 'Undrawn Commitments'

Uncertainty   Economists typically differentiate between 'risk' and 'uncertainty'. Risk exists when a probability based on past experience can be attached to an event, whereas uncertainty exists when there is no objective way to determine its probability

Uncalled Capital   See 'Undrawn Commitments'

Uncommitted Capital   Uncommitted Capital means the capital that the investor has not yet committed, or reserved for commitments to a particular fund opportunity

Undrawn Commitments   The difference between Committed Capital and Paid-in Capital

Value at Risk   The VaR is the maximum mark-to-market loss a given portfolio can suffer for a given time horizon and a given confidence level. For private capital, the VaR measure is based on the implicit assumption that the LP can sell the positions in funds at any time at their current NAV

Venture Capital   Type of financing provided to innovative start-up companies and small businesses believed to have an extraordinary high long-term growth potential

Vintage Year   The year of first draw down of capital for investment purposes; the year in which a fund makes its first investment using the LPs' capital. Various definitions exist for vintage years, for example:

ILPA: 'The year of fund formation and/or its first takedown of capital. By placing a fund into a particular vintage year, the Limited Partner can compare the performance of a given fund with all other similar types of funds form in that particular year.'

CFA Institute's Global Investment Performance Standards: 'Two methods used to determine vintage year are: 1. the year of the investment vehicle's first drawdown or capital call from its investors; or 2. the year when the first committed capital from outside investors is closed and legally binding.'

Cambridge Associates: '[T]he legal inception date as noted in a fund's financial statement. This date can usually be found in the first note to the audited financial statements and is prior to the first close or capital call.'

PitchBook: 'The vintage year is assigned by: (1) year of first investment; (2) if year of first investment is unknown, then year of final close; or (3) if firm publicly declares via press release or a notice on their website a fund to be of a particular vintage different than either of the first conditions, in which case the firm's classification takes precedence'

Vintage Year Peer Group   Private market benchmarks allow comparing performance results by a cohort group of funds formed in the same year – for example, the so-called 'Vintage Year'

Waterfall   See 'Distribution Waterfall'

Yield   Yield sets a minimum distribution level and is used to model income-generating asset types such as real estate or infrastructure. See 'Fixed Returns'

Biography

Thomas Meyer is the managing director of SimCorp Luxembourg s.a.r.l. (part of Deutsche Börse Group). He has held an international career in and out of the financial services, from intelligence officer in the German Air Force to regional CFO of Allianz Asia Pacific in Singapore. He was responsible for the creation of the European Investment Fund's risk-management function with focus on building valuation and risk-management models and investment strategies for venture capital funds of funds. Since 2020, he has been leading the development of SimCorp Dimension's Alternatives Strategy solution.

As director of the European Private Equity and Venture Capital Association, he co-directed the limited partner course delivered by the Private Equity Institute at the Saïd Business School, University of Oxford that led to the EVCA awarded certificate.

He is a Shimomura Fellow of the Development Bank of Japan and was a visiting research fellow at Hitotsubashi University in Tokyo. He studied computer science at the Bundeswehr Universität in Munich and holds a Dr.rer.nat. from the Universität Trier. He graduated with an MBA from the London Business School and an MA from the University of Sheffield's SEAS.

He is the co-author of *Beyond the J Curve* (translated into Chinese, Japanese, and Vietnamese), *J-Curve Exposure*, *Mastering Illiquidity* (all by Wiley), and two CAIA books, which are required reading for Level II of the Chartered Alternative Investment Analyst ® Program. He authored *Private Equity Unchained* (by Palgrave MacMillan).

Bibliography

Aalberts, Edo, Peter Cornelius, and Lucas van der Kamer. 2019. 'Cashflow-Based Investment Strategies and Exposure Modeling'. Paper. AlpInvest. August.

Aalberts, Edo, Peter Cornelius, and Lucas van der Kamer. 2020. 'Cash Flows During Financial Crises'. Paper. AlpInvest. June.

Abrdn. 2019. 'The Commitment Conundrum – Understanding the fine art of private capital fund commitments'. October. Available at https://www.abrdn.com/docs?editionId=73844440-792b-4674-b71e-3f9d15c5eb72 [accessed 28 March 2022].

ACG. 2023. 'Optimal Commitment Pacing'. Alignment Capital Group. Available at http://www.alignmentcapital.com/services/pacing.htm [accessed 3 July 2023].

Ahlin, Victor and Pontus Granlund. 2017. 'Subscription loan facilities in private equity'. Master Thesis in Finance, Stockholm School of Economics.

AnalystPrep. 2019. 'Financial Models'. 16 September. Available at https://analystprep.com/blog/financial-models/ [accessed 28 March 2022].

Anson, Mark. 2013. 'Performance Measurement in Private Equity: Another Look at the Lagged Beta Effect', *The Journal of Private Equity*, 17(1), 29–44. Available at: https://www.jstor.org/stable/43503783

Appelbaum, Eileen and Rosemary Batt. 2014. *Private Equity at Work: When Wall Street Manages Main Street*. New York: Russell Sage Foundation.

Appelbaum, Eileen and Rosemary Batt. 2015. 'CalPERS and Private Equity: A Second Opinion'. The Center for Economic and Policy Research. Guest blog. 9 December. Available at https://cepr.net/calpers-and-private-equity-a-second-opinion/ [accessed 10 January 2023].

Aragon, Lawrence. 2008. 'LPs Are on the Ropes'. peHUB. 7 July. Available at http://www.pehub.com/2008/11/07/lps-are-on-the-ropes [accessed 5 September 2013].

Arnold, Thomas R., David C. Ling, and Andy Naranjo. 2017. 'Waiting to Be Called: The Impact of Manager Discretion and Dry Powder on Private Equity Real Estate Returns', *The Journal of Portfolio Management. Special Real Estate Issue*, 23–43.

Arozamena, Alfredo De Diego, Cristina Polizu, Ming Tang, and James Halprin. 2006. 'CDO Spotlight: Global Criteria for Private Equity'. Standard & Poor's Ratings Direct. January 18.

Artinger, Florian, Malte Petersen, Gerd Gigerenzer, and Jürgen Weibler. 2015. 'Heuristics as adaptive decision strategies in management', *Journal of Organizational Behavior*, 36, 33–52.

Auerbach, Andrea and Alex Shivananda. 2017. 'When Secondaries Should Come First'. Cambridge Associates Insight. August. Available at https://www.cambridgeassociates.com/insight/when-secondaries-should-come-first/ [accessed 20 August 2023].

Aven, Terje. 2015. 'Implications of black swans to the foundations and practice of risk assessment and management', *Reliability Engineering & System Safety*, 134, 83–91. February.

Axelson Ulf, Per Strömberg, and Michael S. Weisbach. 2009. 'Why are buyouts levered? The financial structure of private equity funds', *The Journal of Finance*, 64(4), 1549–1582. 16 July.

Bailey, Jeffrey V., Thomas M. Richards, and David E. Tierney. 1990. 'Benchmark portfolios and the manager/plan sponsor relationship'. In *Current Topics in Investment Management*, Frank J. Fabozzi and T. Dessa Fabozzi (eds). New York: Harper & Row, pp. 71–85.

Baker, Sophie. 2018. 'Rising credit lines sounding alarms for LPs'. *Pension & Investments*. April 2. Available at https://www.pionline.com/article/20180402/PRINT/180409992/rising-credit-lines-sounding-alarms-for-lps [accessed 14 December 2022].

Balyeat, R. Brian, Julie Cagle, and Phil Glasgo. 2013. 'Teaching MIRR to Improve Comprehension of Investment Performance Evaluation Techniques', *Journal of Economics and Finance Education*, 12(1).

Bansal, Saurabh, Genaro J. Gutierrez, and John R. Keiser. Undated. 'Using Expert Assessments to Estimate Probability Distributions'. Available at https://www.smeal.psu.edu/lema/Estimating YieldUncertainty.pdf [accessed 6 July 2022].

Barry, David G. 2022. 'CalPERS Looks to Up Its Private Equity & Infrastructure Investing'. 16 September. Available at https://www.marketsgroup.org/news/CalPERS-Private-Equity-Infrastructure [accessed 6 February 2023].

BCBS. 2001. 'Working paper on risk-sensitive approaches for equity exposures in the banking book for IRB banks'. Basel Committee on Banking Supervision. August.

BCBS. 2005. 'An Explanatory Note on the Basel II IRB Risk Weight Functions'. Basel Committee on Banking Supervision. July. Available at https://www.bis.org/bcbs/irbriskweight.pdf [accessed 14 June 2023].

Belev, Emilian and Dan DiBartolomeo. 2021. 'Practical Applications of Private Equity Benchmarking for Asset Owners and Investment Managers', *The Journal of Index Investing*. Fall.

Belev, Emilian and Thomas Meyer. 2022. 'Measuring Exposure for Limited Partnership Funds', *The Journal of Investing*, 31(6), 36–53. October.

Beutler, Dawson, Alex Billias, Sam Holt, Josh Lerner, and TzuHwan Seet. 2023. 'Takahashi-Alexander Revisited: Modeling Private Equity Portfolio Outcomes Using Historical Simulations'. The Journal of Portfolio Management. Vol 49. No. 7, pp. 144–158. July.

BIS. 2020. 'CRE60 – Equity investments in funds'. Bank for International Settlements. 27 March. Available at https://www.bis.org/basel_framework/chapter/CRE/60.htm [accessed 14 June 2023].

BIS. 2022. 'MAR31 – Internal models approach: model requirements'. Bank for International Settlements. 1 January. Available at https://www.bis.org/basel_framework/chapter/MAR/31.htm?inforce=20220101&published=20191215 [accessed 14 June 2023].

Bitsch, Florian, Axel Buchner, and Christoph Kaserer. 2010. 'Risk, return and cash flow characteristics of infrastructure fund investments', *EIB Papers*, 15(1).

Black, Garrett James. 2018. 'The trillion-dollar question: What does record dry powder mean for PE & VC fund managers?' PitchBook's Private Market PlayBook. March 15. Available at https://pitchbook.com/news/articles/the-trillion-dollar-question-what-does-record-dry-powder-mean-for-pe-vc-fund-managers [accessed 29 October 2018].

Black, Gus. 2015. 'The AIFMD's impact on EU investors accessing Private Equity'. 6 October. Available at https://www.lavenpartners.com/thought-leadership/the-aifmd-impact-on-eu-investors-accessing-private/ [accessed 29 May 2023].

Black, William, Bandile Mbele, Cole van Jaarsveldt, and Johannes Wiesel. 2018. 'Commitment Scheduling for Private Equity Investments', *Financial Mathematics Team Challenge – African Institute of Financial Markets and Risk Management*.

Bongaerts, Dion and Erwin Charlier. 2008. 'Private Equity and Regulatory Capital'. Tilburg University. Discussion Paper. No. 52. May.

Brakman, Steven and Charles van Marrewijk. 2007. 'It's a Big World After All'. CESifo Working Paper No. 1964. April. Available at https://papers.ssrn.com/sol3/papers.cfm?abstract_id=982790 [accessed 1 February 2023].

Brinker, Gijs den and Joris Polman. 2023. 'There is a lot to be said about the returns of private equity'. Het Financieele Dagblad. 3 August.

Brown, Erika and Phyllis Berman. 2003. 'Take My Venture Fund – Please!', *Forbes*. June 23.

Brown, Gregory, Wendy Hu, and Bert-Klemens Kuhn. 2021. 'Private Investments in Diversified Portfolios'. January. Available at https://uncipc.org/wp-content/uploads/2021/02/Asset_Allocation_210129.pdf [accessed 26 March 2022].

Brown, Gregory W., Robert S. Harris, Tim Jenkinson, Steven N. Kaplan, and David T. Robinson. 2015. 'What Do Different Commercial Data Sets Tell Us About Private Equity Performance?' 5 December. Available at https://papers.ssrn.com/sol3/papers.cfm?abstract_id=2701317 [accessed 14 April 2023].

Brown, Gregory W., Robert S. Harris, Wendy Hu, Tim Jenkinson, Steven N. Kaplan, and David T. Robinson. 2020. 'Can Investors Time Their Exposure to Private Equity?' Kenan Institute of Private Enterprise Research Paper No. 18–26, January 22. Available at SSRN: https://ssrn.com/abstract=3241102 [accessed 21 January 2021].

Browne, Kathleen R. 2006. 'Appropriateness and Feasibility of Targeted Diversification in a Private Equity Portfolio'. Master Thesis. Sloan School of Management, Massachusetts Institute of Technology. June.

Buchner, Axel. 2017. 'Risk management for private equity funds', *Journal of Risk*, 19(6), 1–32. August. Available at https://www.risk.net/journal-of-risk/5311701/risk-management-for-private-equity-funds [accessed 9 May 2023].

Buchner, Axel, Christoph Kaserer, and Niklas Wagner. 2010. 'Modeling the Cash Flow Dynamics of Private Equity Funds: Theory and Empirical Evidence', *The Journal of Alternative Investments*, 13(1).

Burgiss. 2020. 'COVID-19 Effects: Recessionary T/A Model Parameters Published'. 30 March. Available at https://www.burgiss.com/news/2020/3/30/covid-19-effects-recessionary-ta-model-parameters-published [accessed 28 November 2020].

Burgiss. 2021. 'Understanding Parameter Sets for Use in the Takahashi-Alexander Forecast Model'. Research. June. Available at https://www.burgiss.com/0602-best-practices-understanding-ta-parameters [accessed 24 April 2023].

Burkhard, Juerg, Matthias Feiler, and Boris Pavlu. 2013. 'Alternatives to the Standard Model under Solvency II: Partial Internal Models'. Swiss Private Equity & Corporate Finance Association. 1 May.

Cardie, J. Heath, Katherine A. Cattanach, and Mary Frances Kelly. 2000. 'How large should your commitment to private equity really be?', *The Journal of Wealth Management*, 3(2), 39–45.

Chen, Siyun, Joseph Priolo, Jerry van Koolbergen, and Claire Mezzanotte. 2018. 'Rating U.S. Collateralized Fund Obligations Backed by Private Equity'. Methodology paper. DBRS. November.

Chernova, Yuliya. 2022. 'Venture Firms Push Fund Caps Out of the Way', *Wall Street Journal*. 18 March. Available at https://www.wsj.com/articles/venture-firms-push-fund-caps-out-of-the-way-11647601201 [accessed 20 May 2023].

Cheung, Lily, Vivek Kapoor, and Chris Howley. 2003. 'Rating Private Equity CFOs: Stochastic Market Cash Flows'. CDO Research Special Report. Standard & Poor's.

Chingono, Brian and Daniel Rasmussen. 2015. 'Leveraged Small Value Equities'. University of Chicago working paper. Available at SSRN: https://papers.ssrn.com/sol3/papers.cfm?abstract_id=2639647 [accessed 2 May 2022].

Chollet, François. 2018. *Deep Learning with Python*. Shelter Island, NY: Manning Publications.

Collan, Mikael. 2012. *The Pay-Off Method: Re-inventing Investment Analysis*. Printed in Great Britain by Amazon.co.uk, Ltd.

Cornel, Jeroen and Julia Wittlin. 2019. 'Constructing Optimized Private Equity Programs'. Black-Rock. November.

Cornelius, Peter, Christian Diller, Didier Guennoc, and Thomas Meyer. 2013. *Mastering Illiquidity – Risk management for portfolios of limited partnership funds*. Chichester: John Wiley & Sons.

Corvino, Giuseppe Leo. 2020. 'Asset allocation and private markets: the need for a cash management strategy'. Preprint. Available at https://www.researchgate.net/publication/340886960_Asset_allocation_and_private_markets_the_need_for_a_cash_management_strategy [accessed 10 March 2023].

Cox, D. R. (1981). 'Statistical Analysis of Time Series: Some Recent Developments', *Scandinavian Journal of Statistics*, 8(2), 93–115.

CSSF. 2021. 'AIFM Reporting Dashboard'. *Commission de Surveillance du Secteur Financier. Luxembourg*. 31 December.

Dawes, Robyn M. 1979. 'The robust beauty of improper linear models in decision making', *American Psychologist*, 34(7), 571–58.

Delgado Moreira, Juan. 2003. 'Probabilistic Forecast'. Presentation. London. Baring Private Equity Partners. March.

de Malherbe, Etienne, 2004. 'Modeling private equity funds and private equity collateralised fund obligations', *International Journal of Theoretical and Applied Finance*, 7(03), 193–230.

DeMiguel, Victor, Lorenzo Garlappi, and Raman Uppal. 2009. 'Optimal versus naive diversification: How inefficient is the 1/N portfolio strategy?', *Review of Financial Studies*, 22(5), 1915–1953.

Demaria, Cyril. 2013. *Introduction to Private Equity – Venture, Growth, LBO & Turn-Around Capital*, 2nd edn. Chichester: John Wiley and Sons.

de Zwart, Gerben, Brian Frieser, and Dick van Dijk. 2012. 'Private Equity Recommitment Strategies for Institutional Investors', *Financial Analysts Journal*, 68(3), 81–100.

Diller, Christian and Christoph Jäckel. 2015. 'Risk in Private Equity – New insights into the risk of a portfolio of private equity funds'. BVCA Research Paper. October.

Dinneen, Pat. 2004. 'Emerging Markets Private Equity: Performance Update'. *IFC Conference*, 6 May. Available at http://www.ifc.org/ifcext/cfn.nst/AttachmentsByTitle/Patricia+Dinneen/$FILE/Panel4-PatriciaDinneed.pdf [accessed 1 February 2006].

Doherty, Michael and Jason Kolman. 2018. 'Introduction to Credit Funds: Basics on How Credit Funds and Private Equity Funds Differ'. Ropes & Gray LLP. Podcast. 27 September.

Doimi de Frankopan, Nicholas. 2009. 'Private equity and the 'new normal'', *IPE Magazine*. December. Available at https://www.ipe.com/private-equity-and-the-new-normal/33378.article [accessed 26 May 2021].

Døskeland, Trond M. and Per Strömberg. 2018. 'Evaluating Investments in Unlisted Equity for the Norwegian Government Pension Fund Global (GPFG)'. Report for the Norwegian Ministry of Finance. January 10.

Duggan, Wayne. 2023. 'A Short History Of The Great Recession'. 21 June. Available at https://www.forbes.com/advisor/investing/great-recession/ [accessed 1 October 2023].

Easterling, Ed. 2004. 'Burying the Myth of Survivorship Bias'. Crestmont Research. August. Available at http://www.eurekahedge.com/Research/News/1028/Burying-the-Myth-of-Survivorship-Bias [accessed 14 April 2023].

EIOPA. 2015. 'Look-through approach'. European Insurance and Occupational Pensions Authority. Rulebook Solvency II. Available at https://www.eiopa.europa.eu/rulebook/solvency-ii/article-2490_en [accessed 9 May 2023].

Ellis, Colin, Sonal Pattni, and Devash Tailor. 2012. 'Measuring private equity returns and benchmarking against public markets', *BVCA Research and Economics*. May 2.

ESMA. 2023. 'Questions and Answers – Application of the AIFMD'. European Securities and Markets Authority. ESMA34-32-352. 14 June. Available at https://www.esma.europa.eu/sites/default/files/library/esma34-32-352_qa_aifmd.pdf [accessed 15 June 2023].

EVCA. 2013. 'Private Equity Risk Measurement Guidelines'. InvestEurope. January. Available at https://www.investeurope.eu/media/1113/evca-risk-measurement-guidelines-january-2013.pdf [accessed 11 May 2020].

Everts, Martin. 2002. 'Cash Dilution in Illiquid Funds'. MPRA Paper No. 4655. Available at http://mpra.ub.uni-muenchen.de/4655/ [accessed 30 September 2011].

Erturk, Erkan, Lily Cheung, and Winnie Fong. 2001. 'Private Equity Fund of Funds: Overview and Rating Criteria'. Standard & Poor's CDO Research.

Espahbodi, Kamyar and Roumi Roumi. 2021. 'Allocation of Alternative Investments in Portfolio Management – A Quantitative Study Considering Investors' Liquidity Preferences'. Degree Project. KTH Royal Institute of Technology, School of Engineering Sciences. Sweden.

Fayvilevich, Greg, Igor Gorovits, Brian Knudsen, Ralph Aurora, and Alastair Sewell. 2018. 'Astrea IV Pte. Ltd.' Fitch Ratings – Fund and Asset Manager Rating Group. June 14.

Fisher, Len. 2009. *The Perfect Swarm – The Science of Complexity in Everyday Life*. New York: Basic Books.

Fleischer, Victor. 2005. 'The Missing Preferred Return'. UCLA School of Law. Law & Economics Working Paper Series, No. 465, 22 February.

Fraser-Sampson, Guy. 2007. *Private Equity as an Asset Class*. Chichester: Wiley & Sons.

Furenstam, Elias and Johannes Forsell. 2018. 'Cash Flow Simulation in Private Equity – An evaluation and comparison of two models'. Umeå University, Spring.

Gelfer, James, Andy White, and Zane Carmean. 2020. 'Basics of Cash Flow Management'. Private Fund Cash Flow Series. PitchBook.

Geltner, David and David Ling. 2000. 'Benchmark and Index Needs in the US Private Real Estate Investment Industry: Trying to Close the Gap'. RERI study for the Pension Real Estate Association, Hartford, CT.

Giannotti, Claudio and Gianluca Mattarocci. 2009. 'The Risk Exposure of Property Cash Flows: Evidence from the Italian Market', *Bancaria*, No. 10. 1 November.

Gillers, Heather. 2022. 'Calpers highlights 'lost decade' for private equity after missing out on $11 billion in gains', *The Wall Street Journal*. 20 September.

Gompers, Paul, Anna Kovner, Josh Lerner, and David Scharfstein. 2009. 'Performance Persistence in Entrepreneurship'. Available at https://www.newyorkfed.org/medialibrary/media/research/economists/kovner/performance_persistence.pdf [accessed 29 September 2020].

Gottschalg, Oliver. 2007. 'Performance assessment: what we know and what we don't know', *Private Equity International*. January.

Gottschalg, Oliver. 2020. 'Initial Insights into the possible impact of the Covid-19 Crisis on Private Equity Cash Flows in 2020'. Unpublished Working Paper. April.

Gottschalg, Oliver. 2021. 'The 2020 HEC-DowJones Private Equity Performance Ranking'. MJ Hudson Report. 25 January.

Grabenwarter, Uli and Tom Weidig. 2005. *Exposed to the J-Curve*. London: Euromoney Books.

Greenberg, Marc. 2015. 'A "Common Risk Factor" Method to Estimate Correlations between Distributions'. Presentation at NASA Cost Symposium (Ames Research Center). 27 August.

Hall, Joseph M. and M. Eric Johnson. 2009. 'When Should a Process be Art, Not Science?', *Harvard Business Review*. March.

Halls, Steven. 2019. 'Average Height for Girls'. 12 August. Available at https://halls.md/chart-girls-height-w/ [accessed 7 September 2020].

Hammond, George, Tabby Kinder, and Ivan Levingston. 2023. 'VCs urge start-ups to delay IPOs after Arm and Instacart hit by volatility', *Financial Times*. 2 October.

Hannover-Re. 2001. 'Hannover Rück SE 2021Solvency and Financial Condition Report'. Available at https://www.hannover-re.com/1855996/2021-solvency-and-financial-condition-report-hannover-ruck-se.pdf [accessed 13 June 2023].

HarbourVest. 2018. 'Rethinking Risk: The Myth of Over-Diversification'. Private Market Insights. November.

Harte, Thomas P. and Axel Buchner. 2017. 'The PE Package – Modeling private equity in the 21st Century'. Presentation.

Harris, Robert S., Tim Jenkinson, and Steven N. Kaplan. 2012. 'Private Equity Performance: What Do We Know?' NBER Working Paper 17874. Available at: https://www.nber.org/papers/w17874.pdf [accessed 14 December 2018].

Heikkila, Tatu. 2004. 'European Single Market and the Globalisation of Private Equity Fundraising: Barriers and Determinants of Foreign Commitments in Private Equity Funds'. University of Illinois at Urbana-Champaign's Academy for Entrepreneurial Leadership Historical Research Reference in Entrepreneurship. Available at https://ssrn.com/abstract=1513780 [accessed 29 September 2020].

Hickman, Richard. 2019. 'HarbourVest Global Private Equity Ltd – Capital Markets Event'. Presentation. 20 June.

Hoek, Henk. 2007. 'An ALM Analysis of Private Equity'. ORTEC Centre for Financial Research. January. Available at http://files.ortec-finance.com/Publications/research/OCFR_App_WP_2007_01.pdf [accessed 2 July 2008].

Hüther, Niklas, David T. Robinson, Sönke Sievers, and Thomas Hartmann-Wendels. 2019. 'Paying for Performance in Private Equity: Evidence from Venture Capital Partnerships', *Management Science,* 66(4).

ILPA. 2011. 'Private Equity Principles'. Institutional Limited Partners Association. Washington, DC.

IPEV. 2018. 'International Private Equity and Venture Capital Valuation Guidelines'.

Inderst, Georg. 2018. 'Infrastructure as an asset class: a brief history', *IPE Real Assets Magazine.* September / October. Available at https://realassets.ipe.com/reports/infrastructure-as-asset-class-a-brief-history/10026752.article [accessed 14 April 2023].

ISDA. 2022. 'Capitalization of Equity Investments in Funds Under the FRTB'. International Swaps and Derivatives Association. January. Available at https://www.isda.org/a/Ht6gE/Capitalization-of-Equity-Investments-in-Funds-Under-the-FRTB.pdf [accessed 13 June 2023].

Jeddy, Aly and Matt Portner. 2018. 'Dry powder in private equity'. McKinsey. April. Available at https://www.mckinsey.com/industries/private-equity-and-principal-investors/our-insights/dry-powder-in-private-equity [accessed 19 October 2018].

Jeet, Vishv. 2020a. 'Modeling Private Investment Cash Flows with Market-Sensitive Periodic Growth'. PGIM Institutional Advisory & Solutions and GIC's Economics & Investment Strategy. October.

Jeet, Vishv. 2020b. 'Measuring the Value of LP Fund Selection Skill – A Fair Comparison Framework'. PGIM Institutional Advisory & Solutions and GIC's Economics & Investment Strategy. April.

Jeet, Vishv. 2020c. 'Building and Maintaining a Desired Exposure to Private Markets: Commitment Pacing, Cash Flow Modeling, and Beyond'. PGIM Institutional Advisory & Solutions and GIC's Economics & Investment Strategy. November.

Jeet, Vishv and Luis O'Shea. 2018. 'Modeling Cash Flows for Private Capital Funds'. Working Paper. Burgiss Applied Research. February.

Jenkinson, Tim, Stefan Morkoetter, Tobias Schori, and Thomas Wetzer. 2022. 'Buy low, sell high? Do private equity fund managers have market timing abilities?', *Journal of Banking & Finance,* 138. May.

Kalra, Raman, Alan Dunetz, Richard Hrvatin, and Richard Green. 2006. 'Going Public with Private Equity CFOs.' Fitch Ratings – Structured Finance. February 6.

Kanabar, Om. 2021. 'Risk Management for Private Equity Investors - a VaR Approach'. Judge Business School, University of Cambridge. 1 April.

Kaplan, Steven N. and Josh Lerner. 2016. 'Venture Capital Data: Opportunities and Challenges'. Harvard Business School. Working Paper 17-012.

Kazemi, Hossein, Keith H. Black, and Donald R. Chambers. 2016. 'Alternative Investments: CAIA Level II'. CAIA Association. Hoboken, NJ: John Wiley and Sons.

Kasumov, Aziza. 2020. 'Stanford endowment chef applies ballet discipline to investment', *Financial Times Fund Management.* 31 October.

Karatas, Tugce, Federico Klinkert, and Ali Hirsa. 2021. 'Supervised Neural Networks for Illiquid Alternative Asset Cash Flow Forecasting'. 5 August. Available at https://doi.org/10.48550/arXiv.2108.02853 [accessed 30 July 2022].

Khan, Faisal. 2019. '9 Black Swan Events that changed the Financial World'. Data Driven Investor. 18 January. Available at https://www.datadriveninvestor.com/2019/01/18/9-black-swan-events-that-changed-the-financial-world/ [accessed 11 May 2020].

Kieffer, Emmanuel, Thomas Meyer, Georges Gloukoviezoff, Hakan Lucius, and Pascal Bouvry. 2023. 'Learning private equity recommitment strategies for institutional investors', *Frontiers in Artificial Intelligence*. 7 February.

Klüppelberg, Claudia, Andreas Kumeth, and Christina Steinkohl. 2010. 'Modelling the Value and Measuring the Risk of Private Equity'. September. Available at https://mediatum.ub.tum.de/doc/1079208/276103.pdf [accessed 9 May 2023].

Knight, Frank H. 1921. *Risk, Uncertainty, and Profit*. Boston, MA: Schaffner and Marx. Houghton Mifflin Company.

Kocis, James M., James C. Bachman, Austin M. Long, and Craig J. Nickels. 2009. *Inside Private Equity – The Professional Investor's Handbook*. Hoboken, New Jersey: John Wiley & Sons.

Koopman, Siem Jan, André Lucas, and Marcel Scharth. 2012. 'Predicting time-varying parameters with parameter-driven and observation-driven models'. Tinbergen Institute Discussion Paper TI 2012-020/4.

Krahnen, Jan Pieter and Martin Weber. 2001. 'Generally accepted rating principles: A primer', *Journal of Banking & Finance*, 25(1), 3–23.

Krohmer, Philipp. 2008. 'Essays in Financial Economics: Risk and Return of Private Equity'. Inaugural-Dissertation zur Erlangung des Doktorgrades des Fachbereichs Wirtschaftswissenschaften der Johann Wolfgang Goethe Universität, Frankfurt am Main. April.

Kshetrapal, Akshat. 2016. 'Identifying sub-categories within the Private Equity taxonomy for buy-out funds'. Master Thesis. Amsterdam Business School. August.

Kumar, Ankit. 2022. 'Why the Private Equity Secondary Market is Poised to Grow – It's now a necessary option for portfolio management'. January 6. Available at: https://www.entrepreneur.com/article/401332 [accessed 2 May 2022].

Kupec, Blazej and Jason Feder. 2022. 'What is private equity co-investing and why consider it?' July. Available at https://www.moonfare.com/blog/private-equity-co-investment#:~:text=Investments%20made%20via%20co%2Dinvestment,and%2010%20percent%20carried%20interest [accessed 26 April 2023].

Lawrence, Michael, Paul Goodwin, Marcus O'Connor, and Dilek Önkal. 2006. 'Judgmental forecasting: A review of progress over the last 25 years', *International Journal of Forecasting*, 22(3), 493–518.

Lee, Ian, Kate Bridge, Maria LoPreiato-Bergan, and Jim Tomczyk. 2023. 'How Do Capital Calls Work?' Blog. Available at https://learn.angellist.com/articles/capital-calls [accessed 24 April 2023].

Lenz, Jimmie, Dominic Pazzula, and Jonathan Leonardelli. 2018. 'Macroeconomic Effects on the Modeling of Private Capital Cash Flows'. FRG Technical Paper. Available at https://www.frgrisk.com/news-and-events/macroeconomic-effects-on-the-modeling-of-private-capital-cash-flows/ [accessed 10 August 2020].

Lerner, Josh and Antoinette Schoar. 2002. 'The Illiquidity Puzzle: Theory and Evidence from Private Equity', *Journal of Financial Economics*, 1(72), 3–40.

Lerner, Josh, Antoinette Schoar, and Wan Wong. 2005. 'Smart Institutions, Foolish Choices? The Limited Partner Performance Puzzle'. NBER Working Papers 11136, National Bureau of Economic Research, Inc.

Lhabitant, François-Serge and Michelle Learne. 2002. 'Hedge Fund Diversification: How Much Is Enough?' FAME – International Center for Financial Asset Management and Engineering. Research Paper No 52. July.

Lhabitant, François-Serge. 2004. *Hedge Funds – Quantitative Insights*. Chichester: John Wiley & Sons.

Loretan, Mico and William B. English. 2000. 'Evaluating Correlation Breakdowns During Periods of Market Volatility'. February. Available at https://www.bis.org/publ/confer08k.pdf [accessed 2 December 2022].

Love, Geoffrey. 2009. 'Praise for Evergreen Funds', *Venture Capital Journal*. 1 December.

Lowe, Richard. 2009. 'Commitment issues', *IPE RA magazine*. March. Available at https://realassets.ipe.com/commitment-issues/31006.article [accessed 13 May 2020].

Lykken, Alex. 2018. 'The pros & cons of long-dated funds'. June 18. Available at https://pitchbook.com/news/articles/the-pros-cons-of-long-dated-funds [accessed 13 May 2020].

Maptrip. 2021. 'How a GPS navigation software calculates the ETA'. Blog. 4 September. Available at https://www.maptrip.de/en/eta-calculation/ [accessed 8 March 2020].

Mascarenhas, Briance and David A. Aaker. 1989. 'Mobility Barriers and Strategic Groups', *Strategic Management Journal*, 10(5), 475–485. September–October.

Mathonet, Pierre-Yves and Thomas Meyer. 2007. *J Curve Exposure – Managing a Portfolio of Venture Capital and Private Equity Funds*. Chichester: John Wiley and Sons.

McGrady, Colin. 2002. 'Pricing Private Equity Secondary Transactions'. Paper. Cogent Partners.

McGuinness, Rob. 2020. 'How to Stress Test Your Foreign Exchange (FX) Risk in the Wake of COVID-19', *Payments Journal*. 22 June. Available at https://www.paymentsjournal.com/how-to-stress-test-your-foreign-exchange-fx-risk-in-the-wake-of-covid-19/ [accessed 29 September 2023].

McKinsey & Company. 2019. 'A turning point for real estate investment management'. November. Available at https://www.mckinsey.com/industries/private-equity-and-principal-investors/our-insights/a-turning-point-for-real-estate-investment-management#/ [accessed 10 March 2023].

McKinsey & Company. 2020. 'A new decade for private markets'. McKinsey's Private Markets Annual Review.

Mende, Jochen, Joseph B. Marks, and Kairat Perembetov. 2016. 'Introductory Guide to Investing in Private Equity Secondaries', *Alternative Investment Analyst Review*. Quarter 3.

Mendoza, Carmela. 2020. 'CalPERS head of PE on why its program has underperformed'. Private Equity International. September 15. Available at https://www.privateequityinternational.com/calpers-head-of-pe-on-why-its-programme-has-underperformed/ [accessed 16 September 2020].

Metrick, Andrew and Ayako Yasuda. 2010. 'The Economics of Private Equity Funds', *The Review of Financial Studies*, 23(6), 2303–2341.

Meyer, Thomas. 2017. 'Applying Artificial Intelligence to Fund Cash-Flow Forecasting'. 4th Private Equity Risk Symposium, Said Business School, Oxford. November.

Meyer, Thomas. 2019. 'Reconciling Alternative Investment Fund and Limited Partner Risk Measurement Approaches'. Unpublished draft script.

Meyer, Thomas and Pierre-Yves Mathonet. 2005. *Beyond the J-Curve*. Chichester: John Wiley and Sons.

Meyer, Thomas. 2014. *Private Equity Unchained – Strategy Insights for the Institutional Investor*. Houndsmill, Basingstoke, Hampshire: Palgrave Macmillan.

Meyer, Thomas. 2020. 'Hidden in Plain Sight – The Impact of Undrawn Commitments', *The Journal of Alternative Investments*, Fall, 1–16.

Meyer, Thomas. 2022. 'Reconciling Limited Partners' Cash-Flow Forecasting with the Look-Through for AIFs', *The Journal of Alternative Investments*, Summer.

Meyer, Thomas. 2023. 'Look-Through'. The Palgrave Encyclopedia of Private Equity. 20 December.

Morgan-Lewis. 2015. 'Fund Size: Targets, Caps, Minimums, and Reductions'. Venture Capital & Private Equity Funds Deskbook Series. Available at https://www.morganlewis.com/-/media/files/special-topics/vcpefdeskbook/fundformation/vcpefdeskbook_fundsize.pdf?rev=db1b607db77945fdacfa7a858d56795d [accessed 30 May 2023].

Morrissette, Mark. 2014. 'Do all US VC's have a hurdle rate before they begin to earn carry? What is it on average?'. Available at https://www.quora.com/Do-all-US-VCs-have-a-hurdle-rate-before-they-begin-to-earn-carry-What-is-it-on-average [accessed 10 April 2023].

Mulcahy, Diane, Bill Weeks, Harold S. Bradley. 2012. 'We have met the enemy...and he is us'. Report. Ewing Marion Kauffman Foundation. Available at https://www.kauffman.org/wp-content/uploads/2012/05/we_have_met_the_enemy_venture_capital_report_kauffman_foundation.pdf, [accessed 18 February 2024]

Munich-Re. 2015. 'Briefing on Solvency II'. Presentation by Munich Re. 30 November.

Murphy, Daniel. 2007. 'A Practical Guide to Managing Private Equity Commitments'. Strategic Research. Goldman Sachs Asset Management. June.

Murphy, Daniel, Juliana Hadas, and James Gelfer. 2022. 'Calling Patterns: Why Private Fund Cash Flow Management May Need to Evolve'. 15 December. Available at https://www.gsam.com/content/gsam/us/en/advisors/market-insights/gsam-insights/perspectives/2022/calling-patterns-why-private-fund-cash-flow-management-may-need-to-evolve.html [accessed 26 April 2023].

Nevins, Daniel, Andrew Conner, and Greg McIntire. 2004. 'A Portfolio Management Approach to Determining Private Equity Commitments', *The Journal of Alternative Investments*, 6(4), 32–46.

Nextvest. 2016. 'Ignoring the Cost of Committed Capital: How PE Funds can Overstate LP Returns by up to 50%'. November 1. Available at https://medium.com/@nextvest/ignoring-the-cost-of-committed-capital-how-pe-funds-can-overstate-lp-returns-by-up-to-50-23b42e6c5558 [accessed 27 August 2018].

Norton, Rorie A. 2020. 'Forming Private Credit Funds: Key Differences in Fund Lifecycle and the Use of Subscription Facilities Versus PE Funds (Part One of Two)'. Private Equity Law Report, 12 May.

Oberli, Adrian (2015). 'Private Equity Asset Allocation: How to Recommit?', *The Journal of Private Equity*, 18(2), 9–22.

O'Hare, Mark. 2008. 'Survivorship Bias – What Survivorship Bias?' Performance Spotlight. March. Available at https://docs.preqin.com/newsletters/pe/SpotlightMarch2008.pdf [accessed 14 April 2023].

O'Shea, Luis and Vishv Jeet. 2018. 'Budgeting for Capital Calls: A VaR-Inspired approach'. Working Paper. Burgiss Applied Research. March.

PACRA. 2005. 'Asset Manager Rating Methodology'. The Pakistan Credit Rating Agency Ltd.

Palnitkar, Arti. 2021. 'Private Equity Valuation'. Thesis, University of Twente, The Netherlands, 26 July.

Pangburn, Leonard C. and Ryan Green. 2021. 'Marin County Employees Retirement Association'. Investor Review, Abbott Capital Private Equity Funds. September 16. Available at https://www.mcera.org/-/media/files/sites/retirement/packets/inv-202109.pdf [accessed 7 March 2022].

Perrin, Ian, Marlow Gereluk, and Marco Szego. 2006. 'SVG Diamond Private Equity II Plc'. Pre-Sale Report. Moody's International Structured Finance, January 26.

Pazzula, Dominic. 2021. 'Optimal Pacing for Private Capital Portfolios'. FRG Technical Paper.

Peterman, Scott, Margaret Niles, Sook Young Yeu, and Anson Chan. 2020. 'Negotiating Private Equity Fund Terms – Key Provisions for PE Sponsors and LP Investors and the New ILPA Model Limited Partnership Agreements'. K&L Gates Presentation. Available at https://files.klgates.com/files/171267_negotiating_private_equity_fund_terms.pdf [accessed 30 May 2023].

Perrin, Ian, Marlow Gereluk, and Marco Szego. 2006. 'SVG Diamond Private Equity II Plc'. Pre-Sale Report. Moody's International Structured Finance, January 26.

Phalippou, Ludovic. 2007. 'Investing in Private Equity Funds – A Survey'. Available at https://papers.ssrn.com/sol3/papers.cfm?abstract_id=980243 [accessed 8 August 2023].

Phalippou, Ludovic. 2008. 'The Hazards of Using IRR to Measure Performance: The Case of Private Equity'. Available at http://ssrn.com/abstract=1111796 [accessed 5 April 2013].

Phalippou, Ludovic and Mark Westerfield. 2014. 'Capital Commitment and Illiquidity Risks in Private Equity'. Netspar Discussion Papers. June. Available at https://www.netspar.nl/assets/uploads/035_Phalippou.pdf [accessed 14 December 2018].

Phillips, Bernard S. 1971. *Social Research Strategy and Tactics*, 2nd edn. Collier Macmillan Ltd, p. 205.

PitchBook. 2020. 'Basics of Cash Flow Management'. Private Fund Cash Flow Series. 4 September.

PitchBook. 2022. 'Allocator Solutions: Cash Flow Forecasting and Commitment Pacing'. Report. 30 March. Available at https://pitchbook.com/news/reports/2022-allocator-solutions [accessed 29 June 2022].

Plender, John. 2023. 'Private equity faces a reckoning after decades of success', *Financial Times*. 11/12 November.

Preqin. 2017. 'Private Capital Performance Data Guide'

Pucker, Ken and Sakis Kotsantonis. 2020. 'Private Equity Makes ESG Promises. But Their Impact Is Often Superficial', *Institutional Investor*. 29 June. Available at https://www.institutionalinvestor.com/article/b1m8spzx5bp6g7/Private-Equity-Makes-ESG-Promises-But-Their-Impact-Is-Often-Superficial [accessed 5 May 2023].

PWC. 2016. 'What's the difference between 'likely and 'probable'?' IFRS Spotlight. September. Available at http://www.pwc.com.au/assurance/ifrs/assets/terms-of-likelihood.pdf [accessed 16 October 2018].

PWC. 2018. 'Illustrative IFRS financial statements 2017 – Private equity funds'. Available at https://www.pwc.lu/en/private-equity/docs/pwc-illustrative-ifrs-financial-statements-2017-private-equity-funds.pdf [accessed 16 October 2018].

Rae, Andrew and Rob Alexander. 2017. 'Forecasts or fortune-telling: when are expert judgements of safety risk valid?', *Safety Science*, 156–165.

Rating Capital Partners. 2002. 'Fiduciary ratings—measuring trustworthiness in the investment management industry'. Presentation. Wiesbaden, RCP & Partners SA.

Reinhart, Carmen M. and Kenneth S. Rogoff. 2009. *This Time Is Different – Eight Centuries of Financial Folly*. Princeton University Press.

Ribeiro, Sandra and Maria João Ferro. 2017. 'Why does Language Matter? Evidence from EU and Mercosur Trade'. Proceedings of the II International Congress on Interdisciplinarity in Social and Human Sciences, 11th–12th May 2017. Available at https://bibliotecadigital.ipb.pt/bitstream/10198/21767/1/CIEO_Paper2.pdf [accessed 20 January 2023].

Richards, Heather. 2020. 'Cash flow planning – What are the pitfalls? And how do you overcome them?' Available at https://www.dynamicplanner.com/cash-flow-planning-tools-pitfalls-and-how-to-overcome-them/ [accessed 27 September 2022].

Ring, Suzi and Lisa Du. 2018. 'Japan waves goodbye to UK as 'gateway to Europe' post-Brexit'. Automotive News Europe. 3 October. Available at https://europe.autonews.com/article/20181003/ANE/181009864/japan-waves-goodbye-to-uk-as-gateway-to-europe-post-brexit [accessed 24 January 2023].

Robinson, David T. and Berk A. Sensoy, 2016. 'Cyclicality, performance measurement, and cash flow liquidity in private equity', *Journal of Financial Economics*, 122(3), 521–543.

Rouvinez, Christophe. 2003. 'Private Equity and Risk – Looking at Diversified Portfolios'. RiskInvest 2003. London, 27 and 28 October.

Rudd, Howard. 2016. 'Why you shouldn't use the triangular distribution'. Blog. 24 July. Available at https://www.howardrudd.net/how-tos/triangular-distribution/ [accessed 3 September 2023].

Ruso, Selman. 2008. 'A Governance-focused Rating System for Closed-ended Funds in Germany'. Diplomarbeit in Corporate Finance at Swiss Banking Institute. 20 October.

Saffo, Paul. 2007. 'Six Rules for Effective Forecasting'. *Harvard Business Review*. July–August.

Saket, Paymun. 2022. 'The Private Equity Pacing Model – 3 Key Challenges Investors Face'. 22 February. Available at https://www.allvuesystems.com/resources/the-private-equity-pacing-model-3-key-challenges-investors-face/ [accessed 26 March 2022].

Samuels, Sarah. 2022. 'Taking Stock: Private Markets (Part Two): The Art of Commitment Pacing and Liquidity Management'. *Blog.* 29 November. Available at https://www.nepc.com/taking-stock-private-markets-part-two-the-art-of-commitment-pacing-and-liquidity-management/ [accessed 3 July 2023].

Schneider, Jerome, Sean Klein, Wade Sias, and Simon Fan. 2022. 'Cash for Calls: A Quantitative Approach to Managing Liquidity for Capital Calls', *The Journal of Alternative Investments*, Fall.

Shepard, Peter, Grace Qiu Tiantian, and Ding Li. 2022. 'Building Balanced Portfolios for the Long Run – A new framework for incorporating macro resilience into asset allocation'. MSCI and GIC research report. 17 October. Available at https://www.msci.com/www/research-report/building-balanced-portfolios/03442287672 [accessed 14 July 2023].

Shen, Junying, Ding Li, Grace (Tiantian) Qiu, Vishv Jeet, Michelle (Yu) Teng, and Ki Cheong Wong. 2020. 'Building a Better Portfolio – Balancing Performance and Liquidity'. PGIM Institutional Advisory & Solutions and GIC's Economics & Investment Strategy. April.

Shen, Junying, Michelle (Yu) Teng, Ding Li, and Grace (Tiantian) Qi. 2021. 'Harnessing the Potential of Private Assets – A Framework For Institutional Portfolio Construction'. PGIM Institutional Advisory & Solutions and GIC's Economics & Investment Strategy. June.

Sidenius, Jeppe and Richard Ballek. 2022. 'Managing diversification in portfolios of funds'. Private Equity Risk Symposium, Said Business School, Oxford. 25 November.

Simon, Hermann. 2007. *Hidden Champions des 21. Jahrhunderts – Die Erfolgsstrategien unbekannter Weltmarktführer.* Frankfurt, New York: Campus Verlag.

Singleton, Geoff and George L. Henshilwood. 2003. 'Developing a Strategy For Private Equity'. Avon Pension Fund Committee. Meeting documents. 28 March. Available at https://democracy.bathnes.gov.uk/celistdocuments.aspx?MID=394&DF=28%2F03%2F2003&A=1&R=0&F=embed$12zAppendix1.htm [accessed 20 June 2019].

Smith, Janet Kiholm and Erin E. Smith. 2021. 'Bias in the Reporting of Venture Capital Performance: The Disciplinary Role of FOIA'. Draft Paper. Available at https://www.lowe-institute.org/wp-content/uploads/2021/05/Draft_2021_VC_paper.pdf [accessed 14 April 2023].

Smith, Terry. 1996. *Accounting for Growth – Stripping the Camouflage from Company Accounts,* 2nd edn. London: Arrow.

Sørensen, Morten, Neng Wang, and Jinqiang Yang. 2013. 'Valuing Private Equity. Network for Studies on Pension, Aging and Retirement'. Discussion Paper 04/2012-041. June 13.

Spliid, Robert. 2015. 'Benchmark Biases in Private Equity Performance (Chapter 15)'. In *Private Equity – Opportunities and Risks,* Baker, H. Kent, Greg Filbeck, and Halil Kiymaz (eds). Oxford University Press: Financial Markets and Investment Series.

Stracke, Don, Oliver Fadly, and Michael Miranda. 2018. 'City of Fresno Retirement Systems – Private Equity Concept and Framework'. NEPC Presentation to Joint Meeting of the Retirement Boards. 24 January 2018. Available at https://foialts.files.wordpress.com/2018/01/nepc-pe-concept-and-framework.pdf [accessed 14 December 2018].

Studer, Michael and Marc Wicki. 2010. 'Private equity allocations under Solvency II.' Partners Group Research Flash. August 2010. Available at: 20100610 Solvency II and private equity FINAL (partnersgroup.com) [accessed 8 April 2021].

Swensen, David F. 2000. *Pioneering Portfolio Management—An Unconventional Approach to Institutional Investment.* New York: Simon & Schuster.

Taleb, Nassim Nicholas. 2007. *The Black Swan: The Impact of the Highly Improbable.* Random House.

Talmor, Eli and Florin Vasvari. 2018. "Risk Management in Private Equity." Unpublished draft script.

Takahashi, Dean and Seth Alexander. 2002. 'Illiquid Alternative Asset Modeling', *The Journal of Portfolio Management*, 28(Winter), 90–100.

Teitelbaum, Richard. 2018. 'One Young Harvard Grad's Quixotic Quest to Disrupt Private Equity'. Institutional Investor. 25 April. Available at https://www.institutionalinvestor.com/article/

b17xwqqjjf71c9/one-young-harvard-grad%E2%80%99s-quixotic-quest-to-disrupt-private-equity [accessed 25 October 2023].

Telos. 2010. 'Fiduciary Management Rating – Deutsche Bank Group – DB Advisors'. June.

Tolkamp, Coen. 2007. 'Predicting Private Equity Performance – The Development of a Private Equity Performance-Forecasting Model for AEGON Asset Management'. Master's Thesis in Industrial Engineering & Management. University of Twente. The Netherlands.

Toll, David M. 2001. 'Private Equity Partnership Terms and Conditions'. Research Report, Asset Alternatives.

Troche, Clemens J. 2003 'Development of a rating instrument for private equity funds'. MBA Management Project Report, NIMBAS Graduate School of Management.

Ungsgård, Oscar. 2020. 'Stochastic Modelling of Cash Flows in Private Equity'. KTH Royal Institute of Technology, School of Engineering Sciences.

van Creveld, Martin. 2022. 'But It Is All We Have'. Blog. Posted on 18 November 2022. Available at https://www.martin-van-creveld.com/ [accessed 18 November 2022].

Vander Elst, Harry. 2021. 'Why you should use bottom-up models in private equity'. 14 April. Available at https://rockslinganalytics.com/why-you-should-use-bottom-up-models-in-private-equity/ [accessed 9 May 2023].

Vardi, Nathan. 2009. 'Did Harvard Sell At the Bottom?', *Forbes*. 24 October. Available at https://www.forbes.com/2009/10/24/harvard-university-endowment-business-wall-street-harvard.html?sh=5e476a3f6c4a [accessed 27 September 2022].

Virtanen, Jussi. 2021. 'Cash flow simulation and model comparison in private credit'. University of Helsinki, Department of Mathematics and Statistics.

Weidig, Tom. 2002. 'Risk Model for Venture Capital Funds'. November. Available at https://ssrn.com/abstract=365881 [accessed 27 September 2022].

Weidig, Tom and Pierre-Yves Mathonet. 2004. 'The Risk Profile of Private Equity'. European Venture Capital Association. January.

Whitten, Gregory, Xiaoyi Dai, Simon Fan, and Yu Pang. 2022. 'Do political relations affect international trade? Evidence from China's twelve trading partners', *Journal of Shipping and Trade*. Available at https://jshippingandtrade.springeropen.com/articles/10.1186/s41072-020-00076-w [accessed 23 January 2023].

Woodman, Andrew. 2023. '*Zombie funds could rise again, but there are antidotes*'. 21 April. Available at https://pitchbook.com/news/articles/PE-VC-exits-zombie-funds [accessed 8 August 2023].

Wright, William Edward. 1977. 'Gravitational clustering', *Pattern Recognition*, 9(3), 151–166. October.

Yan, Ziyou. 2022. 'Simplicity is An Advantage but Sadly Complexity Sells Better'. Blog. August. Available at https://eugeneyan.com/writing/simplicity/ [accessed 29 July 2023].

Zuckerman, Gregory. 2019. *The Man Who Solved the Market – How Jim Simons Launched the Quant Revolution*. Penguin Business.

Index